HEROIC COLONIAL CHRISTIANS

HEROIC COLONIAL CHRISTIANS

COURTNEY ANDERSON
RUSSELL T. HITT
CLYDE S. KILBY
HENRY W. CORAY

Edited with an Introduction by
Russell T. Hitt

J. B. LIPPINCOTT COMPANY
PHILADELPHIA AND NEW YORK

CONTENTS

HEROIC COLONIAL CHRISTIANS

INTRODUCTION

ONLY in the last decade have scholars again turned to study more carefully the lives and writings of some of the greatest minds of American colonial history. The outstanding effort in this direction, of course, is the massive undertaking of the Yale University Press in republishing all the writings of Jonathan Edwards under the general editorship of the late Perry Miller. Paul Ramsey, editor of the first volume, Edwards' *Freedom of the Will*, flatly declares in the introduction that "this book alone is sufficient to establish its author as the greatest philosopher-theologian yet to grace the American scene."

In a new volume, *Protestantism in America*, Jerald C. Brauer, Dean of the Divinity School, University of Chicago, describes Edwards as "one of the greatest intellects America has produced."

Sensing that Edwards and some of his contemporaries are not too well known to this generation, Muriel Fuller, who has had lengthy experience in the New York publishing field, and the editor conferred on assembling a book that would include biographical studies of personalities of the Great Awakening period and later. After many conferences, it was decided that four men stood out—Jonathan Edwards, Gilbert Tennent, David Brainerd, and John Witherspoon.

Both Miss Fuller and her colleague were convinced that earlier liberal scholarship had denigrated Edwards. For example, in a little volume entitled *Benjamin Franklin and Jonathan Edwards*, compiled by Carl Van Doren and published by Charles Scribner's Sons in 1920, this was the appraisal of the great New England divine: "Edwards survives, so far as he may be said to survive at all, outside technical histories of Calvinism and metaphysics, chiefly as a dim figure preaching sermons full of awful imprecations, and hardly at all as a remarkable scientific observer, and one of the impressive mystics of the world."

Courtney Anderson, author of the Edwards study in this volume, would agree with the appellation of "mystic," but he would rate the Northampton preacher as a philosopher equaled by no one in American history unless it be William James. Anderson, a Dartmouth graduate, was chosen to handle the Edwards assignment because of the earlier biography he had written of Adoniram Judson, *To the Golden Shore*.

The holy experiment of the Puritan theocracy had developed into nominal Protestantism by the time Edwards became assistant to his grandfather, the Reverend Solomon Stoddard, in the Congregational Church at Northampton, Massachusetts. But, in December 1734, Edwards lighted the first fires of the Great Awakening, the first religious revival to stir the churches throughout the colonies. Starting with a message on "Justification by Faith," Edwards aroused smug New Englanders by declaring that only those with a vital experience of regeneration could be accepted by a holy God.

"Little wonder," declares Brauer, "people cried out in fear. Either they were damned eternally or they were saved." Without raising his voice or losing his dignity, Edwards continued to hammer home that men could find salvation only by faith in Jesus Christ. The revival spirit spread throughout New England, and eventually all the colonies as well as church leaders in Great Britain were impressed by his majestic preaching. Thousands of men and women, sometimes with great emotion, were converted, and new life came to dying Congregationalism.

Quite unconnected with the events in New England was another spiritual stirring in the Middle Colonies. It began with the forthright ministry of Theodore Frelinghuysen, a Reformed Dutch clergyman, of New Brunswick, New Jersey, who in turn influenced the great Presbyterian theologian-evangelist, Gilbert Tennent, and saw him become a passionate revivalist. Tennent's public ministry was both powerful and polemic. While thousands became ardent disciples of Christ under his ministry, he precipitated a split in the Presbyterian Church that lasted for seventeen years. Later, however, he was instrumental in healing the breach and settled down to a ministry marked by peace and harmony. Tennent, one of the least known of the Great Awakening figures, is included in this volume because he was not only a revivalist but also a great churchman and educator who influenced the stream of evangelical Christianity for several generations.

George Whitefield, an early associate of John and Charles Wesley, helped spark the Great Awakening and brought Jonathan Edwards and Tennent together. A sketch of Whitefield is not included in this volume, but his presence will be felt throughout the book.

David Brainerd, youthful missionary to the Indians of Pennsylvania and New Jersey, caught his vision for the Lord's service in the mounting fervor of the Great Awakening. His intense, self-effacing life, which affected the lives of more Christian leaders than anyone else in the last two hundred years, became known to the world when Jonathan Edwards edited *The Life and Diary of David Brainerd*. Had Brainerd survived his tuberculosis, he undoubtedly would have been Edwards' son-in-law, as the husband of Edwards' daughter Jerusha.

Clyde S. Kilby, chairman of the English Department, Wheaton College, was chosen to write the penetrating study of Brainerd because of his extensive research that has brought to light previously undisclosed material on the young man who sacrificed his life to reach the Indians for Christ.

While the principal force of the Great Awakening was the spiritual strength it gave to the churches of the unborn nation, it is equally true that it cemented the colonies for the revolutionary struggle that was to follow. John Witherspoon, the only clergyman to sign the Declaration of Independence, was both a spiritual figure and one of the Founding Fathers. He lives again in the portrait here presented by Henry W. Coray, Orthodox Presbyterian clergyman and author of several books.

If this volume only succeeds in whetting the appetite of some to read further about these four colonial heroes, the editor and his colleagues will feel their labor has been worth while.

RUSSELL T. HITT

Merion Station, Pennsylvania
February 23, 1966

JONATHAN EDWARDS:
RATIONAL MYSTIC

✿

Courtney Anderson

Paradoxes and measurements

Jonathan Edwards stands with Benjamin Franklin as one of the two outstanding minds in the America of the eighteenth century. Many believe that in another environment he could have become a scientist greater than Franklin. Certainly as a philosopher and theologian he had no peer in his own time. He laid a new kind of foundation for the Calvinism in which he had been born, yet even before his death, the rising flood of history, the turbulent rush of events which were to transform the colonies into the American nation, was carrying him into the backwater of contemporary thought. For his thinking was repugnant to many of the men making a political revolution. So he was brushed aside. Even his congregation rejected and dismissed him. Later, his star began to rise again. Today we recognize him for what he was—one of America's greatest minds—theologian, philosopher and one of the progenitors of the Great Awakening, America's first religious revival.

Thus the paradoxes: The most brilliant philosophical mind of the period devoted itself to establishing a new foundation for a theology which was too frequently dismissed as irrelevant to the needs of the age. Not only that, but this mind applied the most advanced knowledge then available and the newest intellectual and philosophical concepts to re-establish that theology. And not only that, but this logical, precise, analytical mind, scientifically informed in advance of its time, was underneath it all the mind of a mystic. The mind, the intellect, applied its entire powers to explain, to justify, to reconcile, to categorize, to harmonize, to make logical, what the mystic felt. The paradox, the apparent contradiction, between the rationalist and the mystic is so striking that some reject the appellation "mystic"; while others, looking at some of Edwards' sermons, boggle at the word "rational."

That is why the measurements are necessary.

We must take the dimensions of the Jonathan Edwards in his environment and in his time to form any understanding of his thought and the reasons for it. Otherwise he seems all contradiction, admirable but irritating, clear as crystal in thought but often baffling in conclusions.

Here are the simplest major dimensions:

He was born in 1703, he died in 1758. He lived almost all of his life along the lower reaches of the Connecticut River: a hundred-mile-or-so stretch from South Windsor where he was born to Northampton where he was pastor for twenty-three years. His travels were not wide: only as far as New York and Boston.

He was a dutiful son all his life. And that meant *all* his life —for his father died only a few months before he did. He was a loving husband. He was the affectionate father of eleven children.

His father and grandfather were ministers. He went to Yale at the age of thirteen and graduated at seventeen, valedictorian of his class of ten. He was a tutor at Yale for a few years, and briefly a minister in New York. When he was twenty-four, his grandfather selected him to be his assistant in the Northampton church. Two years later, when he was twenty-six, his grandfather died, leaving him in charge. At the age of forty-seven, his congregation dismissed him. A year later he became a missionary to the Stockbridge Indians. Seven years later, he was installed as President of Princeton. A month later, he died.

In the fall of 1703, about the time Jonathan was born, his grandfather Solomon Stoddard of Northampton had urged the use of dogs "to hunt Indians as they do bears." To Stoddard, Indians "act like wolves and are to be dealt with as wolves."

When Jonathan was five, Haverhill, Massachusetts, no more than fifty miles north of Boston, was attacked and razed during Queen Anne's War, which was settled when Jonathan was ten.

He was twenty-one, already a young man, when a party of whites scalped ten Indians in New Hampshire, and were paid a bounty of one hundred pounds per scalp. And he had been five years pastor of the Northampton church, the most prominent church in New England outside of Boston, when George Washington was born on February 22, 1732. He was nearing the end of his life, dismissed from his Northampton church and serving as a missionary to the Stockbridge Indians, when Benjamin Franklin performed the famous experiment with kite and key which proved lightning a manifestation of electricity. This was in 1752, the same year the bell to be known as the Liberty Bell was cast in England and delivered in Philadelphia.

These few bits and pieces of fact tell us something about the times in which he was born, grew up, and lived.

So perhaps we may summarize:

The years of his life were 1703 to 1758, fifty-four years and some months.

The geography of his travels was the valley of the lower Connecticut River, with excursions to Boston and New York.

But the span of his mind was illimitable time and endless space. Here he found God—

". . . but I had as good speak plain, I have already said so much as that Space is God."

". . . for He is the infinite, universal, and all-comprehending existence."

Suppose we try to catch a glimpse of how he came to be what he was.

GENESIS

Jonathan Edwards was the only son, but not the only child, of the Reverend Timothy Edwards and Esther Stoddard Edwards. The time of birth was October 5, 1703. The place was the parsonage in East (now South) Windsor, Connecticut. The parsonage was the first and only parsonage Timothy Edwards ever occupied. In fact, it had been built for him. His congregation was the first and only congregation to which he ever ministered. And he was its first minister.

Before she gave him the boy Jonathan, Timothy Edwards' wife Esther had given him four girls. She was to give him six more girls after the one boy.

Through his mother, Jonathan came into one of the most distinguished family lines in New England, that of the Stoddards. Anthony Stoddard, of the first American generation, had acquired wealth through trade, and status through marriage to Mary Downing, half sister of Sir George Downing and niece of Governor Winthrop of Massachusetts. Anthony Stoddard's son Solomon Stoddard had settled in 1670, eight years after his graduation from Harvard, in the frontier town of Northampton on the Connecticut River. He had married Esther Warham Mather, widow of his predecessor. In addition to the three children by her first husband, she had twelve more by Solomon Stoddard, of whom one was the Esther who married Timothy Edwards and became the mother of Jonathan.

Rarely has a minister acquired such standing and power as Solomon Stoddard did in the Connecticut Valley. He had immense ability and self-confidence. So widespread a network of family relationships grew out of his marriage and the marriages of his children and grandchildren that the result was a virtually tribal, ecclesiastical, social and economic domination over western Massachusetts and northern Connecticut.

In part through this family connection, Jonathan was to gain the best pulpit in New England, and in part through it he was also eventually to lose the same pulpit.

Solomon Stoddard's wife, Jonathan's grandmother, was no whit inferior to her husband. In fact, some considered her his superior. In her long life of ninety-six years, she acquired a tremendous reputation for learning, intelligence, vigor, determination and godliness. So, on his mother's side, no baby could have had a better heritage than Jonathan. Her family was distinguished. She herself was strong, tender, highly intellectual, capable, practical, of great dignity.

On his father's side, Jonathan's ancestry was somewhat different, in that it included an ancestral element that some have thought of as a taint, others as contributing to genius.

Richard Edwards, Jonathan's grandfather, married an Elizabeth Tuttle, mother of Timothy Edwards, Jonathan's father. And the hereditary "taint" was in Elizabeth Tuttle's family. For example: Elizabeth's brother killed her sister with an axe and was hanged for it. Another of Elizabeth's sisters killed her own son.

Elizabeth herself may have been unbalanced in some sense before she married Richard Edwards. Three months after their marriage in 1667, she named under oath, before two magistrates, the man, not Richard, whose child she was to bear. Nevertheless, he did not put her away for many years, even though she was periodically unfaithful, perverse, and given to threats of violence toward her husband.

Jonathan's father Timothy was Richard's first child by Elizabeth Tuttle. He was a witness to his mother's behavior. A long time later he and his sister Abigail were to testify under oath concerning her unwifely conduct and "unamicable carriage" toward her husband.

This testimony was given when Richard Edwards finally filed a petition for divorce from Elizabeth, after twenty-four years of marriage and six children. A petition for divorce was all but unheard of in the New England of the late 1600's. It was refused. Richard persisted. He made a second petition. It was also refused. He persisted. He asked that a committee of ministers be appointed to review his case. This time it was. His plea was heard and he was granted a divorce on scriptural grounds.

Probably Elizabeth Tuttle carried into the Edwards line some actual genetic peculiarity which showed itself as an "erratic" tendency. It appeared in one of Timothy's daughters, and in two of *her* daughters. It appeared in a son of Jonathan's, Pierrepont Edwards. It appeared in Aaron Burr, Jonathan's grandson. It appeared in another grandson. Whether this quality accounts Jonathan Edwards' peculiarly sensitive make-up is hard to say. His intellectual brilliance, no doubt, came from the Stoddard line.

Another character trait in Jonathan was earlier displayed in Richard Edwards' persistence in his intention to marry Elizabeth even after he knew she was several months pregnant by another man; in his persistence in staying married to her for more than a score of years in spite of her flagrant infidelity and "unamicability"; and in his persistence in seeking a divorce once he made up his mind.

This fundamental element of character was a sort of stubborn self-righteousness. It was coupled with a marked insensitivity for the feelings of others and with a lack of respect for the opinion of anyone but himself. Contradictorily, it was also coupled with deep feelings of remorse over what someone else might consider trivial; and, in general, with deep feelings over "things of a spiritual nature." Over such "spiritual" things he could weep easily. He could be overwhelmed with remorse for sleeping during a sermon.

Yet Richard had no hesitation at all in telling other men their faults in the plainest, bluntest language. Once he had made up his mind, nothing could deter him, certainly not the contrary opinion of others.

Richard's son Timothy inherited some of his father's self-righteousness and inability to understand the feelings of those whose views differed from his. He had a picayune sort of perfectionism. As his biographer, Ola Winslow, wrote: "When he memorized his Sunday sermons he did so without the loss of a sentence; when he measured corn on Monday he did it to the last half-pint, 'made the negro sweep it up very clean,' and then measured the sweepings." He was a man of order in the most petty things. He made endless nonessential lists. "His tribute to his own father Richard Edwards ends with a list of seventeen mercies attending the manner of his death, separates his dying words into thirty-five items, works out six ways in which he glorified God at his death, and proceeds to supply numbered particulars under each."

One has a feeling that this attachment to order, to classification, to petty detail, was Timothy Edwards' refuge, his way of repressing deep painful anxieties caused by the pressures he had been placed under early in his life from a wild, erratic, often raging mother and a granitically determined father. Order was his security—painstaking pedestrianism, every step plotted, charted, listed, predictable.

Timothy married Esther Stoddard—a capable, solid, loving woman; some said more capable than he was. They were married on November 6, 1694, four months after Timothy had received his A.B. and M.A. degrees from Harvard. Eight days later they came to East Windsor. A house was built for the couple, the labor donated by the parishioners, the material by Timothy's father. According to tradition, it was the largest, best built, most elaborately appointed house in East Windsor—plain, the second story overhanging the first as was custom. Later, assorted lean-tos were added as the growth of the family dictated.

By his flock Timothy was respected though perhaps not much loved. He was considered learned. His sermons were considered not uneloquent, not unprogressive. He was energetic, loved life and living within his world of minutiae. But originality, independence, the wide sweep of thought and wonder, were not in him.

Nine years after she came to East Windsor Esther Stoddard Edwards gave birth to Jonathan.

THE SCHOOLING OF A PRODIGY

Jonathan's mother gave him love, discipline and care. His four older sisters, one may suppose, gave him the attention a boy may expect from four older sisters. His father gave him a restrained love, discipline, the fussy supervision of a worried mother hen, and much, much instruction.

One of the two ground-floor rooms in the parsonage was called the "parlour." Actually it was a schoolroom, lined on three sides with benches fastened to the wall. School was kept daily for Jonathan, his sisters and various village children—many of them cousins of Jonathan's, children of Abigail, his father's sister, who married Captain Thomas Stoughton.

The schooling was rigorous. It included Latin early, later Greek and Hebrew. It involved great stress on letter-perfect memorization, as we might expect from such a taskmaster as the Reverend Timothy Edwards. His concern for Jonathan is shown in a letter he sent to the boy's mother:

"I desire thee to take care y^t Jonathan dont loose w^t he hath Learned but y^t as he hath got ye accidence, & above two sides of *propria Quae moribus* by heart so y^t he keep what he hath got, I would therefore have him Say pretty often to ye girls; I would also have ye Girls keep what they have Learnt of ye Grammar, & get by heart as far as Jonathan had Learnt: he can help them to Read as far as he hath Learnt: and would have both him and them keep their writing, and therefore write much oftener than they did when I was at home. I have left Paper enough for them which they may use to ye End, only I would have you reserve enough for your own use in writing Letters, &c. I hope thou wil take Special care of Jonathan y^t he dont learn to be rude & naught &c of wch thee and I have Lately Discoursed."

And so forth, through the details of many injunctions: Don't let Jonathan go out into the woods with Tim. Don't let the children stand too close to Tim when he is cutting wood. Be careful the children are not scalded by "wort, whey, water." Do something about Mary's neck. Let Esther and Betty take their powders. Do something for Anne, who is weakly. Don't suckle little Jerusha too long. Take good care of my horse, who "Got a bad wound in Broth^r: Mathers pasture." Take good care of the money in my "Loose Papers" lest it and they be lost. Don't let the children fall in the river if they go across it to meeting. Don't let the cattle get into the orchard and damage the trees. Don't leave the barn open to the cattle. Manure the orchard. Don't let the flax be spoiled. Have a new rope put on the well pole.

All this in a single letter. But along with it, love—love for wife, for children, for God.

"Take care of thyself. The Lord Jesus Christ be with thy Spirit, my dear, and encourage thee to hope and trust in Him, and discover His love to thy soul to Whom I commit thee and all thine and mine, to whom remember my love. And tell my children that I would have them pray daily for their father, and for their own souls, and above all things to remember their Creator and seek after the Lord Jesus Christ now in the days of their youth. God be with you and bless you all. I am my dear, ever thine in the dearest love and affection."

So Timothy Edwards to his wife Esther, concerning his seven-year-old son Jonathan and Jonathan's many sisters.

Precocious as he was, daily stuffed craw-full with learning, one boy in a family of girls, the object of never-ending fatherly adjuration and attention, we might expect Jonathan to be somewhat solitary, somewhat withdrawn, somewhat serious. And so he was.

He had other boys as companions—there were about a hundred houses in the village, and his aunt Abigail near by had seven boys of various ages—but one does not feel that his relations with any of them were very close. In fact, until he reached his early twenties there is no indication that he was really close with any male of his own age.

Not unsurprisingly, at times he was preoccupied with religion. As he wrote many years later:

"I had a variety of concerns and exercises about my soul from my childhood. . . . The first time was when I was a boy, some years before I went to college, at a time of remarkable awakening in my father's congregation, I was then very much affected for many months, and concerned about the things of religion, and my soul's salvation; and was abundant in duties.

"I used to pray five times a day in secret, and to spend much time in religious talk with other boys; and used to meet with them to pray together. I experienced I know not what kind of delight in religion. . . . I with some of my schoolmates joined together and built a booth in a swamp, in a very retired spot, for a place of prayer. And besides, I had particular secret places of my own in the woods, where I used to retire by myself and was from time to time much affected."

But this first religious experience was not enough to relieve him from fear. He still was "uncommonly terrified with thundred, and . . . struck with terror" when he saw a storm rising.

Solitariness coupled with an extraordinary acuteness of observation and curiosity, plus his father's pressure to write, led to his first serious literary composition.

It was probably written in 1715 or 1716, when he was twelve, as the result of a request by an English friend of his father's for information about American spiders. Titled *"Of Insects,"* it is the kind of production which would lead a proud parent of today to believe he had a future scientist on his hands. Benjamin Silliman, early nineteenth-century chemist and geologist, professor at Yale, wrote of Jonathan's essay in the *American Journal of Science and Arts* that the subject "examined, sagaciously . . . , by the philosophical child, remains nearly as he left it." Be this as it may, it is certainly true that we have no better record by any American observer of spiders for a century or so.

Jonathan began by defining and classifying his subject: "These spiders for the present shall be distinguished into those that keep in houses and those that keep in forests upon trees, bushes, shrubs, &c, and those that keep in roten logs for I take em to be very different kinds and natures; there are also other sorts some of which keep in rotten logs, hollow trees, swamps and grass."

He observed: "Nor can any one go out amongst the trees in a dewey morning towards the latter end of August or at the beginning of September but that he shall see hundreds of webbs made conspicuous by the dew that is lodged upon them reaching from one tree & shrub to another that stand at a considerable distance. And they may be seen well enough by an observing eye at noon day by their glistening against the sun; and what is still more wonderfull: I know I have severall times seen in a very calm and serene day at that time of year, standing behind some opake body that shall just hide the disk of the sun and keep off his dazzling rays from my eye and looking close by the side of it, multitudes of little shining webs and glistening strings of a great length and at such a height as that one would think that they were tacked to the sky by one end . . ."

He experimented to see if he could solve the mystery of their web-making: "I plainly perceived a web out from his tail a good way into the air. I took hold of it with my hand and broke it off, . . . but then I perceived another such a string to proceed out of his tail. I now conceived that I had found out the whole mystery." As Jonathan interpreted it, the web is "so exceedingly rare when it first comes from the spider as to be lighter than the air, so as of itself it will ascend in it." And as to the manner of forming the web: "In all probability the web while it is in the spider is a certain liquor with which that great bottle tail of theirs is filled, which immediately upon its being exposed to the air turns to a dry substance and very much rarefies." But if this were so, Jonathan thought a "small drop" ought to be exuded by the spider, and this he could not observe.

Finally, Jonathan drew some necessary moralistic conclusions on his observations as he had been taught to do by his father. These moralizings he placed toward the end of his essay as "Corollaries."

"Coroll: Hence also we may behold and admire at the wisdom of the Creator and be convinced from Providence there is exercised about such little things, in this wonderful contrivance of annually carrying of and burying the corrupting nauseousness of our air, of which flying insects are little collections in the bottom of Ocean where it will do no harm . . .

"Coroll. 2: Admire also the Creator in so nicely and mathematically adjusting their multiplying nature that notwithstanding their destruction by this means and the multitudes that are eaten by birds, that they do not decrease . . ." *

There is no question from this essay and one he wrote perhaps a little later about rainbows that he had the native capability of a scientist. With encouragement, in another environment, he might have been—scientifically, at least—another Benjamin Franklin. But as he himself observed many years later in that private account now called *Images or Shadows of Divine Things*: "Young twigs are easily bent and made to grow another way, old trees most difficultly. So persons in youth are more easily turned than others." In *Images*, the adult Jonathan drew the conclusion "So it is more easy to forsake sin in the beginning than after a long continuance in it."

---

* Spelling and punctuation slightly modernized here and elsewhere.

And the young Jonathan Edwards, the twig, was being sys-
tematically and intensively bent by his father into becoming a
minister. The twig bending had begun almost at Jonathan's
birth. It was to continue, a steady, strong, unintermitting pressure, all through his formative years.

Both of Jonathan's parents gave him love. Yet revolt developed deep in his soul, although he was scarcely conscious of it.
In time it spilled out in his preaching and set a new pattern of
orthodox theology. In his college years, Jonathan demonstrated
his independence of thought in an essay dealing with the nature
of the soul. In this early composition he showed his ability to
reduce opposing arguments to absurdity. It was the beginning,
too, of his penchant for polemics.

YALE: UNSETTLING PHILOSOPHY

Jonathan entered Yale in the fall of 1716, when he was not
quite thirteen. He was a member of a freshman class of ten boys.
At this time Yale was in a "broken and tottering State," as one
of its historians wrote. Some of its students went to school in
Saybrook, some in Weathersfield, some in New Haven.

Apparently Jonathan's class assembled at New Haven. Two
weeks later they moved to Weathersfield, only ten miles from
his home, where they studied under Jonathan's cousin, Elisha
Williams. In October 1718, Jonathan took his residence in the
new college building at New Haven; but a month later all the
class but one returned to Weathersfield. Finally, in June of
1719, the whole college reassembled at New Haven and remained there. In 1720 Jonathan graduated, valedictorian of his
class.

Jonathan was absorbed in the conventional studies of a future
divine: Latin, Greek, Hebrew, geometry, rhetoric, logic, Bible
studies, capped finally by a sort of organized classification of all

learning called the "technologia," taught as "arguments" rather than a compendium of information.

For this, Jonathan was well prepared. In fact, if only through his father's example, his bent was toward classifying, listing, arranging. But in 1717, while he was still at Weathersfield, he was introduced to the work of John Locke in the form of *An Essay Concerning Human Understanding*. The importance of Jonathan Edwards' introduction to Locke can hardly be overestimated. Locke revolutionized his thinking and his life.

Locke demolished the "technologia" for Jonathan. Instead, Locke advanced the idea that the knowledge obtained by every individual is the product of sensory experience. Yet sense experience is not direct knowledge of the world as it is, Locke declared. The senses provide the mind with ideas.

To fourteen-year-old Jonathan Edwards, from whom had come the skeptical mockery of the little essay on souls, the effect of Locke was that of the lifting of an immense burden. As to ideas, "everyone is conscious of them in himself." The mind knows no more than its own ideas. And the great source of them depends upon our sense. This source he called *sensation*. In Perry Miller's words, "Hence Edwards' thought cohered firmly about the basic certainty that God does not impart ideas or obligations outside sense experience. He does not rend the fabric of nature or break the connection between experience and behavior. The universe is all of a piece, and in it God works upon man through the daily shock of sensation."

With this discovery, Jonathan Edwards rejected Puritan scholasticism.

What had he rejected? Or more accurately, what was he in position to examine afresh?

There was the doctrine that men were innately sinful. That God would raise some men out of this state by "grace," and that He would out of His pleasure give grace to certain men and not others. Certain souls were predestined for heaven, others, it would appear, to hell. God being omniscient and omnipotent, no other conclusion was possible, granting the other foundations of Christianity as it had grown up into Protestantism.

But Puritan theologians had worked out an addition to Calvinism that was virtually a doctrine in itself, the "Covenant," or "Federal," theology. The substance of it was that after Adam's fall, God decided of His own free will to make an agreement with men, stating certain terms of salvation which He agreed to abide by. Under these terms, a man might have a fair idea of his standing with God. In this covenant God agreed to go more or less along with human conceptions of justice and right, although naturally He always retained His sovereign right to shed His grace as He pleased. The support for both these doctrines was Scripture as interpreted in certain ways to make it consistent and rational.

So far as standards for admitting individuals into membership in Congregational churches was concerned, certain difficulties made themselves evident. Obviously, full church membership, with all its privileges and responsibilities, ought to be extended only to those who were saved, whose salvation was insured through God's grace. But how was one to know?

The old Congregational principle had been to admit only those who were able to give a profession of their faith. They could not partake of the Lord's Supper unless they could give evidence of their conversion.

As the population increased, as more and more people entered New England who did not feel this certainty, and still more who did not even care, the power and authority of Puritan ministers and churches professing this doctrine began to decline. Here and there ministers raised objections to the doctrine of the innate sinfulness of man and that he was under condemnation. Here and there they offered arguments to show that man does have some free will in all his affairs, including that of the choice of salvation.

At first the churches of New England had combined in one institution all social functions: priestly functions, handing down of civil and criminal law, prophecy, and even in a real sense the exertion of police power. But beginning at about the time of Jonathan's birth, civil government began freeing itself from the church. Public welfare, law, and punishment became matters for the state, for lawyers, judges and policemen. To the clergy, civil government seemed much too lenient. It allowed too many liberties. So, "during the opening decades of the eighteenth century we find the clergy engrossed with the task of making people good." They became essentially moral reformers.

In this situation, the standards for admission to full church membership became a difficult problem. Insisting on the old profession of faith and credible evidence of conversion might keep the churches pure, but it might also keep them small.

There had already been a compromise. Originally, those who could not or would not give a credible account of conversion had been completely barred from church membership. But they wanted their children baptized, as they had been, if only to allay a lingering fear that a child might otherwise be condemned to hell by Original Sin. So, in 1662, a sort of conditional membership was created, a "Half-Way Covenant," to serve such purposes.

Now Jonathan's grandfather Solomon Stoddard, wise, practical and bold, came forth with a solution that went further. He opened church membership and communion to everyone except the "openly scandalous." He declared the communion to be a "converting ordinance," as one of the means of salvation. But the elders, not the congregation, should rule the church. Furthermore, he began to organize regional associations of churches which were to control discipline and the choice of ministers. The whole was Presbyterian rather than Congregational. The Massachusetts government would not countenance it.

But Stoddard had power in the Connecticut Valley through

his many connections. He went ahead to establish the Hampshire Association of Valley churches. In 1705, when his grandson Jonathan was only a baby, Connecticut gave legal blessing to the scheme, as the famous *Saybrook Platform*. The change was to have immense significance for Jonathan Edwards when he occupied his grandfather's pulpit in Northampton later.

The creed itself was supported by a kind of scholasticism. John Locke had freed Jonathan from that scholasticism. He might still believe that God was omnipotent and omniscient, that man was inherently sinful and damnable, that God had predestined only certain ones to receive His grace and His salvation —but the line of supporting reasoning would have to be different.

Within the same years that Jonathan encountered John Locke's *Essay Concerning Human Understanding,* he also encountered Isaac Newton's discoveries, in the form of the *Opticks* and *Principia*.

Newton presented Jonathan with the concept of a universe operating according to laws which can be expressed mathematically. It was a universe of motion and forces, in which every particle attracted every other particle with a force proportional to the sum of their masses and inversely proportional to the square of their distance from each other. Although the equation was workable for only two bodies, presumably the principle held good everywhere. It was a universe in which a body would proceed without deviation in the direction and speed in which it was going unless deflected by some other body or some other force: the new direction being the mathematical resultant of these forces. It was a universe in which the circling of earth and planets about the sun, the fall of a leaf to the earth, and the trajectory of a musket ball were operations of the same law, expressible in the same mathematical formula.

If this were so, Jonathan had to reconsider his ideas about God in the light of the new knowledge. Obviously a God who operated in this way was not a God of whim, whatever else He was. And God was larger, in a sense, than before. And less a person, less like a human being. One had almost a tendency to think of God as "It." And so, *What* or *Who* was God? And how reconcile this God with the God of the Scripture, if Scripture were literal fact?

Perhaps it is not surprising that Jonathan was rather solitary and withdrawn. He was attempting to carry very heavy intellectual freight. But, although he was wrestling with intellectually revolutionary material, this in itself did not account for his holding himself apart. His temperament did that. He had shot up in size—to a weedy six feet plus an inch by the time he reached adulthood. He also was college butler. It was an honor, but portioning out food at one end of the college hall at mealtimes did not bring him closer to the other boys.

And, besides, there was that something in him of his father's and his grandfather's self-righteousness, their lack of tolerance and tact. A minor disagreement with his roommate and cousin, Elisha Mix, led, not to his settling the difference with his cousin, but to a detailed description of his grievances to his father. Timothy Edwards promptly wrote to Elisha's father also, detailing not only Jonathan's grievances but adding some criticisms of his own of nearly everybody in the Mix family.

This characteristic of the Edwards men did not endear Jonathan to his fellow students at Yale. Even when he was not personally involved, he could not help telling others in what respects he found them to blame. He was to reap trouble from it later, for, as Ola Winslow remarks, "Throughout his life he showed the same curious blindness, making no allowance for human resentment of criticism, and continuing to act as if it did not exist."

It is no wonder he made no lifelong friends from his early years. But he had already found his world. It was a world of thought, of ideas, rather than a world of men.

And in that world, he had plenty to do. He was now involved with the theology in which he had been indoctrinated since infancy, with the revolutionary ideas of Locke in the realm of psychology, and with the equally revolutionary ideas of Newton in the realm of nature. And no one knew better than Jonathan Edwards that all three were the same realm. He would have to choose and reject, or to reconcile, or to synthesize. This would be his task for the rest of his life.

Meanwhile, he began the making of notes: on ideas, on the mind, on physics.

A MYSTICAL SOLUTION

Fortunately, something else happened to Jonathan that spared him the inner emotional pain that might have been brought about by the necessity of choosing among, reconciling, or intellectually synthesizing Locke, Newton, and the Calvinist interpretation of Scripture. It might be called a dissolving of the problem.

This was his conversion. It was partly religious, partly spiritual, partly mystical. Apparently it happened when he was seventeen years old. By then, he had graduated from Yale and was in his second year of graduate study in theology. Years later he told about it in his *Personal Narrative:*

"From my childhood up, my mind had been full of objections against the doctrine of God's sovereignty in choosing whom he would to eternal life, and rejecting whom he pleased; leaving them eternally to perish, and be everlastingly tormented in hell. It used to appear like a horrible doctrine to me. But I remember the time very well, when I seemed to be convinced, and fully satisfied, as to this sovereignty of God, and in his justice in thus eternally disposing of men, according to his sovereign pleasure. But never could give an account, how, or by what means, I was thus convinced, not in the least imagining at the time, nor a long time after, that there was an extraordinary influence of God's

Spirit in it; but only that now I saw further, and my reason apprehended the justice and reasonableness of it. . . . And there has been a wonderful alternation in my mind, in respect to the doctrine of God's sovereignty, from that day to this; so that I scarce ever have found so much as the rising of an objection against it, in the most absolute sense, in God's shewing mercy to whom he will shew mercy, and hardening whom he will . . .

". . . But I have often, since that first conviction, had quite another sense of God's sovereignty than I had then. I have often had not only a conviction, but a delightful conviction. The doctrine has very often appeared exceeding pleasant, bright, and sweet.

". . . The first instance that I remember of that sort of inward, sweet delight in God and divine things that I have lived much in since, was on reading those words, I Tim. i.17. *Now unto the King eternal, immortal, invisible, the only wise God, be honor and glory for ever and ever, Amen.*

"As I read the words, there came into my soul, and was as it were diffused through it, a sense of the glory of the Divine Being; a new sense, quite different from any thing I ever experienced before. Never any words of scripture seemed to me as these words did. I thought with myself, how excellent a Being that was, and how happy I should be, if I might enjoy that God, and be rapt up to him in heaven, and be as it were swallowed up in him for ever! I kept saying, and as it were singing over these words of scripture to myself; and went to pray to God that I might enjoy him, and prayed in a manner quite different from what I used to do; with a new sort of affection.

"From about that time, I began to have a new kind of apprehensions and ideas of Christ, and the work of redemption, and the glorious way of salvation by him. An inward, sweet sense of these things, at times, came into my heart; and my soul was led away in pleasant views and contemplations of them.

". . . The whole book of Canticles used to be pleasant to me, and I used to be much in reading it . . . and found, from time to time, an inward sweetness, that would carry me away, in my contemplations. This I know not how to express otherwise, than by a calm, sweet abstraction of soul from all the concerns of this world; and sometimes a kind of vision . . . of being alone in the mountains, or some solitary wilderness, far from all mankind, sweetly conversing with Christ, and wrapt and swallowed up in God. The sense I had of divine things, would often of a sudden kindle up, as it were a sweet burning in my heart."

Jonathan discussed these things with his father, "and when the discourse was ended, I walked abroad alone, in a solitary place in my father's pasture, for contemplation. And as I was walking there, and looking up on the sky and clouds, there came into my mind so sweet a sense of the glorious *majesty* and *grace* of God, that I know not how to express. I seemed to see them both in a sweet conjunction; majesty and meekness joined together; it was a sweet, and gentle, and holy majesty; and also a majestic meekness; an awful sweetness; a high, and great, and holy gentleness.

"After this . . . God's excellency, his wisdom, his purity and love, seemed to appear in every thing; in the sun, moon, and stars; in the clouds, and blue sky; in the grass, flowers, trees; in the water, and all nature; which used greatly to fix my mind. I often used to sit and view the moon for continuance; and in the day, spent much time in viewing the clouds and sky, to behold the sweet glory of God in these things; in the mean time, singing forth, with a low voice my contemplations of the Creator and Redeemer . . .

"Before, I used to be uncommonly terrified with thunder . . . but now, on the contrary, it rejoiced me. I felt God, so to speak, at the first appearance of a thunder storm; and used to take the opportunity, at such times, to fix myself in order to view the clouds, and see the lightnings play, and hear the majestic and awful voice of God's thunder, which oftentimes was exceedingly entertaining, leading me to sweet contemplations of my great and glorious God. While thus engaged, it always seemed natural to me to sing, or chant for my meditations; or, to speak my thoughts in soliloquies with a singing voice."

Of all his experiences at Yale, this mystical religious experience was the most profound emotionally and spiritually, as the discovery of Locke and Newton had been the most profound intellectually. He was to devote the rest of his life attempting to fuse them with Scripture into one coherent whole.

Later in his life, some of his thought was to appear in his sermons. But this was, in a sense, teaching, couched in a traditional form, for auditors who must be considered for what they were in education, background and understanding. He did not tell them all that he thought.

More of his thought was to appear in various treatises, some of them published after his death. These were written to explain, to convince, and often in large part to demolish, the arguments of opponents. In this respect, the old family self-righteousness and tendency to criticize others showed itself.

But the heart of his thought, intended for himself alone and not for publication, he put in private writings. At different times, these took different forms. Some were essays, such as the brief *Of Being*, probably a college work and his first attempt to put his philosophy in writing. Some were writings on natural science, such as *Colours*. One was the lengthy essay known as *Notes on the Mind*. These were all works of his college days. Another was a series of thoughts he continued writing down all his life, the *Miscellanies*. He probably began the *Miscellanies* about 1722, when he was nineteen and preparing to begin his professional life. Another private work of later life was the collection of thoughts edited by Perry Miller and published under the title *Images or Shadows of Divine Things*.

In addition to these, he wrote down at intervals a series of *Resolutions*, the last of them when he was about twenty, and a

Diary, a record of feelings rather than events, in which he wrote sporadically until he was more than thirty.

The importance of these works, and especially the earliest, lies in the fact that Jonathan Edwards seems to have arrived at almost all his intellectual and philosophical conclusions by the time he began his lifelong career as a minister. Once he had formulated his basic conclusions in his early twenties he did not seem to change them. Instead, he spent the rest of his life elaborating them. Thus, instead of speaking of the progression of his thought over the years of his life, it is closer to fact to speak of its blooming or flowering. As a philosopher and theologian, he was formed almost all at once. In Perry Miller's words, "Edwards was not the sort who undergoes a long development or whose work can be divided into 'periods.' His whole insight was given him at once, preternaturally early, and he did not change: he only deepened."

Thus, during the decades of colonial change that resulted in the American Revolution and the establishment of a republic, Jonathan Edwards always remained to one side. It was almost as though he had congealed when he was twenty. Of the political, social and economic changes going on around him he had little comprehension and no approval at all.

Jonathan Edwards never revolted against his father's ideology. Possibly the fact that he had two or three long, severe illnesses during the time a revolt could be expected had something to do with it. During these periods he had a great deal of mothering and fathering, one supposes, and the result might have been a closer and in some ways a more dependent emotional attachment to his parents. We do know that he was very close to his father all his life. Timothy Edwards lived almost as long as his son Jonathan, and during all that time the father and son met regularly every few weeks.

The natural time for revolt would have come when Jonathan first encountered Locke and Newton. Although he was still an adolescent, he grasped their meaning instantly, as almost no one else in his time did. He himself wrote that this was at a time when he was "full of objections against the doctrine of God's sovereignty, in choosing whom he would to eternal life, and rejecting whom he pleased; leaving them to perish, and be everlastingly tormented in hell. It used to appear like a horrible doctrine to me."

Other contemporaries of Edwards, such as Timothy Cutler, rector of Yale, and two tutors and four ministers who had been exposed to the contents of the Dummer Library, were converted to heresy—from the Yale point of view—and went over to the Church of England. Naturally, Cutler and the tutors were dismissed from Yale. But Jonathan Edwards was not swayed from orthodoxy by the Cutler affair and the inquisition that followed. In fact, he may have been strengthened in it.

Not long before Cutler was dismissed, Jonathan had accepted the pastorate of a small Presbyterian church in New York and had gone there. But he certainly knew of the suspicions of Cutler's heresy before he left. He remained in New York less than a year. He was to return to Yale as a tutor in 1724, when he was nineteen. By this time, Yale's emphasis on orthodoxy had become extreme. As Ola Winslow writes:

". . . orthodoxy consisted in complete acceptance of the Saybrook Platform; heresy consisted in any variation therefrom, particularly in the direction of Arminian doctrine and prelatical church government as opposed to Congregationalism. In future all rectors and tutors would be obliged by trustee requirement to declare their orthodoxy in terms of these specifications, and upon the slightest suspicion of deviation therefrom they could be subjected to an examination."

Jonathan hesitated not at all to take this oath.

"For two more very important years in his intellectual development he lived in an atmosphere abnormally sensitive to the slightest breath of heresy, according to trustee definition, walked

an orthodox chalk line in all his thinking, took the responsibility
for buttressing younger minds against any skeptical leanings, and
consciously strove to remove the blot from the college escutch-
eon. What is more important to an understanding of his later
career than even the strengthening of his own allegiance to
'sound doctrine' is that these experiences also developed in him
a protective attitude toward the cause he espoused, with the result that henceforth throughout his life he did not so much proclaim the doctrine as defend it."

But he was an intellectual, a thinker. He had been exposed to
Locke and Newton at a receptive age. His sharp intelligence
could not simply ignore the new ideas. To escape inner pain, he
had somehow to make an acceptable synthesis of the old ideas
and the new. The conversion, with all its relief, its good feelings,
was, one suspects, the emotional and spiritual signal that the
synthesis had been successful.

"The delights which I now felt in the things of religion were
of an exceedingly different kind from those . . . that I had as a
boy; and what I then had no more notion of, than one born
blind has of pleasant and beautiful colours. They were of a more
inward, pure, soul animating and refreshing nature.

"My sense of divine things seemed gradually to increase, until
I went to preach at New York, which was about a year and a
half after they began; and while I was there, I felt them, very
sensibly, in a much higher degree than I had done before . . . I
used to be continually examining myself, and studying and contriving for likely ways and means, how I should live holily, with
far greater diligence and earnestness, than ever I pursued any
thing in my life; but yet with too great dependence on my own
strength; which afterwards proved a great damage to me.

"My experience had not yet taught me, as it has done since,
my extreme feebleness and impotence, every manner of way;
and the bottomless depths of secret corruption and deceit there
was in my own heart."

The synthesis succeeded, but perhaps not completely. One wonders whether there could have been something precarious about it. For, when all his life he attacked contrary views as a means of defending his own, he gave proportionately less space to the presentation of his own as a result. He consciously had two lives of thought: an inner and an outer. As he wrote in his *Diary* on Friday, January 10, 1724, after a passage in the shorthand he used at times: "Remember to act according to Prov. xii. 23, A prudent man *concealeth* knowledge."

GOD AND GOD'S PURPOSE

What was Jonathan Edwards' philosophy at the time he left Yale for good? What were his views?

Intellectually he was a thoroughgoing rationalist. Emotionally and spiritually he was a mystic, suffused with a love for God and the wonder of God's love.

The first question he dealt with in *Of Being* was the basic one of the nature of the universe, using the term in its very broadest sense; and of its causation.

He began with the assumption "That there should be nothing at all is utterly impossible. . . . So that we see it is necessary some being should be. . . . And it is self-evident that there can be nothing in one place as well as in another; and so, if there can be in one there can be in all. So that we see this necessary eternal being must be infinite and omnipresent.

"This infinite and omnipresent being cannot be solid. . . . For solidity is nothing but resistance to other solidities. Space is this necessary, eternal, infinite and omnipresent being. . . . But I had as good speak plain. I have already said as much as that space is God. And it is indeed clear to me that all the space there is, not proper to body, all the space there is without the bounds of the creation, all the space there was before the creation, is God Himself."

Then, how about being, existence, matter?

"Neither can there be any such thing without consciousness. How is it possible that there should something be from all eternity and there be no consciousness of it? It will appear very plain to everyone that intensely considers of it that consciousness and being are the same thing exactly. And how doth it grate upon the mind to think that something should be from all eternity and nothing at all be conscious of it? . . . Let us suppose, for illustration, this impossibility, that all the spirits in the universe be for a time deprived of their consciousness, and God's consciousness at the same time be intermitted. I say the universe for that time would cease to be, of itself; and not only, as we speak, the Almighty could not attend to uphold the world, but because God knew nothing of it."

By deduction Edwards came to the conclusion that *being* was *idea,* or *consciousness* of *idea.* He also reasoned that "the exercising of the infinite power of God is necessary to keep the parts of atoms together . . . and it follows the constant exercise of the infinite power of God is necessary to preserve bodies in being." To Edwards, the world was a real world. He did not attempt to deny objective existence or the laws of nature even though he had come to the conclusion "there is no proper substance but God himself."

By employing the reasoning of Locke and the laws and facts of Newton, the young minister had developed a basic concept that harmonized with orthodoxy. His universe was one of causality, with God—a personal God—being Ultimate Cause. "How impossible it is," he reasoned, "that the world should exist from Eternity, without a Mind."

Edwards also asked himself, what are the purposes of God? He went into this in a discussion of "Excellency" because "There has nothing been more without a definition than Excellency; although it be what we are more concerned with, than anything else whatsoever; here, we are concerned with nothing else."

After considering it as harmony, symmetry and proportion, and then "similarliness of direction," he finally arrived at "The Consent of Being to Being, or Being's Consent to Entity." And among "spirits"—meaning sentient beings—excellence "is in its prime and proper sense, Being's consent to Being. There is no other proper consent but that of *Minds*, even of their Will; which, when it is of Minds toward Minds, it is *Love*, and when of minds towards other things, it is *Choice*. Wherefore all the Primary and Original beauty or excellence that is among Minds, is Love . . .

"As to the proportion of this love—to greater spirits, more and to less, less—it is beautiful, as it is a manifestation of love to Spirit or Being in general . . .

"Seeing God has so plainly revealed Himself to us; and other minds are made in His image and are emanations from Him, we may judge what is the excellence of other minds by what is His, which we have shown is Love. His infinite beauty is His infinite mutual love of Himself. Now God is the prime and original being, the first and last, and the pattern of all and has the sum of all perfection. We may therefore, doubtless, conclude that all that is the perfection of spirits may be resolved into that which is God's perfection, which is love.

"Wherefore all Virtue, which is the Excellency of minds, is resolved into *Love to Being;* and nothing is virtuous or beautiful in Spirits, any otherwise than as it is an exercise, or fruit, or manifestation, of this love; and nothing is sinful or deformed in Spirits, but as it is the defect of, or contrary to, these."

Not only that, but— "As to God's excellence, it is evident it consists in the love of Himself, for He was as excellent before He created the universe as He is now. But if the excellence of spirits consists in their disposition and action, God could be excelled no other way at that time, for all the exertions of Himself were towards Himself.

". . . 'tis peculiar to God that He has beauty within Himself (consisting in being's consenting with His own being, or the love of Himself in His own Holy Spirit), whereas the excellence of others is in loving others, in loving God, and in the communications of His Spirit. . . . And if we take notice when we are in the best frames, meditating in divine excellence, our idea of that tranquility and peace which seems to be overspread and cast abroad upon the whole earth and universe naturally dissolves itself into the idea of a general love and delight everywhere diffused."

Thus Edwards was able to fit his feelings, the product of his conversion, into the entire structure.

"The secret," he was convinced, "is the infinitely exact, and precise, and perfectly stable Idea, in God's mind, together with his stable Will, that the same shall gradually be communicated to us, and to other minds, according to certain fixed and exact established Methods and Laws." Not only was his mysticism an integral part; but with God being the world, the universe, Substance, and Idea, Newton's difficulty in explaining how a force such as gravity could operate across space disappeared, and Locke's concept of a somewhat impersonal God as a First Cause or First Mover, or First Creator, simply vanished into God as everything spatial and everything sentient.

How free is our will?

With this foundation laid, Edwards was ready to approach the difficult problem of man's free will—particularly man's freedom to sin—and God's justice in condemning unsaved sinners to hell. The subject was to absorb him all his life. One of the products some thirty years later was his great book *Freedom of the Will*, of which Perry Miller writes: "Beyond all peradventure, the *Freedom of the Will* is the cornerstone of Edwards' fame; it is his most sustained intellectual achievement, the most powerful piece of sheer forensic argumentation in American literature. It became the Bible of the New England theology, and is considered by logicians one of the few proofs in which the conclusion follows inescapably and infallibly from the premises."

This is true. Yet it is also true that Edwards had worked out the elements as a young man at Yale. The problem was of surpassing importance. For, of all doctrines, that of "Arminianism" was most anathema to orthodox Calvinist theologians.

Jacobus Arminius had been a sixteenth-century Dutch theologian who founded the anti-Calvinist school in Reformed theology. He had pointed out that if God is entirely omniscient and omnipotent, He not only foresees but decides who will sin and be damned, and who will receive grace and be saved. Thus, to Arminius, if the Calvinist view were correct, God had played a rather dirty trick on mankind. In a sense, He created some human beings merely in order to damn them.

The Calvinist position, of course, lay in the statement that "In Adam's fall, we sinned all." All mankind was born with original sin, from Adam's disobedience. Hence all mankind was inherently sinful and under condemnation. Hence men could only be spared punishment by pardon as grace. To Arminians, this meant that God was the author of sin, unless some way could be found to get Him off the hook. And this way was to suppose that God gave man, in creating him, a certain amount of genuine free will, or liberty, to decide for himself. Otherwise, to Arminius, God became a sort of monster.

The tendency of the times in New England and the Colonies was in the Arminian direction. Predestination, to many sincere people, took away any incentive to be moral, to try to do better, to seek salvation. What was the use? God had already decided the issue. So, in a sense, the old Calvinist view, some felt, encouraged immorality or at least laxity in doing good works.

They did not feel this was what a good God meant. He *wanted* men to do better, to be better—and so He had implanted in them liberty, or freedom, of will at least to wish or will to be saved.

Then, if they were sinful, the sin was a free choice, and they were damnable. But they also had freedom to choose salvation.

The Covenant, or Federal, Theology had avoided this problem somewhat. God retained free arbitrary choice of whom He would give grace and whom He would damn, but He had made a compact with men. In the early seventeenth century, in the enthusiasm of trying to make a theocracy in New England, the legalism of this point of view was not so evident as it had become by Edwards' day. He met the problem head on.

First of all, he asserted "that nothing ever comes to pass without a Cause." And there was no more reason "to suppose that an act of the Will should come into existence without a Cause" than "to suppose the human soul, or an angel, or the globe of the whole universe, should come into existence without a Cause." (By "will" he meant also preference and desire and approving, liking, embracing, determining, directing, inclining toward and being pleased with—a will somewhat passive.)

What determines the will? The mind's understanding of what is the goodness, or the agreeableness, of the objects considered determines the will. But the will does not determine itself.

"For if the determination of the Will, evermore, in this manner, follows the light, conviction and view of the Understanding, concerning the greatest good and evil, and this be that alone which moves the Will, and it be a contradiction to speak otherwise; then it is necessarily so, the Will necessarily follows this light or view of the Understanding, and not only in some of its acts, but in every act of choosing and refusing. So that the Will does not determine itself in any one of its own acts, but all its acts, every act and choice and refusal depends on, and is necessarily connected with some antecedent cause; which cause is not the Will itself, nor any act of its own, nor any thing pertaining to that faculty, but something belonging to another faculty, whose acts go before the Will, in all its acts, and govern and determine them."

So . . . a man can do what he wills, but he cannot *will* what he will will. And *this* was freedom, or liberty: "this *liberty,* that I *can* do if I *will.*"

And this, Edwards felt, was the highest liberty conceivable. "No one can rise higher in his conceptions of liberty, than the notion of it which I have explained: which notion is apparently, perfectly consistent with the whole of that necessity of men's actions, which I suppose takes place . . ."

Or, as Locke had written: "How can we think any one freer than to have the power to do what he will?"

And, since something other than a person's will determines what he wills, then what he wills, traced back through all its antecedents, is caused by God. Edwards faced this conclusion squarely in *Freedom of the Will:*

". . . if by 'the author of sin,' is meant the permitter, or not a hinderer of sin; and at the same time, a disposer of the state of events, in such a manner, for wide, holy, and most excellent ends and purposes, that sin, if it be permitted or not hindered, will most certainly and infallibly follow: I say, if this be all that is meant, by being the author of sin, I don't deny that God is the author of sin (although I dislike and reject the phrase, as that which by use and custom is apt to carry another sense), it is no reproach for the most High to be the author of sin. This is not to be the *actor* of sin, but on the contrary, of *holiness.* What God doth herein, is holy; and a glorious exercise of the infinite excellency of his nature. And I don't deny, that God's being thus the author of sin, follows from what I have laid down . . ."

But, he asserted, the same conclusion follows from Arminian doctrines, if God's omnipotence and foreknowledge are admitted. "That it is most certainly so, that God is in such a manner the disposer and orderer of sin, is evident, if any credit is to be given to the Scripture; as well as because it is impossible in the nature of things to be otherwise."

The distinction is that, "If by 'the author of sin,' be meant the sinner, the agent, or actor of sin, or the *doer* of a wicked thing; so it would be a reproach and blasphemy to suppose God to be the author of sin. In this sense, I utterly deny God to be the author of sin; rejecting such an imputation on the most High, as what is infinitely to be abhorred; and deny any such thing to be the consequence of what I have laid down."

What God had done, so to speak, was to create Adam, the progenitor of the human race, with two kinds of principles planted in him. "There was an *inferior* kind, which may be called natural, being the principles of mere human nature; such as self-love, with those natural appetites and passions, which belong to the *nature of man* in which his love to his own liberty, honor, and pleasure, were exercised: these, when alone and left to themselves, are what the Scriptures sometimes call *flesh*. Besides these, there were *superior* principles, that were spiritual, holy, and divine, summarily comprehended in divine love . . . which are called in Scripture the *divine nature*." These are "supernatural" as above "mere human nature" and "depend on man's union and communication with God." Without them, man would still have man's human nature.

The "superior principles were given to . . . maintain an absolute dominion in the heart. . . . And while things continued thus, all things were in excellent order, peace and beautiful harmony . . ."

But, "When man sinned, and broke God's covenant, and fell under His curse, these superior principles left his heart." ". . . So light ceases in a room when the candle is withdrawn; and thus man was left in a state of darkness, woeful corruption and ruin; nothing but flesh without spirit."

So the inferior principles came to rule "self-love, and natural appetite" . . . the "immediate consequence of which was a *fatal catastrophe*. . . . Man immediately set up *himself* and the objects of his private affections and appetites, as supreme; and so they took the place of God"—like fire in a house, they had been a good servant; now they were a bad master.

"Thus it is easy to give an account, of how total corruption of heart should follow on man's eating the forbidden fruit, though that was but one act of sin, *without God's putting* any evil into his heart, or *implanting* any corrupt taint, and so becoming the *author* of depravity. Only *God's withdrawing*, as it was highly proper and necessary that he should, from rebel man, being as it were driven away by his abominable wickedness, and men's *natural* principles being *left to themselves*, this is sufficient . . ."

But why should we, his successors, be deemed sinful, with the original sin?

Because ". . . as Adam's nature became corrupt without God's implanting or infusing any evil thing into his nature; so does the nature of his posterity. God dealing with Adam as the head of his posterity (as has been shown) and treating them as one, he deals with his posterity as having *all sinned in him.* . . . Whereby they come into the world mere *flesh*, and entirely under the government of natural and inferior principles; and so become wholly corrupt, as Adam did."

At times it seemed a gloomy philosophy to Edwards. His private writings are full of self-blame; of consciousness of sin or guilt; of resolutions to pray to be allowed to do better.

Yet his philosophy and theology were intensely realistic. Like his predecessors, he recognized frankly and took into full account the inborn unpretty characteristics of man: his hostilities, his limitations, his beastliness, his selfishness. The Puritans had accounted for these, as did Jonathan Edwards, as a heritage from Adam, a product of original sin, hence innate total depravity.

Later generations as well as his own were to emphasize rather man's good impulses, his perfectibility, his desire to achieve something better. They had a tendency to gloss over the ugly.

We of the middle twentieth century, after two World Wars,

the sadistic extermination of many millions of Jews and other innocent people, the bombs of Hiroshima and Nagasaki, are better able to accept Jonathan Edwards' insistence on the innate depravity of man than the nineteenth century was. That century's mechanistic, simplistic view of inevitable progress and improvement we now see as a limited reading of the facts.

Even the most skeptical of us must agree that in some fundamental sense man's will is *not* free, that thought and will are products as well as producers, links in a complex web that goes out and out and through and through, and back and back, to that Being which is Space, which is Idea, which is Cause, to Whom we give the name God.

To some, the full acceptance of this concept brings joy as it did to Jonathan Edwards—the mystical ecstasy of faith in oneness with God.

And, in Edwards' case, another kind of joy—a fierce joy that he had forged the sharpest, strongest weapons any man ever had for confounding the Arminians, the Deists, the unbelievers, the slack, the hypocrites, the self-satisfied, the merely ignorant. And as weapons will, they were to turn against him.

All these ideas were formed within the ten-year period of Edwards' connection with Yale. His philosophy and theology were fully established by the time he was twenty-two or twenty-three.

We know what his mind was doing during this ten-year period. What was his body doing? He continued studying theology at Yale for the two years after his graduation in 1716. In this period he was converted. It was then that he accepted God as a God of damnation as well as of salvation.

It was during 1722 that the heresy of the rector, Cutler, and the two tutors began to be suspected, and they were discharged the following month.

But by this time Jonathan Edwards was in New York City. He had been called in August of 1722 by a small Scotch Pres-

byterian congregation, a group which had seceded from the first
Presbyterian church and met in a building on William Street between Liberty and Wall. He pleased the congregation but they
were too small to support a minister, and in April of 1723 he
sadly sailed for home.

The experience had been good for him. New York was still a
village. He was still undergoing the religious experience that
had begun a year or so before, and "very frequently used to retire into a solitary place, on the banks of Hudson's River, at some
distance from the city, for contemplation on divine things and
secret converse with God."

Sensitive as he was then, full of tender feelings—and only
eighteen—he formed the first really warm intimate friendship
he had ever had, "where I lived, with Mr. John Smith, and his
pious mother. My heart was knit in affection to those, in whom
were appearances of true piety." This kind of sharing of feelings
was new to Edwards. Twenty years later he was still receiving
letters from John Smith.

He spent the summer of 1723 in East Windsor. Offered a
tutorship at Yale, he turned down a pastorate at Bolton. He
served as Tutor from May of 1724 until the summer of 1726—
two years, which were interrupted by a lengthy, almost fatal illness in late 1725. He had never been robust, but from now on
he was to suffer long illness nearly every year for the rest of
his life.

As Senior Tutor he was addressed as "Sir Edwards." There
was no rector after Cutler's leaving. The student body was en-
larging—from forty his first year to sixty his second. The work
was hard. He was not only a teacher but administrator. He and
his junior, "Sir Treat," handled all discipline except for the most
serious matters. In fact, Edwards was for all practical purposes
in charge of the college much of the time.

The trustees were more than satisfied. A vote in 1725 referred to their tutors' "Extraordinary Services" and added five

pounds to each one's salary. But efficient as he was, taught by his father to handle detail in orderly fashion, he was tired and dejected a good deal of the time.

September 26, 1726, he would write in his *Diary*:

" 'Tis just about three years, that I have been for the most part in a low, sunk estate and condition, miserably senseless to what I used to be, about spiritual things."

But events were already in the making which would result in his leaving Yale and taking the pastorate which he would occupy for the next quarter of a century.

NORTHAMPTON

"They say there is a young lady [in New Haven] who is beloved of that Great Being, who made and rules the world, and that there are certain seasons in which this Great Being, in some way or other invisible, comes to her and fills her mind with exceeding sweet delight, and that she hardly cares for any thing, except to meditate on him—that she expects after a while to be received up where he is, to be raised up out of the world and caught up into heaven; being assured that he loves her too well to let her remain at a distance from him always. There she is to dwell with him, and to be ravished with his love and delight forever. Therefore, if you present all the world before her, with the richest of its treasures, she disregards it and cares not for it, and is unmindful of any pain or affliction. She has a strange sweetness in her mind, and singular purity in her affections; is most just and conscientious in all her conduct; and you could not persuade her to do anything wrong or sinful, if you would give her all the world, lest she should offend this Great Being. She is of a wonderful sweetness, calmness and universal benevolence of mind; especially after the Great God has manifested himself to her mind. She will sometimes go about from place to place, singing sweetly; and seems to be always full of joy and pleasure; and no one knows for what. She loves to be alone, walking in the fields and groves, and seems to have someone invisible always conversing with her."

The name of the young lady in New Haven who was always singing sweetly and full of joy and pleasure was Sarah Pierrepont. Legend has it that this paean of praise was written about her when she was thirteen. The writer, Jonathan Edwards, was then twenty. The year was 1723. He had just returned from New York and is supposed to have written it upon a blank page in a book he was reading. Probably more people have read this encomium than anything else Jonathan Edwards ever wrote except the famous sermon known as "Sinners in the Hands of an Angry God."

Sarah was to become his wife, be mistress of his parsonage and bear him eleven children. She had every qualification for a minister's wife, the first being that she had been born in a parsonage.

Her ancestry was even more impressive than Jonathan's. She was born January 9, 1710, daughter of James Pierrepont and Mary Hooker. The Pierrepont family was of Norman descent. Her father had been born in America, graduated from Harvard, was said to have been the first person involved in the founding of Yale, and was the first minister in New Haven. Her mother was a granddaughter of Thomas Hooker, the great divine who had led the migration to the Connecticut Valley and founded Hartford.

Sarah had beauty and more worldly ease than Jonathan, "and for all her solitary walks and her piety," writes Ola Winslow, "was noted for her charm, her flashing wit, and a gay repartee of which her English cousin Lady Mary Wortley Montague, might have been justly envious."

But before Edwards could marry, he had to have a parsonage. Or, as one occasionally thinks about him, when he got a parsonage he had to woo someone to share it with him.

The parsonage was to be Northampton, that of his grandfather Solomon Stoddard. By 1725 Stoddard had occupied it more than half a century. He had built an ecclesiastical empire. From his capital he ruled Hadley, Hatfield, Springfield, Westfield, Long Meadow, Suffield and Deerfield. He was sometimes called "Pope" Stoddard. An autocrat of a sort, he changed the old Congregational requirements for church membership by offering church membership and communion to everyone who was not "openly scandalous." He justified dropping the old requirement that membership be limited to those who could give a profession of their faith, and communion to those giving evidence of conversion, by the argument that "All Ordinances are for the Saving good of those they are to be administered unto." Hence, communion became a "converting ordinance."

Stoddard had established an essentially Presbyterian power structure in his own church. The elders were to rule over it, not the rank and file, for "The community are not men of understanding." He ruled his church, and he ruled the Hampshire Association of churches. But now he was in his eighties, and knew that he needed help.

In April of 1725 a colleague pastor for him had been voted. In August of 1726 Jonathan Edwards was invited to preach. He seemed satisfactory. In November he was invited "to Settle." His salary was set at 100 pounds. He was given 300 pounds for a homestead, with which he bought a lot on King Street, where he made his home for so long as he lived in Northampton. He was also given two pasture lots totaling fifty acres. Several years later his salary was to be raised to 200 pounds.

Edwards was ordained at the beginning of 1727. Five months later, July 20, 1727, he married Sarah Pierrepont. He was almost twenty-four. Sarah was seventeen. But they were as well equipped for ministerial life as any two young people of their time could be. Both had grown up in parsonages, both had been destined, trained, prepared and indoctrinated for their roles.

Two years later, in February of 1729, Solomon Stoddard died.

Edwards was now in charge of one of the most important churches in New England—certainly in the Connecticut Valley, and by all odds the most important in Western Massachusetts. His position was secure. His congregation of some six hundred respected him and liked his sound doctrine. They liked Sarah. When he fell ill in 1729, they demonstrated their feelings by building him a large barn. By all indications, Jonathan and Sarah Edwards could look forward to a long, secure life in Northampton, like that of his grandfather Stoddard from whom he had, in a sense, inherited it.

George Washington was not yet born. He was not to be born until 1732, the year in which Sarah Edwards bore her third child. Sarah, the eldest child, was born in 1728; Jerusha, the second, in 1731; and Esther, the third, in 1732. Esther was to marry Aaron Burr, first President of Princeton. There were to be eight more children: Mary, Lucy, Timothy, Susannah, Eunice, Jonathan, Elizabeth and Pierrepont. Although the Indian menace had passed, Northampton still showed traces of the dangerous days. The two hundred houses of the town clustered around the fortlike church on top of Meeting House Hill. Remnants of the old trenches and earthworks encircling the settlement were still visible. The fertile fields along the Connecticut River provided food and were the economic reason for Northampton's existence. The river was the real highway to civilization downstream. Roads were horseback trails. Dense forest surrounded the cleared areas. In these were dangers: from wolves, mainly; rarely from an Indian who might take a cow or a scalp.

The minister was the pre-eminent citizen. He embodied education, knowledge, wisdom, to a degree even salvation; and he still carried an aura of the time when he was part of the theocracy —the government behind government. Certainly Solomon Stoddard had been a theocrat, and Jonathan Edwards inherited at least some of the mantle.

Although young, Edwards must have looked the part. He always wore the ministerial black robe in public, and continued with buckled shoes long after buckles had begun to go out of style. He was tall, thin, serious if not solemn, inclined to be sickly.

Edwards was not a minister who made many pastoral visits among his congregation, although he called when asked. The main occupations of his life were study, writing and preaching. He read widely. The kind of books he read was about the same as of any other minister of his time; but, as Ola Winslow says, "Few ministers in either England or America could have matched him in the breadth, the thoroughness, or the amazing industry of his application." The range of his reading was wide, but he was always "the scholar in religion," never the "layman adventuring among ideas." And his scholarship had a weakness: "that he usually had a hypothesis to prove, was committed beforehand to the conclusion, and zealously accumulated material to that end."

Edwards wrote out his sermons for years. When he stood in the pulpit, his sermon was before him in a little hand-stitched booklet, 3⅞ by 4⅛ inches. He was not alone in this practice. Many other ministers of the time made identical sermon booklets. If he did not quite read his sermon, he certainly followed his notes very closely. In this respect he differed from Solomon Stoddard, who had preached from memory—as Jonathan's own father did until he was 70 years old.

Edwards had a quiet way of preaching. He spoke without gesture or movement, each word was distinctly pronounced, his voice was low, his delivery natural, his manner solemn, "looking and speaking as in the presence of God." He looked straight forward over the heads of his hearers as he spoke. In those early years, he was not a "hellfire and damnation" preacher. In fact, his preaching life as a whole, no more than a third of his sermons were of the "imprecatory" kind. More often than not they dealt with the blessedness of communion with God, and with God's love. And even when he moved men to cry out for fear of their souls in later years, he never employed flamboyant, dramatic gestures or a loud voice.

Edwards made his effects by, one must say, his literary skill, even genius of a sort. He led his listeners by the hand from the most familiar things to things less and less familiar—more glorious or more terrible, as the case might be—but always step by step, always getting the concurrence of the imagination as he went along. And so, as he planned, his listeners soon *were* in heaven, or *were* in hell, never realizing how they had been led there.

Along with the artistry—perhaps a part of it, perhaps something else—was a certain "cryptic element," as Perry Miller calls it, which was in everything he wrote. Edwards had decided early in life not "to look as if I was much read, or was conversant with books, or with the learned world"—an ambition he was certainly never to achieve. Yet his sermons often appear childishly obvious in content and conclusion. The form he used was that of all the ministers of his time, as rigid as a sonnet. But into that form he poured the artistry a great poet might pour into a sonnet.

What of his daily life aside from his preaching? All New England ministers were farmers in those days, but Jonathan Edwards was probably less so than most—partly for reasons of health, partly for wish to study. He probably supervised work in the fields and the care and shearing of the sheep he owned. Only a few men in the village were capable of intellectual companionship with him, but he had numerous ministerial visitors.

One of the most frequent visitors was certainly Colonel John Stoddard, Solomon Stoddard's son, the most powerful man in the region, and the wealthiest. Wise, generous, honorable, a gentleman in the old tradition, he had made it his business to be Edwards' counselor and supporter from the beginning. He was one of the few who were able to appreciate Edwards intellectually. Edwards visited Stoddard often; and Stoddard visited Edwards.

In fact, the number of visitors at any one time in the Edwards home is amazing to us with our more isolated family life. There might be a dozen to eighteen at dinner after a meeting. Guests sometimes stayed for weeks. If they fell ill, they had to be cared for until they were well. They came on horseback, and the horses had to be stabled and cared for. When a guest left, Jonathan usually rode a few miles with him to see him well on his way.

Although Edwards did not make as much of pastoral visits as some ministers, he took seriously his duty to teach the Northampton children about religion. Catechizing took a good deal of time. He was thorough. And generous. He wrote fourteen pages to a Suffield girl, Deborah Hatheway, who had asked him for "Some Directions" on how to conduct herself in a Christian way. He took time to prove to a thirteen-year-old boy that a two-inch cube contains eight times as much matter as a one-inch cube—by sawing up pieces of wood in an actual demonstration.

Every evening Edwards tried to spend an hour in conversation with his children before they went to bed and he went back to his study. Letters and other papers preserved show charming details: "Extra pennies for little Jerusha for her diligence in reading," writes Ola Winslow; "pistareens borrowed from Timothy and paid back again; silver spoons thought of and purchased for the daughters before they were old enough to use them properly." There are an "order for the latest style in clergymen's buttons, three pounds paid out for a hat, eleven pounds for a gold locket and chain, sixteen shillings for 'a pare of gold wiers,' bills for spelling books, cables of thread, thimbles, three yards of lute string, a silk handkerchief, a ribbon for Sarah, a broom, a mousetrap, a primer, 'one child's plaything,' one dozen long pipes, grocery lists showing infinite chocolate for the Edwards consumption, the fragment of a letter expressing parental concern over measles, Dr. Mather's bill for two bloodlettings . . ."

There was laughter and merriment in the household as the children grew older; but Jonathan Edwards himself probably did not supply much of it. One feels that laughter at home was permitted, indulged, even approved—but that he himself was not much given to laughter. He was much given to solitary meditation, not only in his study, but afield. He often rode out in the woods to think, sometimes tying his horse to a tree, and walking and contemplating. On these jaunts, he carried pen, ink and paper, or bits of papers and pins. When an idea came to him which he wanted to remember, he pinned a piece of paper to his coat. Sometimes, legend has it, he came home covered with many reminders pinned to himself, all to be unpinned one by one with his wife's help.

This was his life in the early years of his pastorate. Those first five or ten years were to be perhaps the best he ever knew. He had the full approval of his congregation, his doctrine was considered sound, he was making headway, he was becoming known even in Boston.

STODDARD'S SUCCESSOR

In 1731 Jonathan Edwards was invited to give the Thursday Public Lecture at the First Church in Boston. The date was July 8. Boston by now was a big city, with a population of 13,000. To be invited to give one of the Thursday lectures was always an honor, especially for one who lived so far from Boston as Jonathan Edwards did. This particular Thursday fell during Harvard's Commencement Week. The presence of the power and learning of New England, there for the Commencement, made it a greater honor. The fact that he was a Yale man made it more significant, if not more honorific.

For a test was involved. Was Jonathan Edwards a worthy successor to his grandfather Stoddard? His subject was: *God Glorified in the Work of Redemption, by the Greatness of Man's Dependence upon him, in the Whole of it*. The thesis with which the sermon began was: "There is an absolute and universal dependence of the redeemed on God. . . . The redeemed are in every thing directly, immediately, and entirely dependent on God."

The lecture, or sermon, was thoroughly orthodox. He said that "the redeemed have all their good of God . . . and all from the *grace* of God. . . . The grace of God in bestowing this gift is most free. . . . It was what we never did anything to merit." And so on, through a lengthy cataloguing: Man's dependence is now greater on God's arbitrary grace than before the Fall and far more than under the first covenant, through every step of our redemption.

To the delighted conservatives, it looked as if Edwards had given challenge of battle to the death to the Harvard liberals. They may have overlooked that he had gone even further than the conservatives themselves, by omitting the mention or language of the Covenant or Federal Theology. Where he could have used the word "covenant" in the statement of his thesis, he had used the word "contrivance": "The nature and contrivance of our redemption is such, that the redeemed are in every thing directly, immediately, and entirely dependent on God." Although it had been held that grace is from God, but means must be used, Edwards *almost* said grace was immediate without means of ordinances. He did say that grace is not only from God, but is continually maintained by Him, as light is all day from the sun.

There were other expressions used in a new and different way from anything the conservatives had heard: "excellency"; "sensible" considered as an intellectual faculty. To us, with our knowledge of Jonathan Edwards' private writings from his Yale days, his meaning is not so mysterious. But in their delight, this the conservatives overlooked.

The Boston lecture placed Jonathan Edwards in the front rank of New England divines. Its emphasis had been upon the fact that God's bestowal of grace upon individual men is arbitrary; men are entirely dependent upon God for the receipt of it.

But in the lecture, he had not discussed the nature of grace. He did that two years later in a sermon to his people in August of 1733. They were so pleased, the report goes, that they persuaded him to publish it. Perry Miller suspects that "he did considerable rewriting; he could hardly have devised a more carefully constructed sequel to the Boston lecture than the treatise that came off the press early in 1734 bearing the title, *A Divine and Supernatural Light, Immediately imparted to the Soul by the Spirit of God, Shown to be both a scriptural and Rational Doctrine.*"

It seems clear to one considering it from this distance of years that the "Light," viewed subjectively, was a *feeling*—the same feeling Jonathan had experienced in his conversion, his mystical experience.

Edwards considered first what the Light was not. It was not "those convictions that natural men have of their sin and misery." Such a light was "common grace," "natural," "of no superior kind to what mere nature attains to. . . . In other words, common grace only assists the faculties of the soul to do that more fully which they do by nature, as natural conscience of reason will by mere nature make a man sensible of guilt."

But, on the other hand, "in the renewing and sanctifying work of the Holy Ghost those things are wrought in the soul that are above nature . . . those principles are restored that were utterly destroyed by the fall."

Thus, although the Spirit of God may act on the mind of a "natural man," it acts "in the mind of a saint" in a different way, "as an indwelling vital principle."

The Light "does not consist in any impression made upon the imagination." It does not suggest "any new truths or propositions not contained in the Word of God." The arousal of emotion (or in Edwards' language, "affection") of or for religious things is not this Light. "Men by mere principle of nature are capable of being affected with things that have a special relation to religion as well as other things." For instance, Christ's story may have a deep, moving effect, yet an individual "may be affected with it without believing it"—as by "what he reads in a romance, or sees acted in a stage-play."

So, if these are what the Light is not, what is it?

The spiritual and divine Light is "true sense of the divine excellency of the things revealed in the Word of God, and a conviction of the truth and reality of them thence arising." But primarily it is "a real sense and apprehension of things revealed in the Word of God."

The conviction is a consequence of the "true sense" of the things revealed in God's Word, and hence "an effect and natural consequence of this sight of their divine glory."

Edwards declared: "There is a divine and superlative glory in these things. . . . He that is spiritually enlightened truly apprehends and sees it, or has a sense of it. He does not merely rationally believe that God is glorious, but he has a sense of the gloriousness of God in his heart. There is not only a rational belief that God is holy, and that holiness is a good thing, but there is a sense of the loveliness of God's holiness."

"Thus," wrote Jonathan Edwards, "there is a difference between having an *opinion*, that God is holy and gracious, and having a *sense* of the loveliness and beauty of that holiness. There is a difference between having a rational judgment that honey is sweet, and having a sense of its sweetness. A man may have the former, that knows not how honey tastes."

And from "this sense of the divine excellency of things contained in the Word of God," arises the "conviction of the truth and reality of them."

Finally, Edwards raised the question of how the Light is given to men. He believed that it was given directly by God "without making use of any means that operate by their own power or natural force." He did not deny that "natural faculties are used in it. They are the object of this Light: and in such a manner, that they are not merely passive, but active in it." Nor did he deny that "outward means" were involved. For he does not mean "inspiration, where new truths are suggested." This Light is given only by "a due apprehension of the same truths that are revealed in the Word of God; and therefore it is not given without the Word." Nevertheless the Word of God is not the cause, but is used as a means of transmission of the "subject-matter."

"As, for instance, the notion that there is a Christ, and that Christ is holy and gracious, is conveyed to the mind by the Word of God: but the sense of the excellency of Christ, by reason of that holiness and grace, is, nevertheless, immediately the work of the Holy Spirit."

The Harvard lecture, and the sermon on the *Divine and Supernatural Light*, expressed Edwards' theology almost completely, in a highly compressed form, and they delighted his congregation, so we are told.

Yet in them there are statements and implications that in the long run were to isolate Edwards from the main thrust of American thought of his time, and even to alienate him from his own congregation.

For instance: God saves whom He will. The imparting of the Divine Light is the sign of salvation. The Divine Light is a felt experience, rather than an intellectually reasoned conviction, although the experience involves the conviction as well.

Thus, doing good works does not save. Knowing and believing the Bible does not save. Obeying one's conscience does not save. Only a commitment to Jesus Christ saves.

Jonathan Edwards was confident, most of the time, that *he* was saved. He was confident that *he* had received the Light. The Light he was describing was his own conversion of the Yale years. But in describing and defining what the Light was, and by what means it was given, and by what evidence it could be identified, he was also establishing some criteria for determining who was excluded.

For instance: All men who were not familiar with the Word of God were excluded. They must be damned. All men who were familiar with the Word of God, who believed in it, who tried to live by it, who prayed, who attended church faithfully, were also excluded *unless* by His arbitrary will He granted them Saving Grace, which they could recognize by their experience with the Divine Light.

In time, this was to raise a question: If only the few Elect were to be saved, then whom did Christ suffer for? All mankind? Or only the Elect?

Sooner than that, however, the conclusions to which he had come were having an effect on Jonathan Edwards in terms of the day-to-day practicalities of his ministry.

For instance: if the evidence of the Light was a felt experience, then might it not be as important in a sermon to arouse this feeling as an assistance toward Grace, so to speak, as to create intellectual conviction? In fact, was it not *more* important, since feeling came first and intellectual conviction second?

And, if the church were to consist of the Elect, was not the visible expression and testimony of this feeling the true criteria for admission to church membership and to participation in the Lord's Supper? If so, sooner or later, Grandfather Stoddard's loose standard for church membership would have to be tightened.

Revival in Northampton

During Solomon Stoddard's ministry there had been periodic religious revivals when people were stirred and joined the church in numbers. But the last of these had taken place in the year 1718.

Now, gradually, Jonathan's preaching began to have an effect. Late in 1733, the younger people began to be visibly impressed. When he preached specifically about the "evil tendency" of the traditional Sunday evening "mirth and company keeping," they began to change their ways. The following spring, a young man and a young married woman died suddenly and unexpectedly. In the sober mood engendered by these deaths, Edwards "proposed it to the young people, that they should agree among themselves to spend the evenings after lectures in social religion, and to that end divide themselves into several companies to meet in various parts of the town." They did, and religion became a weekday affair as well as a Sunday concern.

By now a great deal had begun to be heard about heterodoxy. People, some respectable, began to doubt the strict Calvinism in which they had been raised. Edwards, always at his best when demolishing the contrary opinions of others, set himself to preach a series of sermons on justification by faith. He was opposed by Israel Williams, Jonathan's powerful cousin, and by other influential members of the congregation. They wanted to keep so controversial a subject out of the pulpit. Jonathan Edwards being what he was in his own nature, as well as taught by his father, the result could be only to harden his determination.

There was also the question: Had Solomon Stoddard been wrong in considering Communion a converting ordinance? In admitting all well behaved people to church membership?

Edwards sought to prove by logic and by citation of chapter and verse the sovereignty of God, His inexorable justice, and that justification can be granted through faith alone. But in the fourth sermon, *The Justice of God in the Damnation of Sinners,* he applied all his talents to preaching damnation. His thesis was, "It is just with God eternally to cast off and destroy sinners." He pointed out that God is infinitely lovely because He has infinite excellence and beauty. He is infinitely honorable. He has infinite authority. He is infinitely worthy to be obeyed. We have an infinite dependence on him. The conclusion?

"So that sin against God, being a violation of infinite obligations, must be a crime infinitely heinous, and so deserving of infinite punishment." In short, the punishment should fit the crime: sin against God is infinite crime; it merits infinite punishment.

But what is sin, or are sins?

First, in his sermon, he gave a long list of classes of sins: pride, enmity, contempt, blasphemy; quarreling, atheism, hardheartedness, wickedness—"breaches of every command, in thought, word and deed; a life full of sin; days and nights filled up with sin" —and more.

These were generalities. But in his application he went into particulars, the sins of the people of Northampton:

"How *many sorts* of wickedness have you not been guilty of? . . . What profaneness and contempt of God has been exercised by you! . . . Yea, you have not only spent the time in worldly, vain and unprofitable thoughts, but immoral thoughts; pleasing yourself with the reflections on past acts of wickedness, and in contriving new acts."

This was only the beginning. For close to ten minutes he enumerated: "What revenge and malice have you been guilty of towards your neighbors? . . . What covetousness has been in many of you! . . . How much of a spirit of pride has appeared in you . . . ? How have some of you vaunted yourselves in your apparel! Others in their riches! Others in their knowledge and abilities! Has it galled you to see others above you! . . . And how have you shewn your pride by setting up your wills in opposing others, and stirring up and promoting division, and a party-spirit in public affairs!

"How *sensual* have you been! Are there not some here that have debased themselves below the dignity of human nature, by wallowing in sensual filthiness, as swine in the mire, or as filthy vermin feeding with delight on rotten carrion? . . . How much of your precious time have you spent away at the tavern, and in drinking companies, when you ought to have been at home . . . !

"And what *abominable lasciviousness* have some of you been guilty of! How have you indulged yourself from day to day, and from night to night, in all manner of unclean imaginations! Has not your soul been filled with them, till it has become a hold of foul spirits, and a cage of every unclean and hateful bird? What foul-mouthed persons have some of you been. . . !

"And what *lying* have some of you been guilty of . . . !"

And so on, and on, until—

"Now, can you think when you have thus behaved yourself, that God is *obliged* to shew you mercy? . . . If God should forever cast you off, it would be exactly agreeable to your treatment of *him.* . . . You have never loved God, who is infinitely glorious and lovely; and why then is God under *obligation* to love you, who are all over deformed and loathsome as a filthy worm, or rather a hateful viper?"

There was much, much more—all delivered in a low, moderate tone without gesture or movement, with a gaze directed at the bell rope, but every syllable spoken with utter distinctness.

It was his most effective sermon in more ways than one. Conversions began, first the young, then their elders. A young woman, a notorious "company keeper," was saved. It was like a "flash of lightning" to the young people.

There were those who agonized, and those who rejoiced. ". . . in the spring and summer following, anno 1735, the town seemed to be full of the presence of God; it never was so full of love, nor of joy, and yet so full of distress, as it was then."

Although there were those who scoffed, the revival spread to South Hadley, to Sunderland, to Hatfield, to West Springfield and Long Meadow, to Enfield, to Westfield.

At the end of May, while the revival was at its height, Edwards wrote an account of what was going on to Benjamin Colman of Boston. Colman had the letter printed and sent copies to friends in England. Later, Edwards reworked the letter and in late 1736 it was published in London as *A Faithful Narrative of the Surprising Work of God in the Conversion of Many Hundred Souls in Northampton, and the Neighboring Towns and*

Villages. By 1739 it had gone through three editions and twenty printings and become a sort of manual of revivalism. As such, it has been used ever since. An abridged version with comments was republished as recently as 1957.

Much of the interest of the *Narrative* consists in two case histories: that of Abigail Hutchinson, a chronically ill young woman who had died before Edwards wrote of her; and Phebe Bartlet, a four-year-old child.

Abigail was a quiet, reserved person who first went through a period of envy of the conversion of the young "company keeper," resolved "to do her utmost to obtain the same blessing," began to search the Scriptures, and then was struck by "an extraordinary sense of her own wickedness," which came on her "as a flash of lightning and struck her into an exceeding terror."

After a few days of prayer, she awakened with a feeling new to her—a feeling of relief and surrender. It grew into "a sweet sense of the excellency and loveliness of Christ in his meekness." She retained this "beatific vision of God" until her death not long after.

Phebe Bartlet, the four-year-old, was first "affected by the talk of her brother, who had been hopefully converted a little before at about eleven years of age." From then on, she listened closely to the religious talk of the older children, and soon began "very constantly to retire, several times a day, as was concluded for secret prayer." But she said she could not find God. Then one day the mother heard Phebe "in the closet" crying, "Pray, blessed Lord, give me salvation! I pray, pardon all my sins!" Later, she told her mother she was afraid she would go to hell. This mood, which included "crying and writhing her body to and fro," continued some days, and then Phebe found relief. She said "with a smiling countenance, 'Mother, the kingdom of heaven is come to me!'" She became "very strict upon the Sabbath," wanted Sunday to come so she could "hear Mr. Edwards preach," was extraordinarily scrupulous about avoiding what she considered sin, and remained in a converted, compassionate spirit up to the time Edwards wrote.

But there were things Jonathan Edwards was to learn about revivals and great emotional upheavals. That spring a weak-minded man named Thomas Stubbins attempted suicide. Later, Joseph Hawley, Jonathan's uncle and one of the most important men in the town, "cut his throat on Lord's day morning." He died immediately.

Reaction set in. By the end of 1735 things had declined nearly to what they had been before. Some of the three hundred souls that had been saved had to be disciplined. The "parties" revived, the "quarrels" resumed.

In the revision of his letter, in November, Edwards described the falling off of enthusiasm following the death of Hawley—even to the compulsion some comparatively untroubled pious persons had to obey the inner urge of "Cut your own throat, now is a good opportunity. Now! Now! So that they were obliged to fight with all their might to resist it, and yet no reason suggested to them why they should do it."

He was already convinced that the experience of grace is an emotional experience rather than an intellectual conviction. Now his clinical observation showed that certain stages took place in it: the bone-deep conviction of God's sovereignty, and then "a conviction of the justice of God in their condemnation," then a deep abject terror. And then the relief, the "conversion," the "grace."

Edwards certainly felt his views on the falsehood of Arminianism were confirmed: Conversion *required* feeling that God was just in damning one. He also learned that, in revivals, what goes up sometimes comes down. There is a waxing and a waning. And it even can be that a person "of weak mind" (as in the case of one attempted suicide) or "prone to the disease of melancholy" (as in the case of Joseph Hawley) may be tempted to suicide and may succeed—through the depression that ought to precede the relief, but sometimes does not. He learned that the arousal of feelings can be attended with dangers. But the risk was worth it. For he had a procedure for helping souls receive saving grace.

THE GREAT AWAKENING: SINNERS IN THE HANDS OF AN ANGRY GOD

To all seeming, the aftermath of the 1735 revival was good—good for Northampton, good for Jonathan Edwards. His church had three hundred new converts. In 1736 a new meetinghouse was built on Meetinghouse Hill, close to the old one, which had been built in 1661. The new meetinghouse, almost twice as large as the old one, was completed for practical purposes in mid-July of 1737. The Sunday next, Jonathan Edwards preached in it, using as text Amos 9:6—"*It is he that buildeth his stories in the heaven,*" linking the raisers' work in creating the building with God's creation.

By now, Edwards was famous all over New England. And farther. His *Narrative* had made him known in England and Scotland. But he had his enemies: those who had opposed his speaking on controversial subjects; some of those whose sins he had pointed out all too openly in his sermons; those who were repelled and even disgusted by the emotional manifestations of revival; those who could not stomach a God who was to be glorified for His arbitrary selection with full foreknowledge of those to be saved and those to be damned.

About this time Edwards' name became attached to an unfortunate document. The Springfield congregation had called a liberal, Robert Breck, to their pulpit. The Hampshire Association opposed his ordination. A council of Boston ministers was convened in October of 1735—but just as Breck rose to answer the charges he was hustled off to jail. In the storm of protest that followed, the Massachusetts General Assembly voted censure against the Hampshire Association for undue interference in parish affairs. By now Breck had been ordained and had taken his lawful place in the Hampshire Association. Edwards' part in the affair had been merely to compose a defense of the Hampshire Association after the Massachusetts General Assembly had voted censure. He was criticized for that action. Perhaps more important, his name was on the document of defense. The Breck case was to cause a bitter church battle later; and much of the bitterness was to be directed against Jonathan Edwards.

But before these bitter seeds could bear their fruit, there was to come the Great Awakening—the watershed between the old and the new in American religious history. The occasion was the arrival of George Whitefield from England for two years of evangelism—1740 and 1741—in America.

Whitefield was only in his middle twenties—he had been born December 16, 1714, in Gloucester, England—but he was a new and revolutionary phenomenon in preaching. At Pembroke College, Oxford, he had come under the influence of the Methodists and John Wesley. After leaving school he had evangelized in Bath, Bristol and other towns. He had spent a short time in America, in Georgia, a few years before, and then had returned to England.

Whitefield's principle, doctrine, or purpose, was essentially the same that Jonathan Edwards had come to—the immediate contact of the Holy Spirit with the human heart. But he applied it in a way that was totally new: powerful pulpit oratory. English clergymen would not welcome him to their pulpits and he began to preach in the open air. At Bristol his clear, stentorian voice reached some 20,000 hearers, and his fervor, pathos, and histrionics broke people down completely. His preaching frequently produced "bodily effects"—fainting, physical collapse, hysteria, weeping, screaming, shouting, trances, convulsions.

Whitefield came to Boston in September of 1740, widely heralded. The papers had printed accounts of his effects on English audiences—and their size—for a year. The adverse accounts were omitted. He remained in New England only a month. He spent the first ten days in Boston, traveled to Northampton and spent four days there, then continued south through Connecticut to Philadelphia.

In Boston he preached to a "vast congregation" at Benjamin Colman's church. He preached to five thousand on Boston Common. He preached to eight thousand in the fields. He was well received by most of the clergy, even by Harvard, though there were doubts.

Whitefield had immense charm, great physical agility, a tremendous voice, and enormous dramatic skill. His method of preaching and his pulpit behavior were completely new to New England. The traditional plan of a New England sermon was to begin with a *Text*, expound the doctrine under a *Proposition*, develop it point by point in logical order, and then conclude with the *Application*, which included Improvements, Illustrations and Inferences. Divisions were named, points under each were numbered, objections were presented by number and answered by number. The structure was almost mathematical. The presentation was solemn.

Whitefield threw all this out the window. He told stories. He drew verbal pictures. He employed a voice of gold, a powerful personal magnetism, and a genius for oratory to the endless repetition of a simplified theology. He spoke without notes, he wept, he laughed, he jumped and gestured.

Lord Bolingbroke considered his oratory "the most commanding eloquence I ever heard in any person." In Boston, Dr. Colman wrote, "How awfully, with what Thunder and Sound did he discharge the Artillery of Heaven upon us?" A few others, who did not advertise their opinions, thought otherwise.

Whitefield arrived in Northampton Friday, October 17. He stayed with the Edwardses and departed on Monday evening. Edwards rode with him as far as East Windsor. During those four days he preached four times from the pulpit at Northampton, once at the Edwards house, once at Hatfield. Saturday morning, as Jonathan requested, he talked with the Edwards children, and prayed with them. Sarah Edwards had borne seven by now, the latest, Susannah, was only a few months old.

Jonathan Edwards, although in accord with Whitefield in principle, objected somewhat to his "enthusiastic views." The revival had some good effects, however—in terms of taverns unpatronized, profanity diminished, and perhaps other sins somewhat lessened. Ministers meanwhile toured on horseback with the speed and regularity of military dispatch-riders.

Although his methods of presentation were not those of Whitefield or Gilbert Tennent, of New Jersey, Jonathan Edwards rode also. It was at the end of one of these rides, on July 8, 1741, when the revival was at its height, that Jonathan Edwards preached the sermon for which he is best known: *Sinners in the Hands of an Angry God*. The place was the village of Enfield, to which he had been invited by its minister, who had found his town unresponsive to the revival fervor.

By now, Edwards had become convinced that the experience of grace or conversion was an inward feeling of solemn relief and exaltation, and that receptivity to it required first the deep anxiety of one's certainty of being damned, and a sense of what damnation might be like, together with an acceptance of God's justice in damning whom He would, and thus his own best course would be to arouse anxiety and fear as a necessary preliminary to conversion.

He chose as his text, "Their foot shall slide in due time." (Deut. xxxii: 35.) He began rather mildly by pointing out how it applied to the wicked Israelites—that they were exposed to destruction like one walking in slippery places. Then slowly drawing his listeners along with him step by step, so that there was no place where they could break off and reject, he began relating it to his unregenerate hearers, starting with—

" 'There is nothing that keeps wicked men at any moment out of hell but the mere pleasure of God.' By the *mere* pleasure of God, I mean his *sovereign* pleasure, his arbitrary will, any more than if nothing else but God's had in the least degree, or in any respect whatever, any hand in the preservation of wicked men one moment."

He emphasized the meaning of his statement, item by item:

"There is no want of *power* in God to cast wicked men into hell at any moment." He illustrated the point by piling up picture after picture. "We find it easy to tread on and crush a worm that we see crawling on the earth; so it is easy for us to cut or singe a slender thread that any thing hangs by: thus easy is it for God, when he pleases, to cast his enemies down to hell . . .

"They deserve to be cast into hell. . . . The sword of divine justice is every moment brandished over their heads, and it is nothing but the hand of arbitrary mercy, and God's mere will, that holds it back . . .

"They are already under a sentence of *condemnation* to hell . . .

"They are now the objects of that very same *anger* and wrath of God, that is exposed in the torments of hell. . . . The wrath of God burns against them, their damnation does not slumber; the pit is prepared, the fire is made ready, the furnace is now hot, ready to receive them; the flames do now rage and glow . . .

"The *devil* stands ready to fall upon them, and seize them as his own, at what moment God shall permit him . . .

"There are in the souls of wicked men those hellish *principles* reigning, that would presently kindle and flame out into hell fire, if it were not for God's restraints. There is laid in the very na-ture of carnal men, a foundation for the torments of hell . . .

"There is no security to wicked men for one moment, that there are no visible means of death at hand. . . . The manifold and continual evidence of the world in all ages, shows that this is no evidence, that a man is not on the very brink of eternity, and that the next step will be into another world. . . . Unconverted men walk over the pit of hell on a rotten covering, and there are innumerable places in this covering so weak that they will not bear their weight, and these places are not seen . . .

"Natural men's prudence and care to preserve their own lives or the care of others to preserve them, do not secure them a moment. To this, divine providence and universal experience also bear testimony. . . . Ecclesiastes ii: 16. 'How dieth the wise man? even as the fool.'

"All wicked men's pains and *contrivance* which they use to escape hell, while they continue to reject Christ, and so remain wicked men, do not secure them from hell one moment. Almost every natural man that hears of hell, flatters himself that he shall escape it. . . . But the foolish children of men miserably delude themselves in their own schemes, and in confidence of their own strength and wisdom; they trust to nothing but a shadow. The greater part of those who heretofore have lived under the same means of grace, and are now dead, are undoubtedly gone to hell: and it was not because they were not as wise as those who have gone to hell . . .

"God has laid himself under *no obligation*, by any promise to keep any natural man out of hell one moment."

Item by item, Edwards proceeded remorselessly, without gestures, without dramatic action, without raising his voice, enunciating with that exquisite clarity of diction so that every word could be heard without possibility of escape or misunderstanding by every person in the audience.

Then Edwards began to pile terrifying image upon image as he approached the Application to his hearers:

". . . thus it is that natural men are held in the hand of God, over the pit of hell; they have deserved the fiery pit, and are already sentenced to it; and God is dreadfully provoked, his anger is as great towards them as to those that are actually suffering the executions of his wrath in hell . . ."

And to his hearers: "That world of misery, that lake of brim-stone, is extended abroad under you. There is the dreadful pit of the glowing flames of the wrath of God . . . and you have nothing to stand upon . . . ; there is nothing between you and hell but the air; it is only the power and mere pleasure of God that holds you up."

Stephen Williams, who was there, described the scene: ". . . and before sermon was done—there was a great moaning & cry-ing out through ye whole House —— What shall I do to be Sav^d — oh I am going to Hell — oh what shall I do for Christ, &c. &c. So y^t ye minister was obliged to desist — ye shrieks & cry^s were piercing & Amazing."

There was more to the sermon as Edwards wrote it and de-livered it on other occasions. But on that July 8 at Enfield, at some point he "was obliged to desist." After "some time of wait-ing," the congregation quieted down. Edwards made a prayer, descended from the pulpit and "discours^d with the people." Some "were hopefully wrought up" and were cheerful and re-ceived comfort. Finally a hymn was sung, a prayer made and the assembly dismissed.

EBB TIDE

If Edwards' purpose was to elicit the visible, audible signs of the inward consciousness of guilt, he succeeded—not alone, for other ministers were doing the same thing, but Edwards was perhaps more effective. For, logician and mystic that he was, he also displayed a literary artistry in this sermon that can fairly be called genius.

All over New England people were deeply moved in the Awakening. Many were well affected and tried to live better lives.

There were undesired effects, too. Sermons were no longer learned, orderly presentations based on principles learned at

Harvard and Yale. As ministers left their home pulpits and preached on the revival circuit, their congregations had new opportunities to compare one with another. Sometimes the home pastor found on his return that he suffered by comparison.

Eventually, the Great Awakening spent itself. Among the permanent results were to be a change in the character of popular preaching, and a growth of various kinds of separatist, individualist churches.

One immediate result was a bitter controversy among ministers, the battle of the conservatives, the "Old Lights" against the radical supporters of Whitefield and his methods, the "New Lights." Eventually, the Governor of Connecticut had to issue a proclamation calling for a day of fasting and prayer in atonement of the "Divisions," "Contentions," "Uncharitableness & Disorder" in religious doctrine and practice.

Although the Connecticut Valley was distinguished by the disorders, Northampton suffered only a little less than the valley as a whole. Edwards, as both participant and clinical observer, set forth some of his conclusions on the significance of what was happening at the height of the Awakening in 1741 as *The Distinguishing Marks of a Work of the Spirit of God*. In 1742, when the fervor abated, he added *Some Thoughts Concerning the Present Revival of Religion in New England*.

Edwards felt that although there was hysteria in what had happened, there was at least as much, or perhaps more, real manifestation of the spirit of God. What had happened should be judged by its effect, and judgment should be made by the rule of Scripture. We should, he wrote, "distinguish the Good from the Bad, and not judge of the Whole by a Part." After all, "a great deal of noise and tumult, confusion and uproar, darkness mixed with light, and evil with good, is always to be expected in the beginning of something glorious in the state of things in human society, or the church of God. . . . When God was about to introduce the Messiah into the world, and a new, glorious dispensation, he *shook the heavens and the earth*, and he *shook all nations*." So, many of the errors could be attributed to youth, ignorance and overenthusiasm. Against the excesses of religious behavior, Edwards balanced the obvious reform on the part of many. In fact, he was inclined to think that "the Latter-Day Glory is probably about to begin in America."

Edwards did not believe ministers should be criticized for frightening listeners. Or, as he put it, "To blame a minister for thus declaring the truth to those who are under awakenings, and not immediately administering comfort to them, is like blaming a surgeon, because when he has begun to thrust in his lance, whereby he has already put his patient in great pain, and he shrinks and cries out in anguish, he is so cruel that he will not stay his hand, but goes on to thrust it in further, until he comes to the core of the wound."

Ministers should not be blamed, wrote Edwards, if their sermons bring about "outcries, faintings and other bodily effects." In many cases, these *are* the influence of God's Spirit. Here, Edwards almost surely had someone special in mind—his wife Sarah, although he was careful to speak of her only as "the person."

This person began to experience religious transports about the time of the 1735 revival, and they had increased in frequency, especially during the Great Awakening. "Extraordinary views of divine things, and the religious affections, were frequently attended with very great effects on the body. Nature often sank under the weight of divine discoveries, and the strength of the body was taken away. The person was deprived of all ability to stand or speak. Sometimes the hands were clenched, and the flesh cold, but the spirit remaining."

Yet the *feeling* of the person was "a clear and lively view of sense of the infinite beauty and amiableness of Christ's person, and the heavenly sweetness of his transcendent love."

Edwards himself was sometimes overcome by a flood of tears,

but there is no question that Sarah Edwards had experiences at least similar to those of "the person." When her husband was away at Leicester early in 1742 and Samuel Buell was filling his pulpit, her ecstasy made the neighbors fear for her life. She was actually, she felt, "faint with joy, while contemplating the glories of the heavenly world."

But, Edwards wrote frankly, such experiences were not necessarily entirely spiritual—"they have something else mixed with them, besides what is spiritual. There is a mixture of that which is natural, and that which is corrupt, with that which is divine." But, then, probably Christians never have in this world experiences "that are wholly pure, entirely spiritual, without any mixture of what is natural and carnal."

A year later, he gave a series of lectures on the same subject. The lectures, these various works, together with his observations on the 1735 revival, and his *Personal Narrative*, which may have been written a few years before the Great Awakening, resulted in the work known as *A Treatise Concerning Religious Affections*. Although it was not published until 1746, several years later, we can think of the substance of it as belonging to the immediate aftermath of the Great Awakening. In it, Edwards tried to bring together everything he had learned by observation, in the context of his theological and philosophical system.

His theme, as he stated in his preface, was, "What are the distinguishing qualifications of those that are in favor with God, and entitled to his eternal rewards? Or, which comes to the same thing, What is the nature of true religion? and wherein do lie the distinguishing notes of that virtue and holiness, that is acceptable in the sight of God."

The doctrine he put forth was, "True religion, in great part, consists in holy affections." And by "affections" he meant "no other, than the more vigorous and sensible exercises of the inclination and will of the soul." He considered that the soul has two "faculties"—one of *understanding*, which is that by which it discerns, views and judges of things; and one which is called *inclination*. If inclination is concerned with actions it governs, it is called *will:* "and the *mind,* with regard to the exercises of this faculty, is often called the *heart.*"

It is the more vigorous and sensible exercises of this faculty that are called the *affections.* Thus the will and the affections are not distinct. The affections are merely more pronounced, more observable, and more strongly felt. And it is precisely here that we find true religion: ". . . true religion, in great part, consists of the affections."

This seemed only natural to Edwards. Affections are "very much the spring of men's actions." And it seemed obvious, that religion can take hold of a man's soul only to the degree that it affects the soul. Certainly the Scriptures place religion in the affections: "fear, hope, love, hatred, desire, joy, sorrow, gratitude, compassion and zeal." But primarily, basically, they "represent true religion, as being summarily comprehended in *love,* the chief of the affections, and fountain of all other affections." And "from love arises hatred of those things that are contrary to what we love." And, therefore, "it clearly and certainly appears, that great part of true religion consists in the affections." Therefore, those who dismiss all religious affections as "having nothing solid or substantial" are in error, and "means are to be desired as have much of a tendency to move the affections"— books, manner of preaching, praying, singing.

But what are the signs that religious affections are truly "gracious"? Well, intensity is not such a sign. Nor are bodily effects. Nor that they cause a person "to be fluent, fervent and abundant, in talking of the things of religions." Nor that they come to a person unbidden by himself. Nor "that they come with texts of Scripture, remarkably brought to the mind." Nor "that there is an appearance of love in them." Nor that a person has "religious affections of many kinds." Nor the fact "that comforts and joys seem to follow awakenings and convictions of conscience,

in a *certain order*." Nor "that they dispose persons to spend
much time in religion and to be zealously engaged in the external duties of worship." Nor "that they dispose persons with
their mouths to glorify God." Nor that people who have them
are "exceedingly confident that what they experience is divine."
Nor that "the outward manifestations . . . are very affecting and
pleasing to the truly godly, and . . . gain their charity, and win
their hearts."

Such a list seems to exclude nearly everything. If these are
not the signs, then what are? Edwards frankly admitted that he
could not present signs which would enable anyone to tell for
certain that someone else was experiencing true "affections," or
even that he himself was. Nevertheless, he was convinced that
there were twelve signs:

—that the affections arise from spiritual, supernatural and
divine influences . . . "not a new faculty of understanding,
but . . . a new foundation laid in the nature of the soul."

—that the object, so to speak, be "the transcendently excellent
and amiable nature of divine things, as they are in themselves;
and not any conceived relation they bear to self, or self-interest."
Not that "self-love, through the exercise of a mere natural gratitude, may [not] be the foundation of a sort of love to God. . . ."
But, " 'Tis unreasonable to think otherwise, than that the first
foundation of a true love to God, is that whereby he is in himself
lovely, or worthy to be loved, or the supreme loveliness of his
nature."

—that the affections be "primarily founded on the liveliness
of the moral excellency of divine things. Or . . . a love to divine
things for the beauty and sweetness of their moral excellency . . ."

—that the mind be "enlightened, rightly and spiritually to
understand or apprehend divine things." Edwards was not anti-
intellectual. He did not divorce head and heart. Spiritual understanding involved a fusion that resulted in almost (or in actual-

ity) a new sense: "A sense of the heart, of the supreme beauty and sweetness of the holiness or moral perfection of divine things, together with all that discerning and knowledge of things of religion that depends on, and flows from such a sense."

—that the gracious affections be accompanied by a "conviction . . . of the reality and certainty of divine things."

—that they be "attended with evangelical humiliation . . . which is a sense that a Christian has of his own utter insufficiency, despicableness, and odiousness, with an answerable frame of heart."

—that they be "attended with a change of nature." This, of course, is conversion. But it must not be temporary, though it may be flawed with some remainder of the "natural temper."

—that they be "attended with the lamblike, dovelike spirit and temper of Jesus Christ; or in other words, they naturally beget and promote such a spirit of love, meekness, quietness, forgiveness and mercy, as appeared in Christ."

—that they "soften the heart, and are attended and followed with a Christian tenderness of spirit."

—that they have "beautiful symmetry and proportion." One's mind harks back to Edwards' youthful writing at Yale. Here he meant a certain balance that is healthy, so to speak; as beautiful as the proportioning of the healthy body, with no one emotion or tendency overrunning its due allotment.

—that the higher the gracious affections "are raised, the more is a spiritual appetite and longing of soul after spiritual attainments, increased." False affections, on the other hand, are self-satisfied.

—that "they cause that a practice, which is universally conformed to, and directed by Christian rules, should be the practice and business of his life," who is the subject of them.

This "twelfth sign" was the one to which Edwards gave most space. It is "the chief of all the signs of grace," and it gives others some clue to a person's sincerity. One who has or displays gracious and holy affections behaves at all times according to Christian rules. He makes the practice of religion his most eminent business. He "persists in it to the end of life"—not seasonally, or Sabbath days, or at certain times, or a few years, but forever. And this practice or conformity is not imposed from the outside in, but grows from the inside out: ". . . the inward principle from whence they flow, is something divine, a communication of God, a participation of the divine nature, Christ living in the heart, the Holy Spirit dwelling there, in union with the faculties of the soul, as an internal vital principle . . ."

And this practice is the chief sign of grace to others "as a manifestation and sign of the sincerity of a professing Christian, to the eyes of his neighbors and brethren."

As John E. Smith, editor of the Yale edition of *Religious Affections,* writes: "In Edwards' time this was a bolder step than might be imagined. He was subordinating the traditional 'immanent grace' to the power of the Spirit as expressed in overt behavior, and he did so without becoming involved in a doctrine of works."

Religious Affections shows Edwards at his most brilliant and perhaps most pleasing. He had brought in the sensationalism of John Locke, which he had learned at Yale; he had used the itemizing, list-making, classificatory bent he had from his father; he had used his own conversion experience; he had shown what was healthy, as he saw it, in the Great Awakening; he had shown the delusive character of some supposed "signs"; and he had arrived at a converted Christian who has been changed from inside out, who has come into communication with the Holy Spirit; and who, as a result, behaves in a Christian way and a healthy way.

It was a great achievement.

EXPULSION

But Edwards had been making more and more powerful enemies. Some of them, members of the Williams clan, were relatives of his. His actions in the next few years would embolden them to open and successful revolt.

In the decades since Northampton's beginning as a primitive frontier outpost, the process of settlement had made the area relatively prosperous. The Williams family and others, in one way or another, had enlarged their property holdings; merchants had become wealthy, sometimes by dubious means. At least by implication, Edwards had attacked their behavior and very attitude in some of his revival sermons. He had pointed out that what they might have considered good business and good morality were precisely the sort of sinful thought and behavior which aroused God's wrath. It was not an agreeable doctrine for a rich man to hear.

At the same time, Edwards himself, in the tradition of Solomon Stoddard and other Calvinist divines, had become something of an autocrat. He was paid well and lived well. Yet there was not enough for his many children, he felt, or the many illnesses. The town, on the other hand, criticized the high living standard of the Edwards family, even their clothing.

With Edwards' familial tendency to make no allowances for other people's viewpoints, these factors alone could breed ill will if uncorrected. But Edwards had gone further. In 1742, toward the end of the Great Awakening, he had introduced a mild sort of covenant into his church. It was not the old Calvinist type of covenant which his grandfather Stoddard had done away with, but merely the expression of a commitment. It was a very reasonable covenant. The signers agreed to renounce evil and seek the Lord. They agreed to refrain from gossip and telling evil stories about others behind their backs, and, perhaps hardest, they promised to refrain from defrauding their neighbors, cheating them out of debts, overreaching, or, in commerce, breaching moral equity. This sort of document, forced on a congregation by a "stiff & unsociable" minister who was so reserved as to seem secretive to all but his closest intimates, was bound to arouse hostility when the revival enthusiasm cooled.

Then, in 1744, came the "bad book" episode.

What apparently happened was that half a dozen boys of the "lower orders" got hold of a manual on midwifery. As the book was passed around, it reached a good many children, including the sons and daughters of some of the most respected people in town. Eventually word of it came to Edwards.

"Granny Books" like this one were certainly a necessity in every locality, and surreptitious reading of them by adolescents must have been going on ever since the Puritans arrived in New England. But Edwards, with monumental incomprehension of other people's feelings, acted in precisely the wrong way. After the service in March of 1744, he asked the congregation to remain. Then he told the story publicly, took a vote to elect a committee of investigation which included Colonel Stoddard, always one of his staunchest supporters—and then read off the names of all the children who were to appear at the investigation, making no distinction between those who might actually have been involved and those who might be mere witnesses. The list included children of the first families of Northampton, some of them children of members of the investigating committee. As if someone had touched a match to it, "the town was suddenly all in a blaze."

In New England churches, at this time, bringing the misbehavior of members to the attention of the church was not uncommon. Adultery, drunkenness, and defamation of character came up in this way fairly commonly. For a century or more such cases had been treated in a standard pattern of rebuke and reinstatement. So, in a sense, Edwards had precedent. But congregations were rebelling against this kind of exercise of pastoral authority. And the children of the "bad book" case were unusually young. And, finally, Edwards, in publicly reading the names for all the town to hear, had made no public distinction between those accused and those not accused.

The parsonage became virtually a court of inquiry as the sons and daughters of the best families were drawn into talebearing. Finally, the three ringleaders—the "town hoodlums," according to Ola Winslow—were singled out, and their confessions were read out in a church meeting. The case was closed officially. But not in effect.

People stopped joining the church. In the revival of 1735, some three hundred had joined the church. In 1741, they had flocked in once again. But between 1744 and 1748 not a single person applied for membership. The suicide of Joseph Hawley, the mild "covenant," the "bad book" case, the pastor's way of life, his all but open criticism of his most powerful parishioners as displeasing to God, his manner and personality—all these had their effect.

This was the time of war with the French and Indians— "King George's War." Northampton was fortified once more. Watch houses were built on the outskirts of town. Saratoga, New York, less than a hundred miles to the west, was burned by French and Indians. A few Northampton residents were killed in surprise Indian attacks. Pastor and congregation alike were concerned with the war. Edwards gave numerous sermons marking particular events in the war, at least one of which was all but a recruiting sermon.

During this period, he saw tragedy within his family. His daughter Jerusha had become betrothed to a young missionary to the Indians named David Brainerd. Late in 1747, Brainerd died in the parsonage. Jerusha had nursed him through the last months, even traveling with him to Boston and returning with him when he was unable to go alone.

Naturally, Jerusha also contracted tuberculosis and died early in 1748, at the age of seventeen, the "flower of the family." Five days after her funeral, her father gave a eulogy of her at the end of his sermon—basically one he had used before on the occasion of the deaths of young people. For once, Edwards showed warmth. He spoke of her sudden death, her virtues, his appreciation of the people's sympathy; and finally, to the young people, in hopes that Jerusha's death might be the beginning of general awakening: "I shall think I had much more Cause to admire God's mercy in such a happy Consequence than to mourn for my own loss tho it is so great."

Brainerd, on his deathbed, had asked Edwards to arrange and edit his private papers. This Edwards did, partly as a biography, partly as a presentation of Brainerd's diary, under the title of *The Life and Diary of David Brainerd*. It was published in 1749, three years after *Religious Affections*, and was a continuing success.

But now, finally, the circumstances were arising which were to cause Edwards to leave Northampton forever.

Since his requiring a modest commitment by his congregation members to their changed intentions, he had gradually come to the conclusion that he could no longer accept his grandfather Stoddard's simple requirement for church membership. He concluded that a condition of church membership must be that the applicant be able to profess a sincere belief in his "renovation of heart"—not merely live morally and have knowledge of church doctrine.

It was a logical conclusion. All the signposts in his experience had pointed that way: his own conversion in the early 1720's, his observations in 1735 and again in the Great Awakening, and the criteria for judging God's grace given in *Religious Affections*. Intellectual knowledge was not enough. A spiritual conversion, even a transformation, was necessary—certainly a prerequisite to receiving Communion.

The fact that his views had been changing in this direction

had been no secret to his fellow ministers for some years, nor to many in his own congregation. But the issue had not been raised openly because for four years no one had applied for church membership. Now someone did.

In December 1748, the application was brought before the parish. Edwards refused to admit the applicant without a public profession of faith, and in February of 1749 made a formal statement to the Church Committee that a difference of opinion existed between him and the people. He asked and was granted permission to print his views. His request granted, he wrote and in 1749 had printed in Boston *A Humble Inquiry into the Rules of the Word of God, Concerning the Qualifications Requisite to a Complete Standing and Full Communion with the Visible Christian Church*. In August Colonel Dwight brought back twenty copies for distribution in Northampton.

Meanwhile Mary Hulbert had applied for admission. She agreed to make an open profession of faith written by Edwards only if the church would consent. The rising public feeling had frightened her. But the committee would not agree.

Now the fat was in the fire. The machinations that followed are impossible to describe with brevity. Edwards was accused of himself wanting to be the judge of what was the satisfactory degree of "Experimental Piety" required for admission to church membership. It was not true, and he denied it. But he was not believed. No one was really willing to listen. For what he *was* accused of, was overthrowing "Mr. Stoddard's rule." And this accusation was true. For his grandfather had opened church membership and Communion to everyone who was not "openly scandalous."

In the beginning Edwards had accepted his grandfather's position—partly, perhaps, through youthful admiration. But his own reasoning, and Locke's, and his own inner experience, and his own observation of others, had brought him to raise the question: "Whether, according to the rules of Christ, any ought to be admitted to the communion and privileges of members of the visible church of Christ in complete standing, but such as are in profession, and in the eye of the church's Christian judgment, godly or gracious persons?" His conclusion: No, they should not. What was necessary was a "credible profession and visibility" of "converting grace or piety." And this required "a profession of real piety." Of course, he had ample Scriptural proof.

But by now the rank and file were irritated with him. The powerful were resolved to get rid of him. And the only person who might have helped him, Colonel John Stoddard, Solomon's son and Edwards' faithful defender and counselor since the beginning of his pastorate, had died in the summer of 1748. Left to stand beside Edwards were only Dr. Mather and Colonel Timothy Dwight—the last of the old gentry.

Israel Williams, Edwards' enemy, fell heir to Stoddard's mantle as commander of the militia and wielder of influence. Amasser of real estate, head of the commerce and land oligarchy, Williams had available as a tool twenty-six-year-old Joseph Hawley, son of the Joseph Hawley who had committed suicide, and a cousin of Edwards. Hawley, a lawyer, melancholic like his father, was eventually to go insane, but not until he had become one of the Massachusetts "Sons of Liberty" and a member of the Stamp Act Congress. At this time, however, he had great drive, with every reason to want to please the commercial oligarchy, and even a personal motive in his brother's having received pastoral censure on account of an affair which had become locally notorious. A third leader of the enemies of Edwards was the town blacksmith, Major Seth Pomeroy. As an old man he too was to play a laudable part at Bunker Hill and in the American Revolution.

These three helped provoke the rank and file and led the resulting movement to oust Edwards. With Stoddard gone, Edwards had no stronger supporter than Colonel Timothy Dwight; but he lived too elegantly, like Edwards, to appeal to the public.

In the local factions, he was on the unpopular side. He was no match for men like Hawley and Pomeroy in the rough and tumble of controversy.

The result was inevitable. Edwards, with his gift for detached clinical observation, saw it clearly. "All that I do & say is watched by the multitude around me with the utmost strictness & with eyes of the greatest uncharitableness & severity and let me do or say what I will, my words & actions are represented in dark colours." But he held his head high, preserved his outward serenity, and preached with steadfastness. Meanwhile, committees of all kinds met. The objective of the Williams group was to get discussion of the case of the minister out of the church and into the town. Here Edwards could not speak to defend himself, and they could pack the meeting.

Edwards, however, insisted that the people read in the *Humble Inquiry* his reasons for his position. Then let those who had read it vote him out if they so pleased. Israel Williams tried to have a refutation of the *Humble Inquiry* written. His half brother Elisha, Edwards' first tutor at Yale, undertook the job but had to go to London. Israel's other half brother Solomon went on with it, but the reply was published only after Edwards had left Northampton.

Eventually, after an initial refusal, Edwards was able to get the town's permission to preach on his principles before the congregation. He preached five public lectures in March of 1750, but those against him stayed away.

In this deadlock, a council of nine churches was finally convened in June. It was packed so far as possible with men opposed to Edwards. The decision was that the relationship between pastor and people be dissolved. The minority wrote a protest, but it had no effect. On June 22, the church voted 230 to 23 to dismiss Edwards. Edwards received the news with his usual calm.

Ten days later, July 2, 1750, he preached his farewell sermon.

The church was packed. A masterpiece of cool logic, the sermon relegated all the fever, the recrimination, the rancor, to history.

"How often have I spoken to you, instructed, counselled, warned, directed and fed you, and administered ordinances among you, as the people which were committed to my care, and whose precious souls I had the charge of? . . . I have spent the prime of my life and strength in labors for your eternal welfare . . . although I have often been troubled on every side, yet I have not been distressed; perplexed but not in despair; cast down, but not destroyed."

Now that his flock had publicly rejected him, his work with them was finished. Therefore was it not appropriate to consider "that time when we must meet one another before the chief Shepherd? When I must give an account of my stewardship, of the service I have done *for,* and the reception and treatment I have had *among,* the people he sent me to: and you must give an account of your own conduct towards me, and the improvement you have made of these *three and twenty* years of my ministry. For then you and I must appear together, and we both must give an account, in order to an infallible, righteous and eternal sentence to be passed upon us, by him who will judge us, with respect to all that we have said or done in our meetings here, all our conduct one towards another, in the house of God and elsewhere, on sabbath days and other days; who . . . will judge us with respect to all the controversies which have subsisted between us, with the strictest impartiality: . . . there is nothing covered, that shall not be revealed . . . and by him whose eyes are as a flame of fire: and truth and right shall be made plainly to appear, being stripped of every veil . . ."

—"Then it shall appear, whether I acted uprightly."

—"Then it will appear, whether the doctrine . . . be Christ's own doctrine."

—"Then it will appear, whether my people have done their duty to their pastor . . . whether I have been treated with that impartiality, candour and regard, which the just Judge esteemed due . . ."

—"Then every step of the conduct of each of us, in this affair, from first to last, and the spirit we have exercised in all, shall be examined and manifested, and our own consciences will speak plain and loud, and each of us shall be convinced, and the world shall know; and never shall there be any more mistake, misrepresentation or misapprehension in this affair, to eternity."

Finally, he appealed to those who professed godliness; to those who were Christless and graceless; to those beginning to awaken; to young people. He reminded each of the day of reckoning, "that your souls might be saved from everlasting destruction." He wished for them "a faithful pastor" able to conduct them "in the way to eternal blessedness."

"And let us all remember, and never forget, our future, solemn meeting, on that Great day of the Lord; the day of infallible and of the unalterable sentence. Amen."

STOCKBRIDGE

And so it was over. And yet not over, for he lingered a while.

He had his house, he had no employment, the town had no minister. He continued to supply the pulpit at ten pounds per Sabbath. He was urged to remain and be pastor of a new, second church. He gave this proposal no serious consideration, but his enemies became more upset than before his dismissal. Some half seriously proposed to establish an academy which he could head. Other offers came—from Canaan, Connecticut; from Lunenburg, Virginia; from Scotland.

He finally decided on Stockbridge, less than sixty miles to the west, about halfway between the Connecticut and Hudson Rivers. Here, beyond the line of the frontier, was a mission to the Indians. He had preached there before. He had been one of the launchers of the mission in 1734, with Colonel John Stoddard. Now he would minister to the Indians. He was essentially unfitted to teach Indians; but at least he might find some leisure to reflect and write; and perhaps some peace away from controversy. If these were his expectations, he could not have been more mistaken.

By late 1751 he was settled with his family in what might be called the "white compound," a village within a village inhabited by twelve white families surrounded by two hundred and fifty Indian families.

The Indians were of two conflicting tribes: the French-inclined Mohawks, the terror of all other Indians, and the Housatunnucks. Previous missionaries' conception of their task had been, so to speak, to Calvinize and Anglicize the Indians, along with completely eradicating Indian customs, ways of living, mode of thought, legends, and language.

The twelve white families mostly were closely related, the half who controlled the town were his personal enemies—members of the same Williams clan which had accomplished his downfall. Ephraim Williams and his family had been one of the first four families to be settled at Stockbridge by the Indian Commissioners in Boston. Abigail Williams, Ephraim's daughter, had married John Sergeant, the first missionary. Ephraim Williams was uncle to Israel Williams, Edwards' most powerful enemy; and to both Solomon Williams and Elisha Williams, who had prepared the reply to Edwards' *Humble Inquiry* in the Northampton dispute. Elisha Williams had just become a member of the London Society for the Propagation of the Gospel, which paid most of the missionary's salary. When John Sergeant died, his widow married Major Joseph Dwight, who was resident in Stockbridge as deputy for the Boston Commissioners. Dwight joined the Williams camp.

The Williams family completely controlled the town, turned money toward their own aggrandizement, and in the Williams way were laying foundations for eventual landholdings.

Edwards was the head of the mission, but helpless to direct it against those who considered the town and mission a profitable investment. Yet he was responsible to the Society for the Propagation of the Gospel, to the Boston Commissioners, who had power to disburse money, and to two congregations.

In this confused situation, Edwards revealed himself as a first-class executive and administrator. A letter written to Joseph Paine, official of the London Society, sets forth the conflict between commercial and religious interest, the waste of public monies, the duplication of effort by rival missionaries, and outlines a plan of centralized effort, with education the main objective, which sounds more like missionary planning a century later than that of pre-Revolution days. There is nothing whatever of the evangelist's point of view in this letter; he might be speaking of a program for a business enterprise. His suggestions are those of a practical man, who faces conditions as they are and acts accordingly.

Gradually, he won the confidence of the Indians. He preached mostly old sermons in English, but his pastoral services were appreciated by the Indians, in spite of his poor command of the Mohawk and Housatunnuck languages.

Edwards also won the confidence of the Commissioners—not so much, perhaps, because of interest in his missionary labors as because of their intense awareness of the necessity for having the Indians on the right side, or at least quiet, in the looming French and Indian War. When the Commissioners realized Edwards' correctness in saying the Indians deeply distrusted Ephraim Williams and Joseph Dwight, they took steps to end the Williams domination.

And only in time. The war broke out in 1754. The warlike Mohawks decamped. Mission work came almost to a standstill for three years. A fort was built around the Edwards house. Here, when several whites were murdered near by in the fall of 1754, came town residents and settlers from the countryside for refuge. Edwards served hundreds of meals, provided pasturage for many horses, and had consumed from his store of West India rum "seven gallons, one quart."

In spite of the fact that hostile Indians were outside the settlement and that the loyalty of the few Christian Housatunnuck Indians who remained inside was always in question, many visitors on horseback still visited the Edwards house. People who would carry letters were always coming and going. And there were many letters. Daughter Sarah had married Elisha Parsons in June of 1750; in November of the same year Mary had married Timothy Dwight of Northampton. Esther had married Aaron Burr, President of the College of New Jersey, which was to become Princeton the summer after the family's removal from Northampton. In fact, in 1756 she returned to visit her parents, carrying her infant son Aaron. And Jonathan and Sarah had a baby of their own in the house—Pierrepont, their youngest and last child, born in April of 1750, in Northampton.

Things continued more or less this way throughout the 1750's. Although the war continued, there were no local Indian uprisings except for one in 1756. Meanwhile, in addition to his teaching and administrative work, and with interruptions due to illness, Edwards found time for writing.

His first Stockbridge work was published in 1752. It was a hangover from the Northampton controversy: a reply to Solomon Williams' reply to his *Humble Inquiry*, titled *Misrepresentations Corrected and Truth Vindicated*. It was all polemic. Perry Miller has remarked of it that "if ever a man was cut into small pieces and run through a meat-grinder, it was Solomon Williams."

Whatever else the book did, it illustrated that, to Jonathan Edwards, attack growing out of a certain self-righteousness and inability to comprehend the feelings of others was most congenial. As Perry Miller has said, "The method is a sustained attack, never a defense; he demolishes at tedious lengths all possible positions of his opponents, including some they do not hold but might hold, and all the time hardly declares his own."

At any rate, whether or not it was the result of *Misrepresentations Corrected*, a few years later, in 1754, Joseph Hawley, who had helped lead the opposition to Edwards, wrote an apology: admitted that he had been wrong and asked forgiveness. Edwards was obliged in fairness to answer, but he did so with reluctance. He still felt pain. But he gave a sort of forgiveness.

THE LAST WRITING

In 1753, still under fire from his enemies in Stockbridge, Edwards began a work he had been thinking about for years— *Freedom of the Will*, generally considered to be one of the greatest philosophical treatises ever written by an American. The ideas it expressed were not new to Edwards. They had been with him all his adult life. In essence, they had been arrived at during the years at Yale. What he did now was to express them in magnificently organized form, and of course polemically, argumentatively. He had a dual foundation for this reasoning: one, proof from Scripture; the other, proof from reason, which meant pretty much Lockian reasoning.

The proof from Scripture included the many examples of God's foretelling of "men's moral conduct and qualities, their virtues and vices, their wickedness and good practice, things regardable and punishable." It included the foretelling by God of "many events which were consequent and dependent on the moral conduct of particular persons, and were accomplished, either by their virtuous or vicious actions," and His foretelling "the future moral conduct of nations and peoples." And, obviously, "unless God foreknows the future acts of moral agents, all the prophecies we have" are not true prophecies at all.

For if God cannot "foreknow, he can't foretell." If He can't "certainly foreknow the future volitions of moral agents, then neither can He certainly foreknow those events which are consequent and dependent on those volitions."

In short, free self-determination (free will) and God cannot exist in the same room. "If there be no absurdity or difficulty in supposing one thing to start out of nonexistence, into being, without a cause; then there is no absurdity or difficulty in supposing the same of millions of millions." So, if there really is free self-determination, then millions of uncaused events must be occurring every day. And the same of volitions, or acts of willing. If these occur uncaused, even in the slightest degree, the world is inherently without order.

Edwards' second proof, that from reason, has delighted philosophers ever since he wrote it. Here he attempts to establish that the principle of causation, or universal necessary causation, applies to the will. By causation, however, he does not mean that one thing causes another in the simplistic sense. Instead, he is thinking of a chain of linked events back to the beginning of time, each dependent on the one or ones before and a necessary antecedent to the ones after. The causation here is a "necessary connection"—"really nothing else than the full and fixed connection between the things signified by the subject and predicate of a proposition." He is thinking, really, of God's whole fabric— "God decrees all things harmonious and in excellent order."

As to this necessary connection, or necessity, there is a difference between a moral and a natural necessity. Moral necessity means a necessity "of moral obligation," or "that apparent connection of things, which is the ground of moral evidence; and so is distinguished from absolute necessity, or that sure connection of things, that is a foundation for infallible certainty." Or it can mean "that necessity of connection and consequence, which arises from such *moral causes*, as the strength of inclination, or motives . . . and such certain volitions and action." Natural necessity, on the other hand, refers only to some natural happening.

By "will" Edwards meant largely inclination, or pleasure toward something, "that by which the mind chooses anything."

By "freedom" or "liberty" he meant a person's being "free from hindrance or impediment in the way of doing, or conducting, in any way as he wills." And its opposite, necessity, for example, "is a person's being hindered or unable to conduct as he will, or being necessitated to do otherwise."

Obviously, then, freedom or liberty can only be ascribed to a *being* that has a faculty or property such as "will," not to will itself. Something with no will can't act according to or against its will. And therefore it doesn't make sense to talk about freedom or liberty as belonging to the will. The will does not have a will. "That which has the power of volition or choice is the man or the soul, and not the power of volition itself."

Thus "free will" can only mean freedom to do what one wills, not freedom to will what one wills. What one wills is caused— by a moral necessity. Thus, in the ordinary sense of the word, any man has freedom of will if that means freedom to do what is his choice. But his choice is something he cannot choose—that is determined, by "necessity" rather than "compulsion."

But if will is determined in this sense, then why praise or blame Heaven or hell? And here, of course, was where Edwards had to justify God to man. It came to, to quote section headings —"God's moral excellency necessary yet virtuous and praiseworth" . . . "Jesus' holiness necessary, yet to be praised" . . . "The case of such as are given up to God to sin, and of fallen man in general, proves moral necessity and inability to be consistent with blameworthiness. Command, and obligation to obedience [are] consistent with moral inability to obey" . . . " 'Sincerity is no excuse' " . . . "It is agreeable to common sense and the natural notions of mankind, to suppose moral necessity to be consistent with praise and blame, reward and punishment."

One after another, Edwards knocked down objections, such as that Calvinism winds up by being fatalism and Calvinism makes God the author of sin. He agreed that in a certain sense, God *is* the author of sin if that means being the "permitter or at least not a hinderer." But He may be the author of sin and yet not be the "*actor* of sin," but, on the contrary, be the actor "of holiness."

Today, most minds can follow the argument well up to Edwards' explanations of how a will conditioned by necessity can be punished by God with flames forever because it wills to do what it must will to do, and how this illustrates the greater glory and holiness of God.

As a boy, Edwards had rebelled against what seemed the injustice of God; as a young man, imbued with Locke, he came to accept it with inner joy and calm, and to consider it justice. But, when it came to questioning the assumptions, his mind was blank. His father had insured that Jonathan Edwards would apply a brilliant critical faculty to criticize everything but what his father had taught him.

He never wrote truer than that a man can do what he wills, but his will cannot will what he wills. That is determined by necessity. And Jonathan Edwards' necessity was, one must conclude, determined by his father. Edwards wrote, in effect, that the will is the whole man choosing, "the very willing is the doing." And the whole Jonathan Edwards, in the later years of his life, was the Jonathan Edwards there had been before, back to 1703. For the critical first dozen years, his father had ruled completely.

Freedom of the Will was published in 1754, under the title of *A Careful and Strict Enquiry into Modern Prevailing Notions of that Freedom of Will, which is Supposed to be Essential to Moral Agency, Virtue, and Vice, Reward and Punishment, Praise and Blame.* In a sense, it was only a building block in a larger structure Edwards never lived to finish. The next block was *The Great Christian Doctrine of Original Sin Defended; Evidences of Its Truth Produced, and Arguments to the Contrary Answered.*

Once again, he was elaborating ideas he had come to long before. And again he wrote a polemic. The facts of sheer observation pointed plainly enough to man's innate depravity. And this depravity, or corruption, is his very nature. By itself, it takes him to ruin. This corruption is not necessarily crime. It is the inner evil which shuts man from God—it is moral corruption. When man sinned originally, and broke God's law, his "superior principles" left him. God withdrew them. And they remained withdrawn through all the generations since Adam, because the whole human race was one. Adam and his posterity *"constitute but one moral person."*

Edwards never lived to see *Original Sin* in print. It was still on the press at the time he died. Nor did he live to see in print another work, *The Nature of True Virtue.* This was not published until seven years after his death.

True Virtue leaves one with a sense that it is unfinished. It simply stops without returning to its initial statements. But this was very late in Edwards' life. He was tired. Nevertheless, Perry Miller judges that *True Virtue*'s "perfection of form shows what he could have done with pure thought had he not for all his life been obliged to sacrifice himself to controversy." Yet one must remember it was he himself who chose to sacrifice himself in controversy. We see it when he was an adolescent at Yale; we see it in his father in another form; we see it in his father's father.

At the same time that he was working on *True Virtue*—which probably was never properly finished—Edwards was also preparing another work, *Concerning the End for Which God Created the World.* Both of these books were certainly intended to be part of, or preparation for, a great project which he had had in his mind all his life. This was to demonstrate "how all arts and sciences, the more they are perfected, the more they issue in divinity." It was to be called, or at least he so called it in his mind, "A Rational Account of the Main Doctrines of the Christian Religion Attempted."

In part, the *End for Which God Created the World* is polemic; in part, it is a presentation from Scripture. But it is also something else, which is partly implied, partly expressed, through all the work of his life. God's end, or purpose, is *"the glory of God"* and it, "when spoken of as the supreme and ultimate end of all God's works, is the emanation and true external expression of God's internal glory and fulness." Edwards confessed "a degree of obscurity" in what he was saying, but it was "an obscurity which is unavoidable, through the imperfection of language to express things of so sublime a nature." He tried using a variety of expressions to communicate what he meant, but fell back finally upon "that glory which the scripture speaks of as the ultimate end of all God's works . . . the internal and essential glory of God itself."

As to man—"the creature"—

"When God was about to create the world, he had respect to that *emanation of his glory* which is *actually* the consequence of the creation, both with regard to himself and the creature. He had regard to it as an *emanation* from himself, a *communication* of himself, and, as the *thing communicated*, in its nature *returned* to himself, as its final terms. And he had regard to it also as the *emanation* was *to* the creature, and as the *thing communicated* was *in* the creature, as its subject.

"And God had regard to it in this manner, as he had a supreme regard to himself, and value for his own infinite, internal glory. It was this value for himself that caused him to value and seek that his internal glory should *flow forth* from himself."

Because God values himself, he "delights in the knowledge, and love, and joy of the creature." And the creature is only happy as he becomes one with God.

"It is no solid objection against God aiming at an infinitely perfect union of the creature with himself, that the particular time will never come when it can be said, the union is now infinitely perfect. God aims at satisfying justice in the eternal damnation of sinners: which will be satisfied no otherwise than with regard to its eternal duration. But yet there never will come that particular moment when it can be said, that now justice is satisfied. But if this does not satisfy our modern free thinkers, who do not like the talk about satisfying justice with an infinite punishment; I suppose it will not be denied by any, that God, in glorifying the saints in heaven with eternal felicity, aims to satisfy his infinite grace or benevolence, by the bestowment of a good infinitely valuable, because eternal: and yet there never will come the moment when it can be said, that *now* this infinitely valuable good has been actually bestowed."

At one time, long before, Edwards had told himself privately that if he had to "speak plain," he would have to say that God is space. He had said that all things are the idea in God's mind, and God is idea: that there is no proper substance but God Himself. He had written in the *Miscellanies* of the Trinity—" 'Tis evident that there are no more than these three, really distinct in God—God, and His idea, and His love and delight. We can't conceive of any further real distinctions."

One wishes that when the young Edwards had read Newton's *Opticks,* he had paid more attention to one sentence. Newton had written about God in the beginning forming "Matter in solid, massy, hard, impenetrable, moveable Particles . . . so very hard, as never to wear or break in pieces; no ordinary power being able to divide what God himself made in the first Creation."

Edwards had given the Power of God, the Idea, as that which forced them to cohere. He had also read what Newton had written:

"Now the smallest Particles of Matter may cohere by the strongest Attractions, and compose bigger Particles of weaker virtue; and many of these may cohere and compose bigger Particles whose Virtue is still weaker, and so on for divers Successions, until the Progression end in the biggest Particles on which the Operations in Chymistry, and the Colours of natural Bodies depend, and which by cohering compose Bodies of a sensible Magnitude.

"There are therefore Agents in Nature able to make the Particles of Bodies stick together by very strong Attractions."

All this Edwards had read.

But had he read the next sentence? . . . *"And it is the business of Experimental Philosophy to find them out."*

Benjamin Franklin placed himself within the tradition that sentence represents. Jonathan Edwards, true son of his father, placed himself outside. For experimental philosophy he substituted experimental piety.

DEATH COMES

By late 1757 Stockbridge was relatively quiet. The Indians who remained at the mission were accepting Edwards' ministrations. The domination of the Williams clan had been at least temporarily scotched. Edwards had a home and several hundred acres of land. Timothy, born in 1738, had graduated from college. Sarah, his oldest daughter, had married Elihu Parsons, and lived near by with her children. Jonathan, Elizabeth and Pierrepont, his youngest children, were with him. His wife and three unmarried daughters were with him. Samuel Hopkins and Joseph Bellamy, both noted theologians and good friends, lived not far away.

Edwards had made a new home, a new career. He was deep in a new study, a *History of Redemption*. He was writing theology in a new way: historically. His plan was to show that history has unity. It is all part of a single plan. "It is one design that is formed." In its oscillations, history nevertheless progressed toward a goal. There had been progress from Adam to Christ, then a falling off, and after that a state of "finishing things off which before had been preparing." Mankind was reaching the threshold of the millennium.

Edwards no longer had his youthful energies. He was tired. But he kept working. Then, all at once, his life was disrupted.

26007

On September 27, 1757, his son-in-law Aaron Burr, first President of New Jersey College, died. Edwards had known New Jersey College for many years. Its trustees were in sympathy with him and he with them. In fact, he had been considered for the presidency in 1748 before Burr was elected. He had been in close touch with the college ever since.

Two days later, September 29, the Board of Trustees voted by an overwhelming majority for Jonathan Edwards to take Aaron Burr's place. Edwards should have felt honored. In a sense, he did. But in another sense he was downcast. He was in no mood for another move. But, on the other hand, he was aware that he might some day be forced out of his post at the mission. His enemies were merely waiting for an opportunity to get rid of him.

Finally, on October 19, 1757, Edwards wrote a letter to the trustees frankly putting forth what he considered his disqualifications to be "Head of Nassau Hall."

He was just beginning to be "comfortable" at Stockbridge. He had serious defects: "I have a constitution, in many respects peculiarly unhappy, attended with flaccid solids, vapid, sizy and scare fluids, and a low tide of spirits; often occasioning a kind of childish weakness and contemptibleness of speech, presence, and demeanor, with a disagreeable dulness and stiffness, much unfitting me for conversation, but more especially for the government of a college."

He was also, he wrote, "deficient in some parts of learning, particularly in Algebra, and the higher parts of Mathematics, and in the Greek Classics; my Greek learning having been chiefly in the New Testament."

Besides, study had long "swallowed up" his mind and had been "the chief entertainment and delight" of his life. He had no wish to exchange this for running a college, nor did his tastes and the low state of his energies fit him for such a task.

Also—and here he described them—he was deeply engaged

in his *History of the Work of Redemption* and was preparing for another, to be called the *Harmony of the Old and New Testament*, "in three parts."

So, he felt somewhat at a loss. Nevertheless, in view of "the greatness of the affair, and the regard due to so worthy and venerable a body as that of the trustees of Nassau Hall," he was obliged to consider the matter seriously. He would neither accept nor reject, but would ask further advice. And he made a condition—which was, in effect, that he must be permitted to pursue his studies while president.

The outcome was a foregone conclusion. His neighboring ministers, including Hopkins and Bellamy, met in council at his request, on January 4, 1758, and decided that the call was from God.

On February 16, 1758, Edwards arrived in Princeton, accompanied by his daughter Lucy. He was inducted into office the same day. Later in the spring, when the President's house was ready, his wife and the other members of his family were to follow him. But they were never to occupy the President's house.

Smallpox had been all but endemic around Princeton for some months, with many deaths. A good many people were having themselves inoculated. Inoculation—not vaccination, which was not discovered until 1796 by Edward Jenner—was hazardous. It consisted in essence of attempting to infect a person with a light case of smallpox from someone who had a light case of it. Edwards had decided long ago that in spite of some objections to it on religious grounds, he would undergo inoculation if the situation warranted. And now he felt the situation warranted. Lucy had caught smallpox the preceding summer in Princeton and had been seriously ill for weeks. So, although he himself was in frail health after an illness during the preceding winter, he consulted the trustees. They consented and he was inoculated. His daughter Esther was inoculated at the same time.

He caught smallpox—"favorably," meaning lightly, at first. Then, when he was improving, "a secondary fever set in, and by reason of a number of pustules in his throat, the obstruction was such, that the medicines necessary to check the fever, could not be administered."

In the fashion of the day, he was told there was no hope. He was puzzled. Then why had God led him to Princeton? But he accepted it.

"And a very short time before he expired," wrote Dr. William Shippen, a physician who attended him, "he spoke to Lucy to ye following purpose, dear lucy it seems to me to be the Will of God that I must shortly leave you, therefore give my kindest love to my dear Wife & tell her that the uncommon Union that has so long subsisted between us has been of such a Nature as I trust is Spiritual and therefore will continue for ever: and I hope she will be supported under so Great a trial and submit cheerfully to the Will of God; And as to my Children, you are now like to be left Fatherless which I hope will be an Inducement to you to seek a Father who will never fail you; & as to my Funeral I would have it to be like unto Mr Burrs, and any additional sum of Money that might be expected to be laid out that way, I would have it disposed of to charitable uses."

He died on March 22, 1758.

Two weeks later, Esther, who had been inoculated at the same time, died of a sudden flare-up of smallpox after she had been thought well. In the same year, on October 2, Edwards' widow Sarah died in Philadelphia, where she had gone to get Esther's two small children. She was buried in Princeton, next to Jonathan, Esther, and her son-in-law Aaron Burr.

FOR THE READER WHO WOULD KNOW MORE

What follows is a guide for the interested reader rather than a scholarly bibliography. Full bibliographies can be found in the books listed. The list is divided into books easily procurable in paperback form, and those which are in hard covers.

PAPERBACK

Biographies and Selections:

Aldridge, Alfred Owen. *Jonathan Edwards,* Washington Square Press, New York, 1964. Critique of Edwards' philosophy.

Faust, Clarence H., and Johnson, Thomas H. *Jonathan Edwards, Representative Selections,* etc., Hill and Wang, New York, 1935 and 1962. Handiest selection of Edwards' writings. Excellent critique and bibliography.

Miller, Perry. *Jonathan Edwards,* a Meridian Book, World Publishing Company, Cleveland, 1959, 1963; originally published in hard covers by William Sloane Associates, New York, 1961. Fine biography of Edwards' mind.

Winslow, Ola. *Jonathan Edwards,* Collier Books, New York, 1949; originally published in hard covers by the Macmillan Company, New York, 1940. The standard biography, a Pulitzer Prize winner.

Background:

Locke, John. *An Essay Concerning Human Understanding,* Gateway Edition, Henry Regnery Company, Chicago, 1956. Somewhat abbreviated.

Miller, Perry, and Johnson, Thomas H. *The Puritans,* 2 volumes, Harper Torchbooks, Harper and Row, New York, 1963; originally published in hard covers by American Book Company in 1938. History, discussion and selections from Puritan writing.

Newton, Sir Isaac. *Opticks,* Dover, New York, 1952.

HARDCOVER

Biography, Discussion and Selections:

Allen, Alexander V. G. *Jonathan Edwards,* Houghton and Mifflin, Boston and New York, 1889. The standard biography until publication of Ola Winslow's.

Elwood, Douglas J. *The Philosophical Theology of Jonathan Edwards,* Columbia University Press, New York, 1960. Relates Edwards to contemporary philosophy and theology.

Ferm, Virgilius. *The Collected Writings of Jonathan Edwards,* Library Publishers, New York, 1953. Useful selection, text modernized.

Townsend, Harvey G. *The Philosophy of Jonathan Edwards,* University of Oregon Press, Eugene, Oregon, 1955. Useful selections from *Miscellanies* and other writings.

Works:

Images or Shadows of Divine Things, edited by Perry Miller, Yale University Press, New Haven & London, 1948.

The Nature of True Virtue, with a foreword by William K. Frankena, University of Michigan Press, Ann Arbor, Michigan, 1960.

Works, ed. by Sereno E. Dwight, 10 volumes, New York, 1829, 1830. The most used complete edition. The first volume is a biography by Dwight.

Works, General Editorship by Perry Miller. In process of preparation and publication, Yale University Press, New Haven, 1957 and years following. When completed, this will be the standard edition of Edwards' works. At this writing, two volumes have been published:

Volume 1, *Freedom of the Will,* edited by Paul Ramsey, 1957 and reprinted 1962.

Volume 2, *Religious Affections,* edited by John E. Smith, 1959.

GILBERT TENNENT:
GADFLY FOR RIGHTEOUSNESS

❧

Russell T. Hitt

When George Whitefield arrived in colonial Philadelphia early in November of 1739 fresh from his preaching triumphs in London, he was greeted by throngs of admirers. True, some of the Church of England clergymen were cool toward him just as their counterparts had been in Britain. But the Dissenters—Baptists, Presbyterians, Moravians and Quakers—welcomed him to their pulpits and their homes.

A towering figure in his flowing black cassock, Edinburgh collar, and white wig, the young Anglican priest, imbued with the enthusiasm of the Methodists, looked considerably older than his twenty-four years. Soon the cobbled streets of the largest city of the colonies echoed with the hoofbeats of horses carrying riders eager to hear the preacher who was soon to become the catalyst of the Great Awakening.

The crowds swelled beyond the capacity of any church in Philadelphia, so Whitefield spoke to six thousand eager listeners from the steps of the courthouse. Again, and from the same vantage point in Penn's "Green Countrie Towne," he addressed an ever-increasing throng. Benjamin Franklin, originally more curious about the way Whitefield could project his voice than in the content of his message, became one of his warm friends.

Soon after his arrival, Whitefield was entertained at dinner by Thomas Penn, colonial proprietor of Pennsylvania and son of the city's founder. After the meal Whitefield "prayed with and gave a word of exhortation to more than a roomful of people, who came . . . to hear the Gospel of Christ."

On Saturday morning, November 10, 1739, after preaching to a packed church, Whitefield dined with the parish minister, then went to his rented quarters to rest briefly and to receive visitors. First to arrive was one who was to play an important part in Whitefield's subsequent ministry: William Tennent, founder and "principal" of the Log College, the only training school for Presbyterian ministers in the Middle Colonies. Whitefield wrote in his *Journal* that he "was much comforted by the coming of Mr. Tennent, an old gray-headed disciple and soldier of Jesus Christ." In the ensuing conversation Whitefield learned that he and his elderly visitor had a common friend in Ebenezer Erskine, founder of the Secession Church in Scotland. As they talked, Whitefield was fascinated with Tennent's description of his unique ministry, the training of nearly a score of worthy young men, including his four sons, for the ministry, in a log building near his church at Neshaminy, some twenty miles north of Philadelphia.

The Tennents were experiencing opposition and ostracism from ministers in their Presbyterian Synod, even as Whitefield had been despised for his "enthusiasm" and evangelism by his brethren in the Church of England. As they communed together, the sixty-six-year-old Tennent and the brilliant young English orator found their hearts knit by a common concern about the deadness of the churches.

"Though we are but few, and stand alone, as it were like Elijah, yet I doubt not the Lord will appear for us, as he did for that prophet, and make us more than conquerors," Whitefield commented in his *Journal* on their conversation.

Joined by Tennent, Whitefield went at three o'clock the same day to preach in the city prison, speaking on the trembling jailer of Philippi. "The place was crowded," the *Journal* declares, "and many wept. Returned home with the Swedish minister and old Mr. Tennent. Conversed with them of the things of God; and in the evening, preached to as large a congregation as there was the night before from the Court House stairs."

Before William Tennent departed from the city, he must have told Whitefield more about his four sons—Gilbert, William Junior, John, and Charles—and also extended him an invitation to visit his church and Log College at Neshaminy. Whitefield said that he was leaving the very next week for New York and en route would visit Gilbert, the old gentleman's eldest son, in New Brunswick, New Jersey.

Three days later George Whitefield and Gilbert Tennent met for the first time. These were the men, who more than any others, would light the fires of the first widespread spiritual movement in America—the Great Awakening. For Gilbert Tennent, spurred by Whitefield's energy, vision and powerful preaching, would become the chief human instrument of the Awakening in New Jersey and Pennsylvania, even as Jonathan Edwards was to fulfill that role in New England. There were many spiritual influences that had prepared Gilbert Tennent for such a role, but without doubt he and Edwards owed much to the visits of Whitefield to the Colonies.

Whitefield had already heard of the famed Jonathan Edwards, but he had never expected to find a man of Gilbert Tennent's spiritual stature and preaching ability in America. In later years Whitefield declared that he had never found a man more to his liking.

It was one o'clock in the afternoon of Tuesday, November 13, 1739, when Whitefield arrived in New Brunswick after riding horseback for a day and a half. He had stopped to preach in Burlington, New Jersey, and had spent the night in Trenton. On that very day he covered the thirty miles from Trenton to New Brunswick in seven hours of hard riding.

Gilbert Tennent actually was thirty-six years old when they

met for the first time, although Whitefield judged him to be forty. Like his British visitor, Tennent was tall—slightly more than six feet—and he was similarly clad in the long black robe of a minister, with white wig and collar. Full-faced and vigorous, Tennent had gray, piercing eyes and a clean-cut jaw. Because he wore a leather girdle around his waist, he was described as a sort of John the Baptist by his contemporaries.

Dr. Samuel Finley, an alumnus of the Log College, described Tennent like this: "In his manners, at first view, he seemed distant and reserved; yet, upon nearer acquaintance, he was ever found affable, condescending, and communicative. And what greatly endeared his conversation was an openness and undisguised honesty; at the greatest remove from artifice and dissimulation, which were the abhorrence of his soul . . ."

In eighteenth-century language Finley attested that Tennent "was tender, loving, and compassionate; kind and agreeable in every relation; an assured friend to such as he esteemed worthy of his regards; and a common patron to all whom he apprehended were injured or distressed . . ."

On that afternoon in 1739 when two of the three key figures of the Great Awakening met for the first time, Gilbert Tennent had been the pastor of the Presbyterian Church of New Brunswick for twelve years. He had already benefited greatly from the teaching of his devout and learned father and had been greatly helped spiritually by his contact with the aged dominie of the Reformed Dutch Church, Theodorus Jacobus Frelinghuysen, who served a nearby parish.

From the start Whitefield was impressed by Gilbert Tennent. "Left Trenton at six in the morning, and reached Brunswick, thirty miles distant, at one. Here we were much refreshed with the company of Gilbert Tennent, an eminent Dissenting minister, about forty years of age, son of that good old man who came to see me on Saturday at Philadelphia. God, I find, has been pleased greatly to own his labours. He and his associates are now the burning and shining lights of this part of America. Several pious souls came to see me at his house, with whom I took sweet counsel. At their request, and finding there was a general expectation of hearing me, I read the Church liturgy, and preached in the evening at Mr. Tennent's meetinghouse; for there is no place set apart for the worship of the Church of England, and it is common, I was told, in America, for the Dissenters and Conformists to worship at different times in the same place. Oh, that the partition wall were broken down, and we all with one heart and one mind could glorify our common Lord and Saviour Jesus Christ!"

Whitefield persuaded Gilbert Tennent to accompany him on the journey to New York. The next morning they were riding horseback together toward Elizabeth and thoroughly enjoying each other's company. The exact conversation was not recorded, but Whitefield's *Journal* reveals some clues: "As we passed along, we spent our time most agreeably in telling one another what God had done for our souls."

Although Whitefield had received his bachelor of arts degree from Oxford University three years earlier and already had become an internationally known preacher, as well as a leader with John and Charles Wesley of the Evangelical revival in England, he had come from a humble background. His parents had operated the Bell Inn at Gloucester. In his "A Short Account of God's Dealings with the Rev. Mr. George Whitefield," the great revivalist confessed: "I can truly say I was froward from my mother's womb. . . . I can date some very early acts of uncleanness. Lying, filthy talking, and foolish jesting I was much addicted to. Sometimes I used to curse, if not swear. Stealing from my mother I thought no theft at all. . . . Cards and reading romances were my heart's delight.

"Whatever foreseen fitness for salvation others may talk of and glory in, I disclaim any such thing . . . yet I can recollect very early movings of the Holy Spirit upon my heart, sufficient to satisfy me that God loved me with an everlasting love, and separated me even from my mother's womb . . ."

Tennent must have told Whitefield something of his own earlier life. His godly father, William, for a time had been a minister in the Anglican Church in Ireland although he was married to Katherine Kennedy, the daughter of a distinguished Irish Presbyterian minister. Gilbert, first of the four sons, was born February 5, 1703, in County Armagh. In 1718, when Gilbert had reached the age of fifteen, the family decided to emigrate to the colonies and set sail for America.

Possibly while crossing the Atlantic Ocean on a sailing vessel, Gilbert Tennent came into a deep religious experience. Undoubtedly his father, who was always close to his four sons, counseled the youth, "who was often in great agony of spirit" because of his great concern about his relationship to God. Finally, as Gilbert Tennent later declared, "It pleased God to give him the light of the knowledge of His glory in the face of Jesus Christ."

Gilbert Tennent had read widely in books of theology. Like his father, he became so fluent in Latin that he could converse readily in that language, discussing doctrine and biblical truth with his father and his brothers. For a time he was so convinced of his unworthiness to become a minister that he spent an entire year in the study of medicine.

But, at about this time, "it pleased God to reveal himself to him with so much clearness and comfort, that all his doubts and sorrows and fears were dispelled, and the Sun of Righteousness arose upon him with healing under his wings."

So thorough had his father's instruction been that—for he had received virtually no other training—Gilbert Tennent was awarded a master of arts degree from Yale College in 1725 when he was twenty-three years old. There is evidence that he spent less than a year at Yale before the graduate degree was awarded. In the same year the Presbytery of Philadelphia licensed him to preach. Shortly thereafter he was called to "supply" the Presbyterian Church at New Castle, Delaware, and then received a call to serve as minister, but departed rather unceremoniously from this opportunity. The records do not disclose the reason for his strange action. For this he was rebuked by the Presbytery before he was permitted to accept an opportunity to start a new church at New Brunswick, New Jersey, and was ordained there in 1727.

After a difficult start in New Brunswick, Tennent came under the benign influence of Frelinghuysen, and began to see a rich response to his preaching. It was at this stage of his ministry that Whitefield came into his life.

The Anglican had listened intently to his friend's story. Then he shared the account of his own early missteps and backslidings that were interspersed by deep spiritual concern and a desire to serve God. Encouraged by friends to continue his education, Whitefield had made good progress for several years, but then had dropped out of school to become a "common drawer" of ale in his mother's tavern. In a spiritual slump for a year and a half, Whitefield finally resolved to enter Pembroke College, Oxford, where he earned his way as a servitor. His resolve to continue his schooling and prepare for the ministry was deepened by Thomas à Kempis' *The Imitation of Christ*. He had also discovered William Law's *A Serious Call to a Devout and Holy Life* and *Christian Perfection*. Then Charles Wesley, a fellow student at Oxford, had placed in his hands *Against the Fear of Man*, the work of August Herman Francke, the German Pietist, and another book entitled *The Life of God in the Soul of Man*. It was while reading this book that Whitefield came across the expression: "True religion is union of the soul with God, and Christ formed within us." Whitefield said, "A ray of divine light was instantaneously darted in upon my soul, and from that moment, but not until then, did I know I must be a new creature."

Now Whitefield wrote in his *Journal* concerning Tennent: "He recounted to me many instances of God's striving with his heart, and how grace, at last, overcame all his fightings against God."

The time passed quickly while the two religious leaders conversed and by noon the two men had covered the twenty-two miles to Elizabeth, where they boarded a boat that took them to New York in four hours.

A Mr. Noble and members of his family hospitably greeted Whitefield and Tennent on their arrival in Manhattan and invited the men to stay with them. That evening Whitefield heard Tennent preach for the first time. The service was held in the Presbyterian meetinghouse. It was an experience Whitefield had not expected. "Then I went to the meetinghouse to hear Mr. Gilbert Tennent preach," he wrote in his *Journal*, "and never before heard such a searching sermon. He convinced me more and more that we can preach the Gospel of Christ no further than we have experienced the power of it in our own hearts. Being deeply convicted of sin, by God's Holy Spirit at his first conversion, he has learned experimentally to dissect the heart of a natural man. Hypocrites must either soon be converted or enraged at his preaching. He is a son of thunder, and does not fear the faces of men. After sermon, we spent the evening together at Mr. Noble's house. My soul was humbled and melted down with a sense of God's mercies, and I found what a babe and novice I was in the things of God. Blessed Jesus, grant I make continual advances, until I come to a perfect man in Thee."

Whitefield had found a preacher whom he felt more than excelled his own great gifts. Though Whitefield's influence upon Gilbert Tennent was incalculable, Whitefield, in turn, was greatly challenged by the Calvinistic theology of his newly-found Dissenter friend.

Gilbert Tennent and Whitefield were warmly accepted by the Reverend Ebenezer Pemberton, Presbyterian minister in New York, but Whitefield was denied the pulpits of both the Church of England and the Reformed Dutch Church. Again Whitefield

took to the fields and great throngs gave him responsive attention. Tennent, on his departure for New Brunswick, invited his
new-found friend to preach for him on the return journey to
Philadelphia.

Whitefield describes his second visit to New Brunswick:
"Tuesday, Nov. 20. Reached here about six last night; and
preached today, at noon, for nearly two hours, in worthy Mr.
Tennent's meetinghouse, to a large assembly gathered together
from all parts; and amongst them, Mr. Tennent told me, was
a great number of solid Christians. About three in the afternoon,
I preached again; and, at seven, I baptized two children, and
preached a third time. Among others who came to hear the
Word, were several ministers, whom the Lord has been pleased
to honor, in making them instruments of bringing many sons to
glory. One of them was a Dutch Calvinist minister, named Free-
ling Housen [*sic*], pastor of a congregation about four miles
from New Brunswick . . ."

Whitefield set out the following day for Trenton in the company of Gilbert Tennent. At the urging of Tennent they stopped
off in Maidenhead to conduct meetings in the Reverend John
Rowland's church. Rowland, one of the Log College alumni,
impressed Whitefield: "Blessed be God for sending forth such
burning and shining lights in the midst of the thick darkness
that is upon the face of this generation," Whitefield wrote in his
Journal. "Thou Lord of the harvest, send forth more such labor-
ers into Thy harvest."

The travelers stayed at Trenton that night, and then set out
the next morning for Neshaminy. At noon, when they arrived,
they found a crowd of three thousand people gathered in the
meetinghouse yard listening to William Tennent preach.

"When I came up, he soon stopped," Whitefield chronicled,
"and sang a psalm, and then I began to speak. At first the people
seemed unaffected, but, in the midst of my discourse, the hearers
began to be melted down, and cried much. After I had finished,

Mr. Gilbert Tennent gave a word of exhortation. At the end of his discourse, we sang a psalm, and then dismissed the people with a blessing. Oh, that the Lord may say Amen to it!

"After our exercises were over, we went to old Mr. Tennent, who entertained us like one of the ancient patriarchs. His wife seemed to me like Elizabeth, and he like Zacharias; both as far as I can find, walk in all the ordinances and commandments of the Lord blameless. We had sweet communion with each other, and spent the evening in concerting measures for promoting our Lord's Kingdom."

Whitefield then had opportunity to learn about the Log College, the school that pioneered the way for the College of New Jersey, later to be called Princeton University. In 1739, however, the Tennents thought of the Log College only as a training station for ministers of the gospel, thus spearheading what came to be known as the "New Side" party in the Presbyterian Church. The "Old Side" ministers were suspicious of revivals and evangelism and regarded the Tennents as a divisive influence in the church.

To avoid the opposition leveled against them, the Tennent party had succeeded in having their churches appointed as a separate Presbytery so that they could train and ordain "New Side" ministers and bring life to what they felt was a decadent denomination.

Whitefield provides us with what is believed to be the only description of the Log College: "The place wherein the young men study now is, in contempt, called *the College*. It is a log house, about twenty feet long, and nearly as many broad; and to me, it seemed to resemble the school of the old prophets. . . . From this despised place, seven or eight worthy ministers of Jesus have lately gone forth; more are almost ready to be sent; and a foundation is now being laid for the instruction of many others."

The British evangelist was also impressed by the crowds of

horsemen who gathered at Neshaminy. "I believe there were nearly a thousand horses. The people did not sit upon them to hear the sermon, as in England, but tied them to the hedges; and thereby much disorder was prevented."

On the following day Whitefield left the Tennents, but there were mutual promises to "remember each other *publicly* in our prayers."

Thus it was that the Tennents and Whitefield became fast friends. Whitefield had great admiration for the elder Tennent but it was Gilbert Tennent whose personality and preaching moved him more than any other man in America. Possessed of great pulpit eloquence and power himself, Whitefield felt dwarfed in the presence of Gilbert Tennent.

This brief contact with the Tennents had sharpened Whitefield's theological insights and intensified his convictions on election and related areas of Puritan theology. Soon he would resist his close friend, John Wesley, for the Arminian view of universal redemption, thus forcing a theological gulf between them that was never closed, despite their personal affection for each other.

Whitefield's energetic evangelism had been like a flame to Gilbert Tennent's oil-soaked torch. The American leader of the evangelistic wing of the Presbyterian Church henceforth was to proclaim ever more boldly the message of renewal.

A better understanding of Gilbert Tennent can be had by reviewing the accomplishments of his family—a family that was both devout and learned. His father William, whose early life story has been unearthed by the capable research of church historian Leonard J. Trinterud, author of *The Forming of an American Tradition*, was born in 1673, probably in Scotland, recent research indicates. On his mother's side, William Tennent was related to James Logan, a colleague of William Penn and a noted American colonial statesman and scholar.

William Tennent was educated at the University of Edinburgh, receiving his master of arts degree on July 11, 1693. Soon after he was licensed to preach by one of the presbyteries of the Church of Scotland, he moved to Ireland and presented his credentials in 1701 to the General Synod of Ulster meeting in Antrim, Ireland. Difficulties within the Scottish Church had caused many Scots to settle in Northern Ireland, although this move did not spare them from ecclesiastical unrest and difficulty. Tennent took no parish in the Irish Presbyterian Church. In 1702 he married Katherine Kennedy, daughter of the Reverend Gilbert Kennedy.

Gilbert Tennent, a son of this union, was born February 5, 1703 and was named after his illustrious maternal grandfather. The very year that he was born, the Irish Parliament passed severe laws against the Roman Catholics and Presbyterians and some of the elder Tennent's relatives conformed to the Anglican Church. For reasons not fully explained, William Tennent himself took holy orders in the Anglican Church of Ireland and accepted an appointment, not as a parish rector but as a chaplain to an Irish nobleman, in 1704.

Three other sons were born to the Tennents: William in 1705; John in 1707; and Charles in 1711. Little is known about specific incidents in the boyhood of the Tennent children, but it was a closely knit family in which prayer and reading of the Word of God were the normal shared experience of the family. The Lord's Day was strictly observed as the Sabbath, which meant refraining from all toil and even innocent amusement. All the Tennent lads were tutored by their father, who trained them to become erudite ministers of the gospel able to hold their own with graduates of the British universities of the Old World and of Harvard and Yale in the New. They were indoctrinated with Puritan theology and morality.

The piety and theological convictions of the William Tennent family were not compatible with the prevailing climate of the Anglican Church. Indeed, William Tennent later affirmed that within that Church they "were conniving at the practice of Arminian doctrines inconsistent with the eternal purpose of God." The Ulster Presbyterians were intensely and polemically orthodox but devoid of piety. The Scottish Church in which the elder Tennent had first been licensed was falling under the influence of the Moderate Party which later became so obnoxious to the Erskines.

Maybe William Tennent, prodded perhaps by his Presbyterian father-in-law and dogged by his earlier Dissenting convictions, became increasingly disenchanted with Episcopal polity. Sometime in 1718, the Tennent family set sail for America. When they arrived in Philadelphia, they were warmly received by James Logan, "agent and secretary of all Pennsylvania."

In due course William Tennent applied to the Presbyterian Synod of Philadelphia, appearing before that august body on September 16, 1718, to renounce Episcopalianism as an unscriptural form of church government. He was accepted by the Synod which ordered its moderator to "give him a serious exhortation to continue steadfast in his now holy profession."

After serving two charges, one at East Chester and one at Bedford, New York, William Tennent moved with his family in 1727 to take a charge in the wilderness of Bucks County at Bensalem, just north of Philadelphia. Five years later he established a new parish in Neshaminy in the same county and there served to the end of his days.

There are many misconceptions about the state of religion in the early eighteenth century in the American Colonies. The settlers in the New World were confronted with all the difficulties of frontier life. The scattered churches were supported by small congregations made up of families living at great distances. The roads were poor and horses provided the only means of transportation. In addition, there was a shortage of trained ministers. Many of those who professed to be properly ordained were renegades from the old country with forged papers.

Trinterud vividly describes the vicissitudes of frontier life caused by poverty, hardship, suffering, and disease that often produced sudden bereavements. Also, there were constant encounters with hostile Indians. These conditions bred callousness, resentment and cynicism. Pioneer life developed coarseness and indecency. Because men were thrown upon their own resources to battle the Indians and elements as they eked out a living, they developed an individualistic spirit that stifled brotherly kindness and mercy and encouraged cruelty and indifference.

The preaching of the day was not very inspiring. Benjamin Franklin remarked that the minister of the Presbyterian Church in Philadelphia spent his time in polemics against other churches or in defending his own position.

This was the situation into which William Tennent introduced his family. There was a time when he was considered for a successor to Timothy Cutler as president of Yale when the latter "defected" from Congregationalism to the Anglican Church, but Tennent was destined to establish a school that would serve the churches of the Middle Colonies in a more modest but still effective way. As a scholar and teacher Tennent had no peer in the Synod of Philadelphia. Motivated by a desire to complete the education of his sons and to train preachers for the expanding population, Tennent began his school in a log cabin near the parish church at Neshaminy.

Not much is known about the event, but Gilbert left his parents' home sometime in 1725 to enter Yale College. After less than a year, he was awarded what was tantamount to an honorary master of arts degree. This concluded his formal preparation for the ministry. When he presented himself as a candidate before the Presbytery of Philadelphia in May 1725, he was well received and was licensed to preach. The records are scanty at this point, but there is some evidence to indicate that he helped his father instruct young ministers even before the Log College was opened. It is significant to note that although he had received virtually no formal schooling, except for his work at Yale, Gilbert Tennent's scholarship and qualifications for the ministry were never challenged. The Presbytery before which he appeared was made up of ministers who had been trained in the major universities of Great Britain or at Yale or Harvard.

William Tennent drilled his students in the ancient languages —Latin, Greek and Hebrew, and in the Bible itself. There were only a few textbooks, and most of these were the works of the great Puritan divines. But William Tennent filled his students with an evangelical and evangelistic zeal almost unknown in the formal, credalistic church of which they were members. Prompted by the Presbyterian practice in the Irish and Scottish churches, the Scotch-Irish majority of the Presbytery of Philadelphia was responsible for the passage of the Adopting Act of 1729 under which all ministers subscribed to the "form of doctrine" contained in the Westminster Confession. Both Gilbert Tennent and his father signed the Adopting Act, but they took no part in the controversy that established the church on a course of confessionalism. They, after the manner of their Puritan predecessors, were more interested in proclaiming the gospel to win men to a vital relationship to Jesus Christ.

"Gilbert Tennent was by far the most conspicuous, and in the history of the period under review, no other name is more frequently mentioned," E. H. Gillett declares in his *History of the Presbyterian Church*. "With a nature incapable of fear, a burning zeal in defense of what he deemed to be truth, a commanding person with powerful delivery, he was destined to exercise, wherever he went, a deep and extensive influence. Yet his charity was sometimes overborne by his zeal. His defense of vital truth assumed unconsciously a defiant tone. In dealing with his equals, he was betrayed into adopting the tone of a superior, and the model which he seemed to favor was far more that which presented to view the sternness of one of the old prophets, than the gentleness of the beloved apostle. He was independent and decided in his judgments; tenacious of his convictions, he was not easily to be moved or persuaded by others . . ."

In subsequent years Tennent demonstrated his continuing loyalty to his father and to the principles the evangelistic party of the church regarded as paramount. Throughout his life he was an enthusiastic supporter of all that his father stood for and hotly contested the attitudes of their "Old Side" opponents. In a few short years this was to flare into the first serious schism in the Presbyterian Church and much of the blame would be laid on Gilbert Tennent.

Like many other men in history Gilbert Tennent's great strength proved to be a weakness. He had learned much from his godly father, but at this stage of his life, he was essentially a crusader in a cause. He had not yet learned the importance of declaring the truth in love. That lesson would come.

After his precipitous departure from New Castle, Tennent was called in the following year to form a new Presbyterian church at New Brunswick, New Jersey. In this charge he was to meet a man who probably influenced him almost as much as his father and Whitefield.

In 1726 Dominie Theodorus Jacobus Frelinghuysen, Reformed Dutch Church minister at New Brunswick, already had established a name for himself when the twenty-three-year-old Presbyterian minister arrived to take up his duties. From the very outset of their acquaintance they recognized in each other a kindred spirit. They found themselves in agreement theologically and in general religious outlook.

Frelinghuysen, a German who had been trained in Holland and ordained by the Reformed Dutch Church, had come to New Brunswick in 1717. There, he found the churches of his denomination spiritually dead and "contented with perfunctory orthodoxy." To the consternation of his parishioners, Frelinghuysen had insisted that only those who had experienced regeneration could partake of the Lord's Supper. Visiting his people on a regular and systematic basis, he enforced strict discipline. Opposition to his ministry was encouraged by Dominie Boel of the New York Reformed Dutch Church who from the start had suspected Frelinghuysen of heresy. But his opposition to the sturdy young minister was of no avail. Instead, a revival broke out in his own church and in nearby Dutch congregations. In time English-speaking churches for miles about experienced renewal. Frelinghuysen was never at a loss for an appropriate verse of Scripture and he was so well versed in the Heidelberg Catechism and the official pronouncements of his church that his opponents were doomed to defeat before they started the move against him.

George Whitefield, when he visited the area later, described Frelinghuysen as "the beginner of the great work in that area." Thus, Frelinghuysen was already experiencing the fruit of forthright preaching.

Gilbert Tennent, however, did not have such success in the early part of his ministry. Frelinghuysen and Tennent participated in a joint Communion service, thereby demonstrating their commonly shared spiritual goals and their oneness in the gospel cause. But Tennent saw no upsurge of life in his congregation even after several months of preaching. In the midst of his despair, Tennent received a letter of exhortation from Frelinghuysen, who had taken the young Presbyterian under his pastoral wing.

Frelinghuysen's letter "excited me to greater earnestness in ministerial labors," Tennent later wrote to Thomas Prince, Jr. "I began to be very disturbed about my want of success; for I knew not for half a year or more after I came to New Brunswick, that anyone was converted by my labors, although several persons were affected transiently.

"It pleased God to afflict me about that time with sickness, by which I had affecting views of eternity. I was then exceeding grieved that I had done so little for God, and was very desirous to live one half year more, if it was His will, that I might stand upon the stage of the world, as it were, and plead more faithfully for his cause, and take more pains for the conversion of souls. The secure state of the world appeared to me in a very affecting light; and one thing among others pressed me sore; viz., that I had spent much time in conversing about trifles, which might have been spent in examining people's states toward God, and persuading them to turn to Him. I therefore prayed to God that He would be pleased to give me a half year more, and I was determined to endeavor to promote his kingdom with all my might at all adventures. The petition God was pleased to grant manifold, and to enable me to keep my resolution in some measure."

Actually Frelinghuysen had not contributed to Gilbert Tennent's theological knowledge. All the Tennents cited and recommended the same literature of evangelical Puritanism. The theological and evangelistic understanding of Gilbert Tennent came from his father. But Frelinghuysen had moved Gilbert Tennent to put into practice all that he had learned at his father's feet.

Tennent's illness proved to be a turning point in his ministry. He arose from his sick bed to fulminate against the nominalism of the church, and declare the unsearchable riches of Christ. One of his first sermons was entitled, "A Solemn Warning to the Secure World." In his preface he defended his unpleasant subject and his harsh method as being "most suitable, necessary, and profitable; considering the general and lamentable security that prevails so exceedingly among the children of this generation." Tennent thus took issue with presumptuous religion that he regarded as an affront to God, as Trinterud puts it.

In subsequent sermons Tennent hammered away at this false security in a dead church. His sermons, hardly palatable by today's standards, nevertheless spoke in terms that eighteenth-century people could comprehend. In a message called "The Legal Bow," Tennent said:

"Being thoroughly convinced by Scripture, reasons, experience, and the universal consent of the most godly, eminent and useful divines of the Protestant Church, as well as by the suffrage of the ancient fathers, of the great necessity of a work of humiliation, or conviction, in order to obtain a sound conversion from sin and Satan, to God and holiness . . . and perceiving . . . the gross ignorance of this important truth . . . and thereby a presumptuous security fatally introduced . . . for hereby they are induced to content themselves with dead forms of piety, resulting from a religious education, and historical faith; instead of seeking after the power and life of Christianity. . . . I say, perceiving and considering the aforesaid particulars, I have thought it my duty to insist frequently upon this subject in the course of my ministry."

Tennent was annoyed by church members who equated belief in the Bible and orthodoxy with saving faith. The battle he was waging was not against a denial of the faith but rather of lifeless profession. While the opponents of his day railed against his revivalism, what they opposed was nothing like what is meant by that term today. Tennent did not hold "revival meetings" that appealed to the emotions of his listeners and had for their goal instantaneous conversions. Actually, he knew nothing of such an approach. The "appeal" used in modern evangelism would have been strange to him.

In the style of the older English Puritans, Tennent developed what has been called the preaching of "convictions." He believed that no one could be saved without experiencing the terror that he was not a Christian. Sometimes this agony of soul would continue for weeks and months. It was not uncommon for some poor souls to wrestle in spiritual depression for as long as two years or more. But Tennent preached the solid truth that it was possible for a true believer to know for himself that he was a Christian.

Thomas Prince, Jr., of Boston, a contemporary of Tennent's, described him thus: "I found him a man of considerable parts and learning; free, gentle, condescending: and from his own various experiences, reading the most noted writers on experimental divinity, as well as the Scriptures, and conversing with many who had been awakened by his ministry in New Jersey where he then lived, he seemed to have as deep an acquaintance with the experimental part of religion as any person I ever conversed with; and his preaching was as searching and rousing as any I ever heard. He [aimed] directly [at] their hearts and consciences, to lay open their ruinous delusions and show them their numerous secret, hypocritical shifts in religion, and drive them out of every deceitful refuge wherein they made themselves easy, with the form of godliness without the power."

Now Tennent began to observe tangible results when he preached. The rough men of the frontier wept as they came under conviction. Others groaned and cried out. By 1729 there were many who had turned to Christ and described the joy that accompanied their new experience of vital Christianity. Already the Great Awakening had begun in Presbyterian churches.

While most historians agree that Gilbert Tennent was the chief figure in the Great Awakening in Pennsylvania and New Jersey, at least two of his three brothers were also men of great stature. In the interaction of the lives of the four Tennent sons, much further light is cast upon the forces which made Gilbert Tennent a man of great faith. Particularly striking are the strange events of John's conversion which were recorded after his death by Gilbert Tennent:

"His conviction of his sin, danger and misery, was the most violent in degree of any I ever saw. For several days and nights together he was made to cry out in the most dolorous and affecting manner, almost every moment. The words which he used in his soul-agony were these:

" 'O my bloody, lost soul! What shall I do: Have mercy on me, O God, for Christ's sake.'

"Sometimes he was brought to the very brink of despair, and

would conclude, surely God would never have mercy on such a great sinner as he was. And yet his life was unstained with those scandalous extravagances by which too many in their youth are ensnared. His natural predominant sin was rash anger; and the worst I ever knew him guilty of was some indecent haste in this way, on account of which he was afterwards exceedingly humbled, and against which he became very watchful.

"His passionateness cost him many a deep sob, heavy groan, and salt tear. After it pleased God to confer His grace upon him, he was remarkably altered in this particular, and gained in a great measure an ascendancy over his besetting sin. While under conviction his distress was such as to induce him to make an open confession of his sins to almost all that came near him, and also to beg their prayers in his behalf at the throne of grace. And this he did in the most earnest and beseeching manner. His dolorous groans and vehement importunity were such as greatly to affect even strangers who came to see him. And he earnestly and frequently begged of God that He would humble him to the dust, and beneath the dust."

Thus Gilbert Tennent quaintly described the soul distress of one close to his heart. This type of conversion was common in the experience of those who came under the influence of the Tennent family. Strange as these experiences are to contemporary believers, these are bona fide accounts of spiritual events in the eighteenth century. Gilbert describes further developments in his brother John's conversion:

"One morning when I went to see him, I perceived a great alteration in his countenance; for he, who an hour before had looked like a condemned man going to be put to some cruel death, now appeared with a cheerful, gladsome countenance, and spoke to me in these words:

" 'O brother, the Lord Jesus has come in mercy to my soul. I was begging for a crumb of mercy with the dogs, and Christ has told me that He will give me a crumb.'

"Then he desired me to thank God in prayer, which I did more than once. He also requested me to praise God by singing part of a psalm, which I complied with, and sang the 34th. It was indeed surprising to hear this person singing the praises of God with more clearness, energy, and joy, than any of the spectators who had crowded in on this extraordinary and solemn occasion. . . . The consolations of God had such an influence on him, that about an hour or two afterwards, he walked thirty yards to see his brother William, who was then extremely sick, nigh unto death, and thought by most to be past all human hope of recovery. He said he must see his brother, to tell him what God had done for his soul, that he might praise God on his account before he died. And when he entered the room where his brother was lying, his joy appeared to overflow, and he addressed him in the following words:

" 'O brother, the Lord has looked with pity on my soul. Let the heavens, earth, and sea, and all that in them is, praise God!'

"But being exposed too soon to the cool air, he fell into a fever, and then called in question that eminent discovery of God's love which he had experienced. But it was not long before he was again comforted; and from this time a great change in his conversation was manifest."

Although John Tennent was the third son, he entered the ministry just four years after Gilbert, accepting a call to the Presbyterian church in Freehold, New Jersey. His ministry, though extremely fruitful, lasted only two years. His death came when he was only twenty-five years old.

Even stranger spiritual experiences were recorded about William Tennent, Jr., the second brother. After Gilbert had left the family home at Neshaminy to serve the New Brunswick church, William, who was two years younger, asked permission to continue his theological studies under the tutelage of his eldest brother. The aged father granted this request, commending his son to the favor and protection of God.

After studying with his brother for some time, William was about ready to present himself as a candidate for the gospel ministry. His intense application to his studies apparently caused him to contract a serious illness which soon left him as emaciated as "a living skeleton." Despite the fact that he was attended by a physician who had become his good friend, William continued to sink. Elias Boudinot, a contemporary, describes the strange events which followed:

"He was conversing with his brother [Gilbert] in Latin on the state of his soul, when he fainted and died away. After the usual time he was laid out on a board, according to the common practice of the country, and the neighborhood were invited to attend his funeral on the next day. In the evening, his physician and friend returned from a ride in the country, and was afflicted beyond measure at the news of his death. He could not be persuaded that it was certain; and on being told that one of the persons who had assisted in laying out the body thought he had observed a little tremor of the flesh under the arm, although the body was cold and stiff, he endeavored to ascertain the fact. He first put his own hand into warm water, to make it as sensible as possible, and then felt under the arm, and at the heart, and affirmed that he felt an unusual warmth, though no one else could.

"He had the body restored to a warm bed, and insisted that the people who had been invited to the funeral should be requested not to attend. To this the brother [Gilbert] objected as absurd, the eyes being sunk, the lips discolored, and the whole body cold and stiff. However the doctor finally prevailed, and all probable means were used to discover symptoms of returning life. But the third day arrived, and no hopes were entertained of success but by the doctor, who never left him night or day. The people were again invited, and assembled to attend the funeral. The doctor still objected, and at last confined his request for delay to an hour, then to half an hour, and finally to a quarter of an hour.

"He had discovered that the tongue was much swollen, and threatened to crack. He was endeavoring to soften it, by some emollient ointment put upon it by a feather, when the brother came in, about the expiration of the last period, and mistaking what the doctor was doing for an attempt to feed him, manifested some resentment, and in a spirited tone, said:

" 'It is shameful to be feeding a lifeless corpse,' insisting with earnestness that the funeral should immediately proceed.

"At this critical and important moment, the body, to the great alarm and astonishment of all present, opened its eyes, gave a dreadful groan and sank again into apparent death. This put an end to all thoughts of burying him, and every effort was again employed in hopes of bringing about a speedy resuscitation. In about an hour the eyes again opened, a heavy groan proceeded from the body, and again all appearance of animation vanished. In another hour life seemed to return with more power, and a complete revival took place to the joy of the family and friends . . ."

William Tennent's recovery was slow. In an account written after the illness, a chronicler describes the amnesia he suffered:

"His sister [presumably Gilbert's wife], who had stayed from church to attend him, was reading in the Bible, when he took notice of it and asked her what she had in her hand. She answered that she was reading the Bible. He replied, 'What is the Bible? I know not what you mean.' This affected the sister [sic] so much that she burst into tears, and informed him that he was once well acquainted with it. On her reporting this to the brother, when he returned, Mr. Tennent was found, upon examination, to be totally ignorant of every transaction of life previous to his sickness. He could not read a single word, neither did he seem to have any idea of what it meant.

"As soon as he was capable of attention, he was taught to read and write, as children usually are taught, and afterwards began to learn the Latin language under the tuition of his brother. One day, as he was reciting a lesson in Cornelius Nepos, he suddenly started, clapped his hand to his head, as if something had hurt him, and made a pause. His brother asking him what was the matter, he said that he felt a sudden shock in his head, and now it seemed to him that he had read that book before. By degrees his recollection was restored, and he could speak the Latin as fluently as before his illness . . ."

More eerie than the events surrounding his illness and recovery were William Tennent's recollections of his experiences while he was in the state of suspended animation. His own words give a graphic account:

"While I was conversing with my brother," said he, "on the state of my soul, and the fears I had entertained for my future welfare, I found myself, in an instant, in another state of existence, under the direction of a superior being, who ordered me to follow him. I was accordingly wafted along, I know not how, till I beheld at a distance an ineffable glory, the impression of which on my mind it is impossible to communicate to mortal man. I immediately reflected upon my happy change, and thought, 'Well, blessed be God! I am safe at last, notwithstanding all my fears.' I saw an innumerable host of happy beings surrounding the inexpressible glory, in acts of adoration and joyful worship; but I did not see any bodily shape. . . . I heard things unutterable. I heard their songs and hallelujahs of thanksgiving and praise with unspeakable rapture. I felt joy unutterable and full of glory. I then applied to my conductor, and requested leave to join the happy throng; on which he tapped me on the shoulder, and said, 'You must return to earth.' This seemed like a sword in my heart. In an instant, I recollect to have seen my brother standing before me, disputing with the doctor. . . . The three days during which I had appeared lifeless seemed to me not more than ten or twenty minutes. The idea of returning to this world of sorrow and trouble gave me such a shock, that I fainted repeatedly. . . . Such was the effect upon my mind of what I had seen and heard, that if it be possible for a human being to live entirely above the world and the things of it, for some times afterwards I was that person . . ."

Twelve months after he had fallen ill, William Tennent had fully recovered from his illness and he began to preach with great zeal and power like his brothers, Gilbert and John. When John died in 1732, the congregation at Freehold, New Jersey, called William to be their minister. He served in that pastorate until his death forty-four years later.

Charles, youngest of the four Tennent brothers, seems to have been the least distinguished of the family, yet he identified himself with the fervent preaching of the New Side party which Gilbert headed. Whitefield conducted meetings in the church that Charles served at Whiteclay Creek, Delaware, and there was a great upsurge of revival in the community.

References to Gilbert Tennent's home life are sparse. Presumably he was married in the early part of his New Brunswick ministry. In all likelihood, it was his wife who helped nurse William Tennent, Jr. back to health, but neither her name nor other facts about her have been preserved. She died sometime between Whitefield's second visit to the Middle Colonies in April 1740, and his return to that area in November of the same year. Whitefield, then preaching on Staten Island, describes his meeting with the bereaved husband:

"Tuesday, Nov. 4. I was much refreshed with the sight of Mr. Gilbert Tennent and Mr. Cross. The former has lately lost his wife, and though dear unto him, yet he was enabled with great calmness to preach her funeral sermon, whilst the corpse was lying before him. This put me in mind of Melancthon, who, at the news of his wife's death, said, 'My Kate, I'll come after thee ere it be long.' Since his wife's decease, Mr. Tennent has been in the West Jerseys and Maryland, and told me how remarkably God had worked by his ministry in many places."

Whitefield concluded the entry for November 4 by again expressing his great admiration for Tennent: "Passed the remainder of the evening in hearing Mr. Tennent give an account of his late excursion. Oh, he is a humble minister of the gospel! May I follow him as he does Christ. Amen."

Yet despite these glimpses into Gilbert Tennent's tender love for his wife and the qualities of humility and Christ-likeness which Whitefield found so appealing, Tennent often exhibited a severity that he lived to regret.

The Old Side ministers of the Presbyterian Church continued their opposition to the revivalism espoused so passionately by Tennent, leader of the New Side. He regarded all criticism as attack upon the work of the Lord. Certainly not all of those associated with the Old Side party were as lacking in Christian character and concern as the firebrand of New Brunswick imagined. It was also true that the Tennents had concern for proper church order as well as for practical piety and evangelism.

In 1734 Gilbert Tennent made an overture to the Synod of Philadelphia, requesting a more careful examination of candidates for the ministry as well as for those partaking of the Lord's Supper. Frelinghuysen's influence upon him was quite evident in this action. The overture was favorably received, and Tennent himself could not have penned an admonition more solemn and searching than that contained in the official action taken by the Synod.

Shortly after this, Tennent became involved in a squabble that added to his reputation as a controversialist. A Harvard-trained New Englander named David Cowell was examined and installed by the Presbytery of Philadelphia in the Presbyterian Church at Trenton. Tennent was not at all pleased with the way his brethren had conducted the examination of the newly installed minister, who apparently had indicated that the chief motive of religion was man's happiness. This shallow view of Christianity only underlined the suspicions Tennent had concerning the state of the clergy. He became convinced that many of his brethren in the ministry had never experienced regeneration, and felt that this was the basis for most of the opposition to the Great Awakening. The Old Side leaders, in part at least, also recognized the deadness of the church, but they thought the antidote was a bolstering of the confessional position. They had succeeded in getting the Adopting Act passed in 1729, which compelled all ministers to subscribe to the doctrines contained in the Westminster Confession. In essence, the battle was between those who favored strict confessionalism versus those who stressed spiritual renewal in working for purity and power in the church.

There was enough truth in Tennent's approach to the matter for him to gain a wide hearing. His uncompromising preaching was a challenge to the whole religious life of the church. His biblical messages stressed God's holiness and the perfection of the law of God, that men could be redeemed only by consciously owning up to their spiritual bankruptcy and claiming the grace of God through faith. This kind of preaching shocked those who had taken it for granted that they were Christians. The only response they could give to such a message was either acquiescence to Jesus Christ as Lord and Savior or deny it completely. Many fought back with bitter animosity. By this time Tennent had abandoned the generalized preaching that was the fashion of his day and had followed Frelinghuysen's example of close, personal preaching coupled with intensive and searching counsel.

Tennent wrote Whitefield telling him of his program:

"Since you were here, I have been among my people dealing with them plainly about their souls' state in their houses; examining them one by one as to their experiences, and telling natural people the dangers of their state; and exhorting them that were totally secure to seek convictions; and those that were convinced to seek Jesus; and reproved pious people for their faults; and, blessed be God, I have seen hopeful appearances of concern amongst a pretty many in the places I belong to."

Tennent felt that there were four classes of men:

1. Those genuinely converted, with the comfortable assurance of being God's children.
2. Those earnestly seeking conversion.
3. Those who needed help but were not awakened to need.
4. Rebellious, headstrong sinners.

Gilbert Tennent never encouraged demonstrations of emotion in his meetings, although on more than one occasion there were those who cried out or groaned in their spiritual distress. His brother William insisted that there be no fainting or outcries in his meetings, and he tended to stress the love of God more than judgment in his sermons. In some instances there were excesses in some of the meetings of the revivalists, such as unusual body motions, but none of the Tennents favored such behavior. The opponents of the revival made much of any excesses that did occur and used them as arguments against the New Side party.

Controversy between the two groups within the Presbyterian Church grew more and more violent. Gilbert Tennent felt that the university-trained subscriptionists—those who favored close adherence to the Westminster Confession—disdained the men who had been trained at the Log College. No doubt family loyalty and the crusade for vital piety were mixed motives in Gilbert Tennent's heart. The righteous wrath that was building up inside him was released in the sermon he preached at Nottingham, Pennsylvania, on March 8, 1740, entitled "On the Dangers of an Unconverted Ministry."

Trinterud describes it as a "carefully wrought polemic of such devastating efficiency, it accomplished too much." In essence, Tennent declared that the opponents of the revival demonstrated by their attitudes and actions that they were unregenerate. He accused "unconverted ministers of preaching on law and duty, which was actually preaching salvation by works."

Actually Tennent's propensity for controversy sometimes threatened to extinguish the fires of the Great Awakening. The return visit of Whitefield in April 1740 undoubtedly helped save the day to onward sweep of revival. Whitefield aligned himself with the Log College men, although this intensified the distrust of the Old Side party for his ministry. Whitefield, having suffered considerable clerical opposition himself, was disposed to agree with Gilbert Tennent in his attack upon the "unconverted ministry."

Tennent and his party were aided also by Jonathan Dickinson, respected Presbyterian leader of northern New Jersey, when he preached his sermon on "The Witness of the Spirit," on May 5, 1740. Dickinson thus joined the party of renewal by stressing the fact of assurance of salvation—the doctrine strongly espoused by the New Side leaders.

That same month the disciples of Whitefield erected a huge wooden tabernacle for him in Philadelphia because the crowds were too large for the existing churches. Furthermore, some churches were closed to him. The battle in ecclesiastical circles, however, did not stem the tidal wave of revivalism. Most of the lay people throughout the Colonies warmly accepted the ministry of the Tennents and Whitefield. The chief opponents were the Anglican clergy and the Old Side ministers of the Presbyterian Church.

In the spring of 1740 Whitefield again visited Tennent in New Brunswick. The first evening he was there, the revivalist preached to two thousand eager listeners. In the entry of his *Journal* dated Sunday, April 27, Whitefield writes: "Was told last night by Mr. Gilbert Tennent, of two that were savingly brought home by my ministry, when here last. . . . Preached morning and evening to near seven or eight thousand people. In the afternoon sermon, had I proceeded, the cries and groans of the congregation would have drowned my voice. One woman was struck down, and a general cry went through the assembly. We collected both times upwards of 20 pounds sterling for my orphans. At night a woman came to me under strong convictions. She told me she had often been somewhat moved; but now, she hoped God had struck her home. She cried out, 'I can see nothing but hell!' Oh that all were in as good a way to heaven."

The influence of Tennent upon Whitefield is seen in the statement a few days later when Whitefield was visiting Woodbridge, New Jersey. "I dealt very plainly with the Presbyterian clergy, many of whom, I am persuaded, preach the doctrines of grace to others, without being converted themselves. No doubt some were offended: but I care not for any sect or party of men. As I love all who love the Lord Jesus, of what communion soever; so I reprove all, whether Dissenters, or not Dissenters, who take His Word into their mouths, but never felt Him dwelling in their hearts."

On another occasion that same spring when Whitefield was speaking at Amboy, New Jersey, he had some unexpected visitors: "After sermon, my dear brother and fellow laborer, Mr. William Tennent, coming to fetch me, I passed over a ferry with him and his brother Gilbert, who also came to Amboy to meet me. With them I set out for Freehold, twenty miles from Amboy, the place where God has more immediately called Mr. William Tennent. Oh how sweetly the time did glide on, and our hearts burn within us, when we opened the Scriptures, and communicated our experiences to each other! Our Lord was with us, as with the two disciples going to Emmaus. About midnight, we reached Freehold, and about two in the morning, retired to rest."

Whitefield conducted a preaching tour of New England in the fall of 1740 and for the first time met Jonathan Edwards, whose preaching had been stirring that region. Edwards was deeply moved by Whitefield's preaching, and his British guest was thrilled by the experience of speaking in the Edwards pulpit at Northampton, Massachusetts. On his return, Whitefield stopped off in New Brunswick and urged Gilbert Tennent to make a preaching tour of New England.

"He (diffident of himself) was at first unwilling, urging his inability for so great a work," Whitefield mentioned in his *Journal*, "but afterwards, being convinced it was the divine will, he said, 'The will of the Lord be done.' . . . I cannot but think he will be a burning and a shining light. It being the last time we should be together for a long season, we thought it best to spend some time in prayer together. Mr. Gilbert was our mouth to God. Many were greatly affected. About eleven o'clock we parted in tears, but with full assurance that we should see and hear great things before we met again."

Gilbert Tennent had been deeply involved in the controversy within his church. He still felt the loss of his wife. Perhaps the preaching mission to New England would be a relief from the events that had brought him so much sorrow. Whatever may have been his personal reason for making the trip, it proved to be a great spiritual success.

"At that time there was but little intercourse between the middle and eastern colonies," wrote Archibald Alexander in his book on the Log College, "and no ecclesiastical connection between the Presbyterian and Congregational churches."

Thus, the visits of Whitefield, the British Anglican-Methodist, and Tennent, the Presbyterian, into Congregational territory started something. The preaching tours were successful as evangelistic endeavors, but even more significant was the welding of the Great Awakening into a spiritual movement that swept all of the Colonies from New England to Georgia. It meant a closer relationship between New Englanders and Princeton in later years. Politically, the Great Awakening was to bind all the Colonies together and prepare the way for the national unity that was to come later.

Whitefield was received by a large section of the New England clergy, but Gilbert Tennent was virtually unknown. He took off alone for Boston in the dead of winter, realizing that when he reached his destination there would be neither friend nor acquaintance to greet him. Something of the character of the man can be gleaned from the spirit in which he undertook this assignment, once he was convinced that it was the right thing to do.

Tennent arrived in Boston on December 13, 1740, and began a series of meetings that continued for three months. He was soon preaching every day with extraordinary power and success. One of those greatly impressed by his manner of preaching was the Reverend Thomas Prince, author of *The Christian History:*

"It was," he declared, "both terrible and searching. It was for matter, justly terrible, as he, according to the inspired oracles, exhibited the dreadful holiness, justice, law-threatening, truth, power, and majesty of God, and his anger with rebellious, impenitent, and Christless sinners: the awful danger they were in every moment of being struck down to hell, and damned forever, with the amazing miseries of that place of torment.

"By his arousing and scriptural preaching, deep and pungent convictions were wrought in the minds of many hundreds of persons in that town [Boston] and the same effect was produced in several scores, in the neighboring congregations. *And now was such a time as we never knew.*

"The Rev. Mr. Cooper was wont to say, that more came to him in one week, in deep concern, than in the whole twenty-four years of his preceding ministry."

When Tennent preached at Harvard there were scattered responses from the students, but when he spoke at Yale, half the school body professed faith, according to contemporary reports.

Tennent described his New England tour in a letter to Whitefield: "In my return home, I have been preaching daily; ordinarily three times a day, and sometimes oftener: and through pure grace, I have met with success much exceeding my expectations. In the town of Boston there were many hundreds, if not thousands, as some have judged, under soul-concern. When I left the place, many children were deeply affected about their souls, and several had received consolation. Some aged persons in church communion, and some open opposers were convinced. Divers of young and middle aged were converted, and several Negroes.

"The concern was more general at Charlestown. Multitudes were awakened, and several had received great consolation; especially among the young people, children and Negroes. In Cambridge, also, in the town and in the college, the shaking among the dry bones was general, and several of the students have received consolation."

But Tennent stirred up opposition in New England as he had in New Jersey and Pennsylvania. Dr. Timothy Cutler, former rector of Yale College and now an Episcopal minister in Boston, had nothing good to say about either Whitefield or Tennent: "It would be an endless attempt to describe the scene of confusion and disturbance occasioned by him [Whitefield]. . . . After him came Tennent, a monster, impudent and noisy, who told them they were all damn'd, damn'd, damn'd; this charmed them, and in the most dreadful winter I ever saw, people wallowed in the snow night and day for the benefit of his beastly brayings, and many ended their days under these fatigues. Both of them carried more money out of these parts than the poor could be thankful for."

Lies were told against the two evangelists. Thomas Clap, the bitter little man who was then president of Yale, and who later expelled Brainerd for a petty offense, spread the story that Jonathan Edwards had told him of a scheme in which Whitefield planned to bring godly young men from England to be trained at the Log College, then sent to New England for service in the churches. This plan was to follow the visits of Whitefield and Tennent in an effort to supplant all the clergy of New England. Edwards denied the story and Clap later backed down on the authenticity of the yarn.

Whitefield and Tennent were unmoved by such attacks and

whisperings. They were propelled by a sense of divine mission. History soon would vindicate them.

Tennent returned from his triumphs in New England to his greatest personal and party defeat. The years of bickering between the Old Side subscriptionists and his own burgeoning New Side group had flared into a conflagration. Tennent more than anyone else had precipitated the controversy that now split the Presbyterian Church in two.

In an effort to assure the ordination of graduates of the Log College and others sympathetic with evangelism, Gilbert Tennent and his associates had succeeded in forming their own preserve within the Synod—the Presbytery of New Brunswick. One of the first acts of New Brunswick Presbytery, which annoyed the Old Side leaders, was the licensing of John Rowland, a Log College man, and dispatching him to fill a vacancy within the bounds of Philadelphia Presbytery. As a countermeasure, the Old Side subscriptionists passed a rule that a committee of Synod which they controlled should examine candidates for the ministry as well as a committee of the Presbytery.

Tennent regarded this as a direct slap at the work of the Log College. The Old Side group also voted to establish an officially sponsored school, or seminary, thus ignoring the Log College operation. Many of the Old Siders resented Whitefield's conducting of meetings wherever he was called upon to speak. They regarded this as an intrusion into territory in which the Presbyterian Church had first rights. Old Side attitudes were not helped by the fact that Whitefield and the Tennents were so closely allied.

When Gilbert Tennent flayed his brethren in his widely discussed Nottingham sermon in which he had questioned the regenerate state of his opponents, Whitefield not only agreed with these sentiments, but added his own judgments against those who opposed revival. The Tennents had popular support which only added bitterness to the hearts of their opponents.

When Tennent criticized the acceptance of David Cowell by the Presbytery of Philadelphia and his installation in the Trenton church, his challenge added fuel to the flames. Both Tennent and Cowell were called before the Synod in 1738. After hearing testimony from both sides, the Synod reported that agreement had been reached and that both men had been "arguing over a subject on which neither had clear ideas." For a time Tennent seemed to be satisfied with this judgment, but upon reading the minutes, he declared his dissatisfaction and asked that the case be reconsidered. When this was refused, Tennent publicly branded opposing ministers of the Synod as heretics.

While Tennent was guilty of a judgmental spirit and extreme harshness, there was some justification for his position. Irreligion and coldness characterized much of the church. Furthermore, his experiences with Whitefield and Frelinghuysen and the success of his own forceful preaching had made him eager to see more evidence of vital Christianity. Nearly all the Log College men were experiencing revivals in their churches, and the New Side party was in the ascendancy. Had Tennent shown more love and respect for those who differed with him, instead of inveighing against them, much heartache could have been avoided and there probably would have been no division in the church. Controversy threatened the very spirit of the revival that Tennent espoused.

Gilbert Tennent was the leader in the battle, receiving support from his family and friends. His brother William tended to be more retiring and less contentious even though he was equally successful in evangelism and biblical teaching. Yet it must be said that Gilbert's forceful ministry finally prodded the sleeping church into fervent life.

But now he was to be confronted with a crisis in the church that he had provoked. When the Synod of Philadelphia met May 27, 1741, the Old Side forces were marshaled for decisive action. Robert Cross, leader of the antirevival Old Side faction, presented a "Protestation" against the "irregular" practices of Tennent's New Brunswick Presbytery. Cross demanded complete capitulation or schism. Since only half the members of Synod were present at the meeting, the Tennent party was outnumbered and outmaneuvered. The Synod ended up by expelling the New Brunswick Presbytery, thereby splitting the church.

Actually this decision, which caused a breach in the church for seventeen years, was the final major action of the waning Old Side forces. The controversy belatedly broke Tennent's spirit. Dejected and self-critical, he told Jonathan Dickinson in a letter written in February 1742 that he had "mismanaged" and could not justify his own "excessive heat of temper." In a time of "great spiritual desertion," he confessed, "I have been given a greater discovery of myself than I think I ever had before."

Tennent, in the perspective of time, had come to realize that he had seen the issues only as black and white. Now he acknowledged that some of his own cohorts, particularly James Davenport, had hurt the cause of the revival by excesses that he could not conscientiously endorse.

Jonathan Dickinson, highly respected in the church and soon to be named first president of Princeton University, tried to work behind the scenes for reunion. The Old Side group was asked to withdraw the "protestation" and to have continuing relations with New York Presbytery. Ultimately, when the Synod of Philadelphia met in 1742, Dickinson succeeded in getting a committee appointed to work for a healing of the breach. But Tennent was unwilling to make a full enough retraction to satisfy the Old Side leaders. The Old Siders were intransigent. Dickinson then issued a pamphlet favoring the revival movement, thereby lining up his following in New York Presbytery with the Log College men. The Old Side responded by becoming more virulent in their verbal attacks. But the public generally was with the New Side. The Old Side had had its day, crushed by the juggernaut of the Great Awakening.

Gilbert Tennent had served the New Brunswick church for sixteen years, and when he received a call to serve a Presbyterian congregation made up of New Side sympathizers in Philadelphia, in May 1743, he gladly accepted it. Although the church was geographically within the bounds of Philadelphia Presbytery, Tennent recognized that his opportunities would be greater in the chief city of the Colonies. Soon thereafter his Presbytery of New Brunswick and New York Presbytery voted to form the Synod of New York, making two Presbyterian Churches in the New World.

Bit by bit the animosities began to fade. Some of the Old Side ministers actually formally recognized the Great Awakening as "a work of God's glorious grace." The New Side gradually brought the excesses of revivalism under control. The Log College had ceased to function because of William Tennent's advancing age. He resigned his pastorate in 1742 and two years later offered the Log College property for sale. In May 1746 he died.

The passing of the Log College and the great need for ministers, occasioned by throngs of new converts of the revival, made the establishment of a new college mandatory. A group of ministers and laymen had formed a committee to raise funds for a new school, but New Jersey's Governor Lewis Morris, an Anglican, had rejected their request for a charter. John Hamilton, later interim governor, was friendly to Jonathan Dickinson, so, on October 22, 1746, he signed a charter for the College of New Jersey, later to be known as Princeton College. Elected first president was Dickinson and among the trustees were four Log College men: Gilbert Tennent, his brother William, Samuel Blair, and Samuel Finley, later to serve as Princeton's fifth president. Classes were opened in May 1747 in Dickinson's home in Elizabeth.

Many times evangelism and theology find separate advocates but this was not true of the men most greatly used in the Great

Awakening. Gilbert Tennent was a churchman and theologian as well as evangelist. He never for a moment questioned the importance of an educated ministry. When he and Samuel Davies were appointed by the new college board to raise funds in Great Britain, Tennent accepted with alacrity. Davies, who had heard of Tennent's harshness, was reluctant to travel with him, but after they had been together on the trip he became a warm admirer. In Davies' diary there was a telling entry: "Mr. Tennent, my father and friend, rose to pray at 3 A.M."

In Great Britain Tennent on more than one occasion was questioned sharply about his sermon, "On the Dangers of an Unconverted Ministry." He found that the Old Side had many friends abroad, although few in Britain were favorable to creedal subscription. The fund-raising excursion was a success, however. In the year they were abroad, Tennent and Davies collected four thousand pounds, a sizable sum for that day, plus additional funds for scholarships.

Back in the New World, funds were gathered for the college in the churches of the Synod of New York. New England leaders, like Jonathan Edwards, stood with the New Side men in the fund-raising effort. Soon students from New England were flocking to Princeton. Jonathan Edwards became third president after the untimely deaths of Dickinson and his successor, Aaron Burr. Yale particularly felt the effects of the opening of the new college, graduating only twelve students as the class of 1746. In 1755 Yale appointed a New Side Presbyterian as college pastor and professor of divinity. Shortly thereafter a revival broke out in the New Haven institution.

New Side Presbyterians were initiators of the reawakened spiritual concern for the Indians. Among those who had responded to this missionary call was David Brainerd. Tennent's contacts while abroad provided the funds which financed the continuing work among the Indians directed by Brainerd's brother John.

To the credit of Tennent and the Log College men the narrow spirit of denominationalism and provincialism had cracked in the sweeping tide of the Great Awakening.

As Tennent moved into his second and final pastorate, the days of controversy were coming to an end. Most of his congregation, which had met first in Whitefield's huge tabernacle, were people who had been converted in the Anglican preacher's Philadelphia meetings.

Tennent himself grew mellower in spirit and gradually became more polished in his dress and more literary in his preaching style. "The fiery edge of his zeal had worn off, and he had found by experience that neither people nor ministers were ever rendered better by vituperative attacks from the pulpit or the press," Archibald Alexander wrote in his book about the Log College alumni. Now Tennent had become a man of peace.

One of his first projects was to build a new church at the corner of Arch and Third Streets in downtown Philadelphia. He approached Benjamin Franklin, who had published his "Nottingham" sermon, for names of prosperous Philadelphians. Franklin instructed him to call on everyone of note in the city. This he did and soon funds were in hand for the erection of a handsome church.

In a sense Tennent had "arrived" when he came to Philadelphia, a city of 20,000 souls. It was nearly as large as Dublin or Edinburgh or even Bristol, the second city of England. There was wealth in the colonial capital and many of the substantial citizens were building fine homes. No doubt the Quaker belief in nonresistance had given the city a certain benignity of spirit.

Tennent had remarried. The lady, whose maiden name had been Cornelia DePeyster, was seven years his senior, and the widow of one Matthew Clarkson. This apparently was a happy marriage, ended only by Mrs. Tennent's death in 1753 when she was fifty-seven years old. If there were children by either of Tennent's first two wives, they must have died in infancy. There are no records of any surviving children.

By his third wife, a widow named Sarah Spafford, Tennent had three children: Albert, who was lost at sea; Elizabeth, who died when she was a child; and Cornelia, who married a Philadelphia physician named William Smith. It is noteworthy that his third child bore the same name as his second wife!

With the death of Jonathan Dickinson in 1747, the task of bringing about the reunion of the rival Presbyterian Synods fell to Gilbert Tennent. Thus, the man who had been most responsible for the schism now became the chief advocate of peace in bringing the two factions together again. Tennent was a committed churchman and he had grieved over the division that he, more than any other, had precipitated.

A long dissertation of 141 pages, entitled *Irenicum Ecclesiasticum*, was the means Tennent used in convincing his brethren of the need for reuniting the Presbyterian Church. His efforts at healing the breach and his conciliatory spirit won the day.

On May 29, 1758, the reunited church met in his church in Philadelphia, and Tennent was elected moderator. Actually, during the seventeen-year interval the Synod of New York with which Tennent and Dickinson were affiliated had become the true Presbyterian Church. Indeed it was the most active church in the American colonies. The ranks of the Old Side ministers had decreased from twenty-five to twenty-two while the New Side men had increased from twenty-two to seventy-two.

Tennent's irenic spirit coupled with the fact that he now read his sermons from his Philadelphia pulpit caused some to feel that his greatest days of ministry were over. His messages in the early days had been filled with fervency. He had been a man on horseback, a crusader on fire. Now he was one who had made peace with his brethren. There are always those who find a fighter more attractive.

In these final years of his life Tennent developed an ecumenical spirit, undoubtedly stemming from the influence of White-field. This spirit was evident in the message he delivered at the dedication of the new church:

"All societies which profess Christianity and retain the foundation principles thereof, notwithstanding their different denominations and diversity of sentiments in smaller things, are in reality but one Church of Christ but several branches (more or less pure in a number of points) of one visible kingdom of the Messiah, whose honor and interest rightly understood, is one and the same."

His move to Philadelphia had involved Gilbert Tennent in the political arguments of the day. Although in his earlier years he had dealt exclusively with religious issues, he began to preach on current social and political problems. In 1744, for example, he preached against prostitution. Later he spoke twice celebrating the victory of the British and Colonial forces over the French. In the citadel of Quakerism he even preached in favor of defensive warfare and later promoted the new Association for Defense.

But his interest in revivals and his joy at the conversion of sinners continued unabated. When a revival of religion broke out in the fledgling College of New Jersey in 1757, he was eager to hear about it, and his brother William sent him a lengthy account of just what occurred.

In the last three years of his life, Tennent was too feeble most of the time to preach. His last published message, "A Sermon on the Nature of Religious Zeal," was given on January 27, 1760. The flickering candle of his life slowly grew dimmer, and finally, in 1764, the flame was extinguished forever. Gilbert Tennent was dead.

In the course of the funeral sermon delivered by Dr. Samuel Finley, fifth president of Princeton, some evidence of Tennent's greatness is revealed. He had continued to find new vistas in his exploration of the grace of God.

"He had an habitual unshaken assurance of his interest in re-deeming love for the space of more than forty years," Finley declared, "but eight days before his death he got a clear and more affecting sense of it still. And though he lamented that he had done so little for God, yet he triumphed in the grace of Jesus Christ, who had pardoned all his sins, and said his assurance of salvation was built on the Scriptures, and was more than the sun and the moon."

Thus the strong man of the Great Awakening went to his rest.

"As a preacher few equalled him in his vigorous days," Finley, a Log College alumnus, declared. "Did he set himself to alarm the secure sinner, Hell from beneath was laid open before him and destruction had no covering; while the heavens above gathered blackness and a tempest of wrath seemed ready to be hurled at the guilty head."

Stern prophet, foe of spiritual complacency, evangelist, scholar and gadfly for righteousness—Gilbert Tennent was all of these. In riper and perhaps wiser years, he diligently pursued peace and unity, but not, however, until he had opened up the floodgates of the Great Awakening and brought vitality to the greater part of the colonial Church.

DAVID BRAINERD:
KNIGHT OF THE GRAIL

❦

Clyde S. Kilby

The young enthusiast

On a Monday early in September 1742 a disconsolate young man named David Brainerd slipped silently into the woods outside the trim little village of New Haven. As a criminal, he was bound for prison if apprehended. But he was not a common criminal—the law he had broken was one largely custom-made for him by the legislature of the Colony. The authorities were eager to make an example of him and thus quickly erase a practice which they feared might spread. Like the tinker of Bedford eighty years earlier, Brainerd was to be arrested for unlawful preaching. John Bunyan had gone to prison for this offense and it looked as if Brainerd might do the same.

So, warned by his friends, the young man took to the woods. It was to be months before he could safely visit Yale's campus again. Sitting in the quiet of the September day while the light sifted through the leaves overhead and brought out the early colors of autumn, he solemnly contemplated the strange events of the previous three years. It had been that long since he had somewhat hesitantly, for fear of the corruptions of college life, traveled the twenty-odd miles from his birthplace near Haddam down to New Haven to enroll as a freshman at Yale College.

His first two years at Yale had been eventful but not extraordinary. Contemplating the ministry, he had tackled his Latin and Greek, natural and moral philosophy, metaphysics, mathematics, oratory, and the rest, with such determination that he was soon the leading scholar. He had succumbed to none of the coarser temptations of college life, such as drinking, card playing, firing guns, bell ringing, and rowdiness,[1] * but, as he had feared, his ambition to excel in his studies not only interfered with the holy life he diligently desired but also affected his health. Toward the close of his first year he began to spit blood and was advised by his tutor to return home for a total rest. It was more than two months before he again returned to his studies.

Not only did David Brainerd's greatest joys originate in religion but so did his greatest sorrows. In the interval of his absence from Yale George Whitefield, after phenomenal preaching campaigns through other sections, had come to New Haven. Though he had not the opportunity to see him, Brainerd found great comfort from reports of his visit and felt his soul refreshed and knit to Whitefield's doctrines and zeal.[2] But this admiration for an unseen firebrand became the cause for Brainerd's expulsion from Yale in the middle of his junior year and the cause for his furtive visit in the woods to avoid being arrested and imprisoned.

Much more than a local incident, Brainerd's experience actually marked one extreme of a great religious cycle. One need not go farther than New Haven itself to find a good example of what was occurring throughout New England. Almost exactly a century earlier 111 men had met together in this village and adopted a constitution based, as they sincerely believed, directly and solidly on the Bible. In order that the purity of religious life might be maintained, not only was a strict way of holiness prescribed but methods were provided for punishing heresy. Sometimes these Puritans are accused of quixotic idealism, as if

* Superior figures refer to Notes at the end of this Section.

they did not know man, but it was their sure recognition of the innate and devious evil in man which made them desire to elevate a standard before his eyes and conscience.

In due course the seemingly inevitable occurred. The relatively pure religion of the beginning lost its resiliency and stiffened into powerless forms. Instead of warmth there tended to grow up a correct but chilly routine with often spiritual paralysis. It was against this background that George Whitefield had burst upon New England and set up oppositions that were to have a lifelong effect on the young fugitive in the forest.

Brainerd was trapped between forces generated by George Whitefield and "enthusiasm" on the one hand and Rector Thomas Clap of Yale College on the other. To David Brainerd, beginning his third year at Yale, the wave of the future was clear enough. It was the wave carrying the zealous Whitefield, not the receding wave represented by Rector Clap and other leaders at Yale. Brainerd and some other students felt that the decay of orthodoxy was like a bad tooth which needed a great deal of drilling if indeed not extraction.[3] There was little hope of gaining back the pristine holiness desired so long as men like Thomas Clap were in control. Nothing could be done but sidestep these ecclesiastics and strike directly at the problem. As a consequence, some of the young men at Yale began imitating the enthusiastic evangelism of Whitefield, going where they would and ignoring liturgical and ecclesiastical precedents.

Despite strong efforts of college and civil authorities to prevent it, a group in New Haven decided to secede and establish a church conforming more nearly to their evangelical convictions. Some of the more daring showed their contempt for the Old Lights, as the conservative faction was called, by heckling them as they preached. There seems little doubt that David Brainerd was among the ringleaders of this movement. He and others not only left the established church but paraded their derision of the status quo by going freely to unlicensed churches and by preaching "enthusiasm" in dissenting pulpits wherever they could find them. Brainerd later confessed his "indecent heats," and Jonathan Edwards acknowledged that the young man not only kept company with the radicals but was himself filled with the spirit of nonconformity.

The rub was that administrative power at Yale, as elsewhere, rested in the Old Lights. Consequently the Yale trustees, following Whitefield's visit and the ensuing zeal, adopted strenuous regulations providing punishment for students who, asserting that the tutors, trustees, or Thomas Clap were "unconverted, unexperienced and unskillful guides in matters of religion," refused to submit to their authority, and went about "day and night, and some times for several days together . . . in the town of New Haven, as well as in other towns, and before great numbers of people, to teach and exhort, much after the same manner as ministers of the Gospel do in their public preaching." [4] Much of this was directed straight at David Brainerd, who had been heard to say that Tutor Chauncey Whittelsey had "no more grace than a chair" and who had preached as charged by the trustees. That Brainerd was a principal in the disorders is clear enough from one regulation which prohibited the admission of men over twenty-one to the freshman class. Brainerd had been past this age at admission and was one of two such students specifically mentioned by the trustees as troublemakers.

Not only did the Rector of the University have the trustees on his side but also the governor of the Colony and most of the legislature. They passed laws against outsiders preaching within a parish except by consent of the minister and a majority of the parish. Doubtless in these procedures many of these gentlemen recalled the long, bitter, and bloody conflicts of a century before in England when religious toleration had disappeared first under the Puritans and later under the anti-Puritans. Freedom of religion both in England and New England had suffered eclipse for years.

Oddly enough, David Brainerd himself, by the time when he would normally have been graduated from Yale, had come to a complete about-face concerning "enthusiasm" in religion. Not of course that he ever retreated from his deep and impelling motive to serve God with all his strength. He wrote the trustees a letter of abject and total apology for what he had said about Whittelsey, assuring them of his change of mind. He apologized to the trustees and student body and to any he had been accused of maligning even though he himself had no recollection of it. One might at first suppose this was Brainerd's way of wheedling the trustees into granting his degree, but, in truth, throughout the rest of his life he reiterated his adamant antagonism to all forms of enthusiasm in religion.

Bitter and malignant things were done on both sides in this controversy, but it should not be forgotten that the stakes were high. It is easy to be broadminded where the risk is small. Men are intolerant over high and important values, not passing and insignificant ones. Yale, like nearly all other educational institutions of the Colonies, was established by men who primarily desired the spread of pure and undefiled religion. The population as a whole was religious minded. It was not unusual to see public burnings of what Christians regarded as sinful things—jewelry, fine clothes, wigs, books intended for entertainment, and the like. Of the twenty-four men in Brainerd's class at Yale only three did not have Biblical given names. Brainerd's own brothers were named Hezekiah, Nehemiah, John, and Israel, and his sisters were Dorothy, Jerusha, Martha, and Elizabeth. The place names in Brainerd's diary read like Scripture itself—Judea, Bethlehem, Hebron, Lebanon, Sharon, Canaan, and the like. That was the sort of world to which both David Brainerd and Thomas Clap belonged, however great their opposition to one another in the Yale dispute. It was a world in which Christians tended to take their religion seriously.

David Brainerd's thoughts as he walked through the woods

outside New Haven that day in September 1742 were directly concerned with his antagonism to Rector Clap and the laws against unfettered preaching which the Old Lights had brought into being. This is clearly revealed by his *Diary*. But indirectly his thoughts reverted to the whole twenty-four years of his life. His early years had not been particularly different from normal. Even at the early age of seven or eight he had been deeply concerned for his soul and terrified at the idea of death.[5] He had seen death, for his father had died when David was nine and his mother died just before he became fourteen. David blew hot and cold on religious matters, suffering through the long and tortuous process which he regarded all his life as the only way to salvation. Like John Bunyan, he saw the door to heaven as very narrow and much easier to miss than to enter.

If we go directly to Brainerd's diary, we discover that his struggle against God was more aggressive than Jonathan Edwards' account suggests.[6] "I found in me great struggles, heart-risings, and horrid enmity against God. I often quarreled with God for laying the guilt of Adam's sin to me, whereas I never so much as consented to the commission of it. I wished God had let me alone to stand for myself and not abuse me at that rate, to punish me for what another man had done, and which 'twas impossible I should help, so long after. I charged God with cruelty and injustice and thought he delighted to oppress and crush poor mortals."

Brainerd also quarreled with Adam and thought him a fool for eating of the forbidden fruit and then neglecting to take of the tree of life before he was driven out. Scores of times he wished there were no God or else another God equal in power with whom he might join forces. "I longed to pull the Eternal God out of his throne and stamp him under my feet, more than ever I did to be avenged on any enemy in my life." He was enraged at the idea of God's sovereignty and the injustice of God's making a creature and then subjecting him to everlasting punishment.[7]

It is sometimes true that the very violence of such antagonism is the best antidote to its continuance. One morning when Brainerd was walking through a thick grove of hazels, he realized that it was self-interest rather than the glory of God he had been seeking; that God had no obligation to reward any man with salvation for his good works. "I saw that I had been heaping up my devotions before God, fasting, praying and pretending, and indeed really thinking at some times, that I was aiming at his glory whereas I never once truly intended his honour and glory but only my own happiness." All his thoughts and deeds now appeared as a "vile mockery" and "self worship." [8]

This new state of mind continued from Friday morning until the following Sunday evening of July 12, 1739, when he was again, near sunset, walking through the same thick hazel grove. He felt himself lost, totally helpless, melancholy, and unable to communicate with God. In this condition suddenly "unspeakable glory seemed to open to the view and apprehension of my soul, so that I stood still and wondered and admired. By the glory I saw, I don't mean any external brightness, for I saw no such thing, nor do I intend any imagination of a body of light or splendor somewhere away in the third heavens, or anything of that nature. But it was a new inward apprehension or view that I had of God; such as I never had before, nor anything that had the least resemblance of it. This was something, I knew, that I never had seen before or any thing comparable to it for excellency and beauty. 'Twas widely different from all the conception that ever I had had of God or things divine before. I had now no particular apprehension of any one Person in the Trinity, either the Father, Son or Holy Spirit, but it appeared to be divine glory and splendor that I then beheld. And my very soul rejoiced with joy unspeakable to see such a God, such a glorious divine Being, and I was inwardly pleased and satisfied that he should be God over all forever and ever. My soul was so captivated and delighted with the excellency, the loveliness and the greatness and other perfections of God, that I was even swallowed up in him, at least to that degree that I had no thought, as I remember at first, about my own salvation or scarce that there was such a creature as I. Thus the Lord, I trust, brought me to a hearty desire to exalt him and set him on the throne . . . as the King and Sovereign of the universe."

This transcendent joy and wonder continued unabatedly for perhaps an hour before he was able to bring reason to bear upon the experience, and even then the inward glow continued. "I felt myself in a new world and everything about me discovered a different aspect from what they were wont to do." [9] Now seeing with new eyes the "infinite wisdom, suitableness, and excellency" of the way of salvation, he was astonished at the ignorance and folly of his former views.

Before this experience, Brainerd, at nineteen, had spent a few months farming on land he had inherited from his father. Yet, even as he plowed fields and repaired fences, he increasingly knew that not earth but heaven called and that he would sin greatly unless he became a dedicated spirit. After his hazel-grove experience his way was abundantly clear. In God's everything he had discovered his own nothingness. He proposed to himself that as long as he lived he would, so far as in him lay, become God's witness to others. To carry out this intention, however, meant going to college, and thus it was that he went down to Yale in September 1739.

After his expulsion from Yale, more than two years elapsed before Brainerd took up his first missionary appointment. During that period he studied under Jedediah Mills, a Yale graduate of 1722 who was then pastor at Ripon, a few miles west of New Haven. He was licensed to preach and the day following preached his first regular sermon.[10] Soon he joined his good friend Joseph Bellamy, and together they lived and preached in a barn used as a church and together went out to preach to the Indians along the Housatonic River near the village of Kent. Brainerd traveled widely and preached wherever he could, including clandestine and felonious appearances in and near New Haven. Most important of all, he accepted the invitation of the Honourable Society in Scotland for Propagating Christian Knowledge to become a missionary to the Mahican Indians of eastern New York.

With the Mahicans at Kaunaumeek

One would suppose that young Brainerd, after his long and bitter bout with God and his subsequent conversion, after a good education in which he had excelled, after more than a year of apparently successful itinerant preaching under varying circumstances, after many days of fasting and prayer and a search for "ministerial qualifications," and after accepting an invitation from a missionary society, would have gone forth stalwart and determined. Yet never did any missionary enter upon his duties with less heart. "I set out on my journey towards the Indians . . . loth to give up all for gone." [11] The record of arrival confirms the bleak image of anticipation. "I rode to Kaunaumeek . . . where the Indians live, with whom I am concerned, and there lodged on a little heap of straw; was greatly exercised with inward trials and distresses all day; and in the evening, my heart was sunk, and I seemed to have no God to go to." [12]

For months following Brainerd was to go through some of the greatest inner torments of his life. In December, after his arrival at Kaunaumeek in April 1743, he wrote his brother John, then a student at Yale, "The whole world appears to me like a huge vacuum, a vast empty space, whence nothing desirable or satisfactory can possibly be derived." [13] So far as the *Diary* is concerned, the Indians get hardly a mention, and one might suppose that Brainerd was not a missionary at all but only a young man far removed from society and the situations customary to him, a young man suffering illness of the body and more severe illness of the spirit.

He had been sent by the Society in Scotland not to the Delaware Indians in Pennsylvania as originally planned but to the Mahicans. Kaunaumeek was about twenty miles southeast of Albany. Brainerd lived with a Scotsman and his wife a mile and a half over "the worst of roads" from his Indians. "My diet," he wrote, "consists mostly of hasty-pudding, boiled corn, and bread baked in ashes, and sometimes a little meat and butter. My lodging is a little heap of straw, laid upon some boards, a little way from the ground; for it is a log-room, without any floor." [14] The Scots wife could hardly speak English, the white people were generally profane, and the Dutch in the neighborhood were busily pressing their claim to the land and ready to drive out the Indians. They were therefore antagonistic to the young missionary. Writing to his commissioners, Brainerd described the place as "sufficiently lonesome and unpleasant, being encompassed with mountains and woods and six or seven miles from the nearest village." [15] After three months with the Scotsman, Brainerd concluded he needed to be nearer the Indians and therefore moved into one of their wigwams pending the erection of a little house among them.

He found the Mahicans friendly. These Indians possessed a fine physique and had a somewhat redder skin than western Indians. Both the men and women painted their faces and tattooed totemic symbols on their cheeks. The men liked to wear a colorful braided band around their heads and a mantle of feathers. Among other changes brought about by their contact with whites was the gradual substitution of clothing for animal skins. Their practice of polygamy and their rather loose system of divorce were also in process of change. In war they were treacherous and known for coming upon their enemies unawares. Their woodland adeptness is depicted, rather romanticized, in James Fenimore Cooper's *The Last of the Mohicans*.

Brainerd found these Indians quite tractable, owing to the good influence of John Sergeant, a Yale graduate who was doing excellent missionary labor at Stockbridge, Massachusetts, twenty miles to the southeast, where the "tribal fire" or headquarters of the Mahicans had long been located. His chief fear was that the Indians might become prejudiced against Christianity either by his own unwitting errors or by the conduct of careless white settlers with whom they sometimes came into contact.

Brainerd had hardly begun his labors before he was on the long journey to New Jersey, the first of several such visits, to get permission from his commissioners to establish a school among the Indians, with his interpreter, John Wauwaumpequunnaunt, as schoolmaster. Within a few weeks after his return the school was under way. He spent a large portion of the winter studying the Mahican tongue under John Sergeant at Stockbridge, going down on Mondays and returning at the end of each week. Like Jonathan Edwards, Brainerd did not make a very good language student, perhaps not from lack of ability but because he felt it was not "spiritual" enough. He learned to pray with the Indians in their own tongue and translated some Psalms as well as forms of prayer he had composed. He taught them to sing Psalms so that the religious services might not be without music. His own chief labor he considered to be preaching the gospel, and one of his great joys was to see his Indians occasionally in tears over their spiritual needs.

Actually Brainerd's diary for this period, as at others, is a record not of outer, but of inner events. And for months that record is one of unfathomable spiritual melancholy and the sense of personal vileness such as perhaps was never written by a missionary before or since. "I verily thought I was the meanest, vilest, most helpless, guilty, ignorant, benighted creature living.... Almost all the actions of my past life seem to be covered over with sin and guilt; and those of them that I performed in the most conscientious manner now fill me with shame and confusion, so that I cannot hold up my face.... Sometimes my soul has been in distress on feeling some particular corruptions rise and swell like a mighty torrent, with present violence; having at the same time ten thousand former sins and follies presented to the view, in all their blackness and aggravations." [16] Such are the stock in trade of Brainerd's feelings week after week.

Some change for the better took place after he had completed his little cabin. The seven weeks' labor on it, together with the autumnal gathering of the winter's hay for his horse, took his mind partially off conditions, and when he was finally able to move into the cabin there were at least faint murmurs of pleasure. "I have a house, and many of the comforts of life to support me," he says, and later, "My state of solitude does not make the hours hang heavily upon my hands." [17] Even his uncomfortable food situation does not greatly upset him when he finds, as on one occasion, that he has no bread and nobody to send the ten or fifteen miles necessary to procure it. He makes do with some Indian meal, molding it into little cakes and frying them.

It was a year of illness, sometimes very severe, but there seemed to be no direct relationship between his bodily illness and his mental depression. The winter was unusually cold and stormy, but Brainerd never let bad weather or outward conditions daunt him. He was little bothered by a special report sent to Kaunaumeek all the way from Stockbridge through the governor to say that there was danger of an Indian uprising. Once he became lost in the forest between Stockbridge and Kaunaumeek and was forced to spend the night on the ground, and again, on the same road, he fell into the icy water of a creek.

Yet the winter was broken by some carefully concealed and yet apparent upheaval from outward circumstances in Brainerd's life. There was some temptation which appeared to pull him away from his intended life of holiness and separation. It may have been the temptation to marry Jerusha, daughter of Jonathan Edwards. It is possible that he had met her in September 1743 at the Yale Commencement where he had first made acquaintance with her father. Jerusha had been only fourteen then, yet it was not unusual for a girl of that age to think seriously of marriage. We know that he and Jerusha had become engaged, and we know that Jerusha was perfectly willing to live the life of a missionary's wife, yet for years Brainerd appears to have fought a battle concerning marriage. Could he have fallen that winter for some young woman in Stockbridge in whom the temptation was less spiritual than in Jerusha's case? On December 8 he wrote, "I have not been so much beset by the world for a long time; and that with relation to some particular objects which I had thought myself dead to," and on December 24 he exclaimed, "O that God would . . . save me from the hour of temptation!" [18] Other similar entries in his diary suggest his grief. Doubtless we shall never know precisely what it was, but that Brainerd went through some greatly upsetting experience during his winter at Kaunaumeek is clear enough.

It seems no accident that at the end of this conflict, whatever it was, he found it convenient to explain the difference between a regular and an irregular self-love. The former is supreme love to God, uniting God's glory and the soul's happiness into a common bond. An improper self-love, on the other hand, is one separating man's happiness from God's glory. Love of a man for a woman is in itself a pleasing passion, yet if a man seeks simply the pleasant experience for its own sake, rather than keeping the passion inside the love proper, he will discover it an evil. All experience outside God, declared Brainerd, is of necessity more or less improper experience. Here Brainerd may have been considering one question which vexed him during the rest of his life, whether to marry and settle down in civilization as a pastor or to remain a wandering missionary. Warm and reiterated offers to Brainerd of a pastorate were in themselves a sort of continuous temptation. He had the reputation, young as he was, of being an excellent preacher.

During this winter Brainerd began mentioning his wish to be like the angels. Perhaps such a desire was connected with his victory over whatever temptation had beset him. In the spring a day came when he could say, "I thought that I then enjoyed a heaven as far exceeded the most sublime conceptions of an un-regenerate soul; and even unspeakably beyond that I myself could conceive at another time." He appeared to have overcome the bitterness he had felt toward Rector Clap and other authori-ties at Yale, the strongest known particular sin of his life. "I could not have spoken a word of bitterness, or entertained a bit-ter thought against the vilest man living." [19] He had devoted many days, usually Thursdays, throughout the winter to fasting and prayer and the radical attempt to root out every sin and reach a state of perfection before God.

Thus ended the first year of Brainerd's missionary service. There had been no great revival among his Mahicans, but they had been persuaded to lay aside their "idolatrous sacrifices" and their "heathenish custom of dancing and hallooing." He hoped also that they were in some measure weaned away from their besetting sin of drunkenness.[20] Actually he had persuaded the Indians at Kaunaumeek to remove to Stockbridge and come un-der the guidance of the missionaries there. Many of the Ma-hicans urged him to remain with them, but he told them that others must be allowed to hear the gospel. His attachment to them, so apparently casual elsewhere in the account, is perhaps best indicated by his comment on his last sermon to them, "I had so much to say to them, that I knew not how to leave off speak-ing." [21]

WITH THE DELAWARES IN PENNSYLVANIA

Brainerd entered upon his second missionary labor with even less enthusiasm than the first. "Having received new orders to go to a number of Indians on Delaware River in Pennsylvania . . . I this day took all my clothes, books, etc., and disposed of them. . . . Rode several hours in the rain through the howling wilderness, although I was so disordered in body, that little or nothing but blood came from me. . . . My heart, sometimes, was ready to sink with the thoughts of my work, and going alone in the wilderness, I knew not where." [22]

His destination was the vicinity of eastern Pennsylvania where the Lehigh River joins the Delaware River. On the long journey southward from Kaunaumeek, Brainerd stopped at Minnisink, on the northeastern border of Pennsylvania, where his offer to an Indian king to instruct his people in religion was greeted with a scornful laugh. In a long harangue the king's viceroy inquired of the missionary why Indians should become Christians when Christians were greater liars, thieves, and drunkards than Indians. Finally calmed a little, the viceroy offered to hear Brainerd further on some return visit provided no effort be made to press religion.[23]

Two days later Brainerd arrived wet, fatigued, lonesome, and disconsolate at Hunter's Settlement. His first Sabbath morning there was the gloomiest he had ever experienced. It appeared that every circumstance conspired against him and he felt banished from the sight of God. The Indians he found scattered. He had no adequate interpreter. He felt the temptation to give up, with an alternative hope of dying on the job. "To an eye of reason," he wrote, "everything respecting the conversion of the heathen is as dark as midnight," yet he hoped in God for "the accomplishment of something glorious" among them.[24] Without waiting for a single day to pass, he began preaching, addressing himself both to the Indians and to the Scotch-Irish and Germans making up the little community. He began by living at the home of Alexander Hunter and riding the three miles across the wooded hills to his Indians. He had been welcomed by the Indian king and allowed to preach at will in his house.[25]

As in many other places, the Indians were in process of being driven from their lands. Two years before Brainerd's arrival a great majority of the Delawares had gone eighty miles westward to Wyoming and Shamokin, where Brainerd was later to follow. These Indians had been served for a long period by devoted Moravian missionaries, including a spectacular and effective journey through all these parts by Count Nicholas-Louis Zinzendorf and his followers. Most of the Indian leaders by now knew the difference between white mercenaries and men like Brainerd and Zinzendorf.

A reader of the diary is led to wonder whether Brainerd ever quite accepted this district as his ultimate missionary field. He arrived in early May, but it was the last of November before he built his house near the Indians. There is not much indication that he seriously attempted to learn the Delaware language. His translator was Moses Tinda Tattamy, a Delaware landowner who had been fond of the bottle but was experienced in translation both for earlier missionaries and for the government of Pennsylvania. Actually the year proved to be one of travel, for Brainerd made no fewer than seven trips that occupied almost five months, not counting his frequent preaching at Hunter's Settlement and to the Irish fifteen miles to the southwest at Craig's Settlement.

He returned in May to Newark for his ordination. In September he spent three weeks in New England visiting friends, possibly including Jerusha Edwards, and recuperating. In November he was two weeks absent for the Presbytery meeting in New York. In the spring he was absent five weeks on a 600-mile horseback journey to New England, seeking a helper for his missionary labors and, possibly fully as important, breaking the terrible loneliness of the wilderness. He had hardly landed back among the Delawares before he left for Philadelphia to enlist the aid of the governor in persuading the chief of the Six Nations to allow him to go as a missionary to the Indians on the Susquehanna. The previous October a pastor friend named Eliab Byram, Tattamy, two other Indians, and he had made a ten-day trip northwest through a "hideous and howling wilderness" (where his horse had to be killed after it had broken its leg on the rocks) to Wapwallopen on the North Branch of the Susquehanna, where the friendly Indians postponed their autumn hunting trip a couple of days to listen to Brainerd and then invited him back in the spring.

This trip not only encouraged Brainerd as a missionary but also improved his health. Despite sleeping on the ground inside bark shelters while wolves howled around them, Brainerd "scarcely ever enjoyed more health." A second trip in May took him and Tattamy to the main stream of the Susquehanna and then a hundred miles along the river while they visited seven or eight different tribes and Brainerd preached through different interpreters. Actually the Susquehanna was then the home of a great number of Indian tribes which had been pushed westward all the way from central New York and northwestward from Virginia and North Carolina.

Brainerd later traveled south to Juniata where, among others, he met a zealous Indian reformer who manifested great anxiety over the degeneraton of his people. Though Brainerd still regarded Indians as "savages," he was much impressed with this Indian's manifest eagerness to benefit his people.[26] On his second trip Brainerd suffered an ague which was accompanied with great pains and a "great evacuation of blood." He fully expected for awhile that he would die.

Brainerd closed the work among the Delawares with little to show for his efforts. He had prayed earnestly for some mighty display of God's power but none had appeared. He had seen some evidences of the moving of the Spirit when he preached to the whites at Hunter's and Craig's Settlements. And once, at the neighboring town of Neshaminy, scores or even hundreds in an audience of three or four thousand had been deeply affected and mourning for their sins. Interpreter Tattamy and his wife had shown some signs of God's hand upon them. But still Brainerd wondered if he were not wasting the funds of the Scots missionary society which supported him.

He had found many of these "savages" cynical toward the white man. They were ready, and often astonishingly able, to defend their way of life as compared with his. What Brainerd saw was a gun-and-gospel civilization with all of its heartbreaking tensions and anomalies. He saw Indians who had frequently been outrageously cheated of their lands by white men, often with alcohol as chief agent. Even worse, he had seen the disintegration of ancient tribal customs and religion where the collision of the old ways with the new commonly resulted in stalemate or indifference. Even the efforts of the chieftains of the Seven Nations to maintain a semblance of dignity was beset by the apathy of Indians who drowned their troubles in alcohol or sometimes connived with unscrupulous whites to cheat other Indians farther west of their furs and land. In one dramatic instance Brainerd found Indians who were prevented from turning to the gospel by threats from their powwows [medicine men] to enchant and poison them. To demonstrate their powerlessness he challenged the powwows to bewitch and poison him.[27]

It was mostly a year of illness for the missionary and even more pronounced a year of recurring melancholy. The wilderness in which he lived, his separation from like-minded friends, and his seeming failure with the Indians—together with his native tendency to depression—made it perhaps the worst year of his life. The death wish was strongly upon him. After a bleak night in which, on his way home from Newark, he had become lost in the wilds for some hours while at the same time suffering severe pains, he came to a home where a corpse was laid out, and as he looked on the body, he "longed that my time might come." In early February he had what he described as a hellish experience—unfortunately one omitted by Jonathan Edwards from the *Diary*—which made him "long for the grave more, unspeakably more, than for hid treasures." A few days later he said, "I could see myself dead and laid out and enclosed in my coffin and put down into the cold grave, with the greatest solemnity but without terror." [28] Once at least he suffered the deep feeling that there is no God. His only encouragements were his habitual trust in God and his occasional ability to preach in the Spirit's power. At the end of April he was so ill that he was unable effectually to read, pray, or meditate, and so came to the conviction that it was absolutely necessary to "divert" himself "by all lawful means." This belief is reaffirmed sporadically throughout the rest of his life, yet we never learn what the diversion is. Most likely it was simply leisurely horseback riding.[29]

Thus ended seven years of Brainerd's life since he had first offered himself to God for the ministry. The summer as a farm owner, those bittersweet years at Yale, and now a year each with the Mahicans and the Delawares—all were past. Whatever one may think about Brainerd's neglect of his health, whatever may be said of his waxing and waning emotions, in respect to his duty Brainerd was like an Arthurian knight who never forgets his vigil, his basically clear, pure trust, and the necessity of eternal obedience.

Now, at twenty-seven and with only two and a half years to live, the young man had come a discouragingly short distance on his way to the Grail. Or so it seemed to him. Had the Almighty granted his death wish in that winter of 1744–45, David Brainerd would have forfeited the great manifest missionary success that was in the offing.

AT CROSSWICKS

Starting with the very day of David Brainerd's arrival at his third Indian post, at Crossweeksung, or as we now call it Crosswicks, in New Jersey, eighty miles southeast of his former work, there began one of the most remarkable visitations of the Holy Spirit in the history of the Christian church. Brainerd repeatedly acknowledged that he himself was not the primary agent. Though he preached and prayed as never before, at the same time he stood as much amazed as everybody else at the supernatural character of events.

Conditions for such a movement of the Holy Spirit could hardly have been worse. The Indians in the vicinity were widely scattered, living two or three families together over a territory of thirty-six miles. They were the ragtag who had not followed the westward migrations and were often engaged as tinkers or even as beggars on the outskirts of white villages. Many of them had run into debt through their excessive drinking. The whole territory was being overrun by an influx of ambitious white immigrants.[30] On Brainerd's part, he came in without "the least hope," his mind depressed, his spirits "extremely sunk," and his bodily strength at low ebb. One could hardly have concocted a situation less calculated to result in anything good.

When Brainerd arrived at Crosswicks on June 19, 1745, he found no men, only four women and a few children. After he had preached to them, they immediately went as far as fifteen miles away to tell others what they had heard. Brainerd began to preach daily, and the number of Indians steadily increased. Though some of these Indians had been enraged at an earlier effort of Tattamy to say something about Christianity, there was now no sign of opposition, but rather, from the beginning, a steady and serious attention that eventually grew into tears, repentance, and Christian joy. Indians gathered from as much as twenty miles away and most of them remained on the spot. On one occasion when food was much needed for the group it seemed providential that three deer were killed almost within sight of the camp. As the revival continued into August, Indians came from as far away as forty miles.

Brainerd was asked to preach twice a day. There was manifest evidence of great concern. The Indians found their spiritual needs taking precedence over everything else. A divine tenderness so affected them that a few words from the missionary might bring them to tears and often to outright sobbing and groaning over their sins. On one occasion almost the entire audience of forty were "pierced with the tender and melting invitations of the Gospel" and cried bitterly over their spiritual condition. A little later the distress of the Indians was so great that some lay on the ground and moaned incessantly. Brainerd noticed that Indians coming in for the first time were often quickly overcome with penitence and that white people who came out of curiosity or even to jeer were quickly subdued and penitent.

Brainerd himself was amazed at what was happening and saw the working of the Spirit as "the irresistible force of a mighty torrent or swelling deluge" which bore down everything before it. "Old men and women, who had been drunken wretches for many years, and some little children, not more than six or seven years of age, appeared in distress about their souls, as well as persons of middle age." The converts of one day would go to their unconverted friends in a successive meeting and take them by the hand and tenderly tell them of the joy of salvation.

One skeptical young Indian woman who had come apparently to mock the proceedings was promptly sobered as Brainerd began to preach and before he had concluded she was like one "pierced through with a dart, and cried out incessantly." Even after the service was over she prayed earnestly as she lay on the ground oblivious of her surroundings. Brainerd listened intently and heard her saying, in her Indian tongue, "Have mercy on me, and help me to give Thee my heart." She remained in this condition for many hours. Brainerd felt that no atheist could have withstood the power of God on this occasion. Indians who had not long before made the welkin ring with their drunken feasting and dancing now cried out for salvation.

The immediate change in the lives of those converted was a great comfort to Brainerd. They were humble, devout, and

tender of conscience. One morning Brainerd found a female con-
vert downcast and he inquired the cause. The woman said that
the evening before she had been angry with her child and then,
fearful of having sinned, she had awakened before daylight and
wept for hours. On one occasion the group most distressed about
their sins consisted of old men who wept and cried aloud so
earnestly that no one could doubt their anxiety.

Brainerd noted that he had never seen God work so independ-
ently of normal means. Little preaching was necessary. He
simply talked quietly to the people and then looked in glad astonishment on the work of the Lord among them.

Sometimes worn out from his preaching and having to retire
exhausted to his quarters, Brainerd found that the Indians often
remained behind for hours to pray and worship. He was convinced that some of them if possible would have remained
twenty-four hours at a time in religious services. Once an Indian
woman came to the meeting reluctantly, was duly touched by the
Spirit, and afterward insisted on going forty miles to her husband in order to bring him under the influence of the Gospel.

As the number of converts increased, Brainerd, after first making very sure of the reality of their salvation and of their Christian walk, began to baptize them. Four and a half months after
he first reached Crossweeksung he had baptized forty-seven Indians of whom about half were children. Of the adults baptized
one was almost eighty years old and two others were middle-
aged men "who had been remarkable even among the Indians
for their wickedness." One indeed had been a murderer, and
both were notorious for bad temper and drunkenness.

Even in this happy situation Brainerd could not help but remember former great expectations that had proved abortive, so
he was often suspended between hope and doubt. But this time
he need not have doubted, for the power of God was to manifest
itself for a whole year and reverberate to distances unthought of.
"I never saw the work of God appear so independent of

means. . . . I discoursed to the people on what I hoped had a proper tendency to promote conviction; but God's manner of working upon them appeared . . . entirely supernatural and above means . . . so that I seemed to do nothing, and indeed to have nothing to do, but to stand still and see the salvation of God. . . . The Lord appeared to work entirely alone, and I saw no room to attribute any part of this work to any created arm." [31] Such was the tenor of Brainerd's account. His attitude was commonly that of the astonished observer. There seemed to be no subtlety of plan, no skillful arranging, no proportioned circumstances, only prayer and more prayer, plus a mild urgency on the preacher's part. Sometimes "the face of the whole assembly would be apparently changed almost in an instance, and tears and sobs become common among them." On a day in January the first service was listless and the people seemingly indifferent, but at a later service on the same day the very first prayer was accompanied by a remarkable descent of God, and Brainerd felt compelled to depart from his usual caution and press for a speedy acceptance of salvation.[32]

The power of occasions is often mentioned by Brainerd. "There was scarcely three in forty that could refrain from tears and bitter cries. . . . Some few could neither go nor stand, but lay flat on the ground . . . crying incessantly for mercy. . . . Old men and women, who had been drunken wretches for many years, and some little children, not more than six or seven years of age, appeared in distress about their souls, as well as persons of middle age. . . . Some of the white people, who came out of curiosity . . . were also much awakened. . . . Sundry old men were also in distress for their souls, so that they could not refrain from weeping and crying out aloud; and their bitter groans were the most convincing as well as affecting evidence of the reality and depth of their inward anguish." [33]

When he went from house to house on a January day to converse with Indians about their spiritual condition, "divers persons wept . . . and appeared concerned for nothing so much as for an interest in the great Redeemer." Sometimes the baptismal services proved a powerful means of awakening the onlookers. At times the spirit came with "ravishing comfort." In one instance a group of fifteen strange Indians, several of whom had never attended a religious meeting before, were in less than one week brought to serious spiritual attitudes, and "one very rugged young man, who seemed as if nothing would move him," finally trembled and wept.[34] And so it went month after month.

Long since cured of enthusiasm, Brainerd looked with a rational eye at the situation and was adamant in explaining to his audiences the steps to true salvation. After nine months of revival he said: "So far from thinking that every appearance and particular instance of affection amongst us has been truly genuine . . . I am sensible of the contrary; and doubt not but there have been some corrupt mixtures, some chaff as well as wheat especially since religious concern became so common and prevalent here." [35]

In the midst of the Great Awakening, Brainerd recapitulated his thoughts upon what was happening. First, said he, the revival had begun at a time when he was extremely depressed in both body and mind and when he, supposing his work largely a failure, was thinking of resigning from the missionary society that supported him. Secondly, that it was solely the work of God seemed manifest from the manner in which from fantastically small beginnings the Indians themselves had spread the good word and brought together their relatives and friends to hear the Gospel. Thirdly, he noted that the cynicism and taunting of ungodly whites had little effect. Fourthly, he felt God had provided not simply an efficient interpreter but one who himself knew the power of God and therefore could reinforce the Christian message. Fifthly, the awakening was taking place through the simple preaching of divine grace and love rather than by "harangues of terror." (One wonders what Brainerd thought of

Jonathan Edwards' *Sinners in the Hands of an Angry God*.)
All physical manifestations in the revival had been commensu-
rate with genuine afflictions of the soul and without real similarity
to "those convulsions, bodily agonies, frightful screamings and
swoonings, that have been so much complained of in some
places." Lastly, the converted Indians had both a remarkable
doctrinal understanding and, on the practical side, had quit their
drunkenness and running into debt and had begun to live by
principles of justice and honesty.

Strangely, a similar revival was under way at Brainerd's former station in Pennsylvania. He had returned there for a visit
because of the low state of his health, and the Holy Spirit went
with him. One great victory was the baptism of interpreter Tattamy and his wife and children. Tattamy had been known far
and wide both for his astuteness and his drunkenness, and his
conversion was a powerful witness to other Indians. Tattamy
had actually received his "comfort" six months earlier, but Brainerd was seldom in a hurry with his converts.

As word of God's visitation at these places spread abroad,
great numbers of both Indians and whites came. Generally they
looked on with quiet awe and many were saved. Others became
rude, especially white men, and tried to disrupt the meetings.
Some told outrageous lies about Brainerd, such as that he intended to trap the Indians and sell them to the British as slaves.
One group of Indians took a bitter delight in taunting others
who wept over their sins. But, as time went on, the tide of salvation moved so powerfully that Brainerd became fearful the very
unpopularity of not being a Christian might lead some to the
mere appearance of grace rather than to genuine conversion.

Brainerd often preached three times a day, and once the service ran for eight hours. Observing the revival, he felt he must
never again allow circumstances to cause him to doubt the power
of God. Brainerd steadfastly taught his audiences that conversion must be the final step in a process that involved a develop-

ing realization of one's hopeless condition before God. To be doubly sure that the Indians understood what Christianity was, he thoroughly catechized all converts and was delighted with the depth of spiritual knowledge he uncovered. He was particularly careful with respect to baptism and even more to the administration of the Lord's Supper. For the latter he felt it desirable first to consult his commissioners and then to give his converts minute instructions concerning its meaning. The Indians had by this time established their own village, and Brainerd went from house to house for private teaching and encouragement of his people.

So the Great Awakening gradually subsided. Brainerd had baptized eighty-five Indians, some of them his Pennsylvania people, and including a murderer-conjurer. Brainerd reported that "paganism" and idolatrous practices had almost entirely disappeared and that the Indians' besetting vice of drunkenness was all but wiped out. Their marriage customs had become Christian and they were living together in a spirit of Christian love. He had gathered the Indians into one place near Cranberry, fifteen miles from Crosswicks, for better Christian fellowship, education, and agriculture. He had brought in a schoolteacher, who began instructing about thirty young people during the day and fifteen married people in the evenings.

Was there ever a more fruitful missionary labor in the same length of time? Best of all was the conviction that the work was not primarily the missionary's but God's. One cannot read his account without feeling, in Brainerd's words, that it was sufficient "to convince an atheist of the truth, importance, and power of God's Word." [36]

Brainerd somehow managed two more trips, both discouraging in their outcome, into the interior, each about forty days in length. He apparently entertained the idea that perhaps his real missionary work should be somewhere along the Susquehanna in the vicinity of Juniata and Shamokin, Pennsylvania, or even farther west, a country "where the devil now reigns in the most eminent manner." On the second trip he was desperately ill, coughing and spitting blood and with a fever which often kept his clothes wringing wet all night and made it almost impossible for him to sit on his horse during the day. Yet on this trip he decided to press far down the West Branch of the Susquehanna almost to the center of Pennsylvania. One cannot read this section of his *Diary* without feelings of pity, wonder, admiration, and at times aversion. Yet it was precisely Brainerd's willingness to ignore every hindrance to the prosecution of a spiritual ideal that struck fire in the souls of so many who later read the *Diary*.

LAST DAYS

Brainerd arrived home from the second Susquehanna trip on September 20, 1746. He attempted to carry on his usual activities among his Indians, including the construction of a house for himself at Cranberry, but his *Diary* evidences only too clearly his increasing illness. On November 3 he wrote: "Being now in so weak and low a state that I was utterly incapable of performing my work, and having little hope of recovery, unless by much riding, I thought it my duty to take a long journey into New England, and divert myself among my friends, whom I had not seen for a long time." [37] Perhaps he knew in his heart that it was his farewell as a missionary. Before leaving he visited one by one the homes of his Indians and exhorted them to faithfulness. "I scarcely left one house but some were in tears," he reported.

At Elizabeth, New Jersey, he was confined almost four months among his friends and very ill. The following March he made a brief visit to Cranberry, then returned to Elizabeth where he performed the marriage ceremony for Jonathan Dickinson, first president of the College of New Jersey (later Princeton University), and assisted in examining his own brother John who was to become his successor with the Indians in New Jersey. In April he was invited to the home of Jonathan Edwards in Northampton, Massachusetts, and on April 21, the day following his birthday, he set out. He was so ill that he could ride but slowly, yet he expected that the exercise of riding would benefit him. Doubtless he noticed the loveliness of the greening countryside, but there is no hint of that in his *Diary*. The same feeling of vileness beset him at times and with it the same longing for holiness and heaven.

After stopping at Haddam to visit his kinfolk, he arrived at Northampton. What would one not give for a glimpse of his meeting with Jerusha Edwards? It has been generally assumed that David and Jerusha were already engaged, but an entry in the journal of Esther, Jerusha's sixteen-year-old sister, appears to indicate that this may have been their first meeting. Esther says that Brainerd "is likely to become a member of this family it seems. Soon after coming to Northampton he displayed strong affinity for Jerusha, our sister of seventeen, who was soon inoculated with his high spiritual views, and deeply interested in his Indian work." Esther goes on to say that in his missionary labors Brainerd has had "no domestic attention, no home care, no one to hold him back from over exertion," and that it is his intention, provided he recovers, "to take a female helpmate back with him." She adds the interesting remark: "I am pretty sure this kind of love would never satisfy me. I believe he loves her more because she will make a good missionary, than for any other reason." [38]

If David and Jerusha had just met for the first time, the friendship must have ripened fast, for on June 9, on the advice of physicians that riding would do him more good than anything else, she accompanied him all the way to Boston. It was for them a four-day journey, and one can imagine them winding over the hills and fording the little streams and talking together.

David had felt much better on the trip, but shortly after ar-

riving in Boston he became desperately ill with lung hemor-
rhages. For several weeks he remained in critical condition, yet
able to carry on conversations, in Jonathan Edwards' phrase,
with "many eminent characters . . . some of the first rank; who
showed him uncommon respect." [39] Particular inquiry was made
of the needs of his Indians in New Jersey, and contributions were
given for the school there and for Bibles to be distributed among
the Indians. He and Jerusha Edwards, this time accompanied
by David's youngest brother Israel, who had come to Boston
because of David's low condition and also to bring him word
of their own sister Jerusha's death, again took horse and spent
the larger part of a week returning through the countryside to
Northampton. Esther Edwards reported, "Jerusha has just returned from her sojourn in Boston with her sick charge. . . .
Never was so much idolatry bestowed on mortal man. . . . She
actually almost worships the ground he treads upon." [40]

His brother John came, bringing David's diary, with which
he occupied himself for some time in rereading and emending,
having been persuaded by Jonathan Edwards that it must not
be destroyed.

David now began the lengthy routine expected in those days
of a dying Christian. He wrote his final letters. He talked
warmly of Christ and of his longing for death. He called in the
children and servants of the Edwards household and after exhorting them to holy living said, "I shall die here, and here I
shall be buried; here you will see my grave, and do you remember what I have told you." He spoke lovingly to Jerusha. He
continued busy and on the night of his death talked with his
brother John about the welfare of their Indians. At daybreak on
October 9, 1747, he died, at the age of twenty-nine.

Esther wrote in her journal that at the funeral "dear Jerusha's
illuminated face was a study. She was rapt up no more in the
living. . . . For exactly nineteen weeks, day and night, she has
cared for this sick man; and she is only eighteen." Three days

later a crowded church heard Jonathan Edwards preach the funeral sermon and lay David Brainerd to rest. Esther wrote that "the October foliage, full of glory, seemed Nature's expression of the triumphal conclusion of his life's years." [41]

Five months and two days later Esther made another entry: "This day our dear Jerusha died at eighteen. If as she and her sainted David, and we all believe, has gone to her Father's House, she has already joined the holy company. . . . They have been separated only five months. Though I doubt whether he has ever been absent from her thought and longing love. . . . We shall lay the frame of this ministering angel side by side with that of the man who breathed out his life almost in her arms." She ventured a quaint and touching additional note: "This is what the world calls St. Valentine's day, though I have been taught to think it all folly. Being a girl, I suppose, I could not help remarking the coincidence." [42]

THE MAN OF FEELING

Did any man ever write as much and reveal as little about his humanity as David Brainerd? The *Diary* is concerned with Brainerd the saint, the *Journal* with Brainerd the busy missionary, yet both are distressingly incomplete about Brainerd the man. Jonathan Edwards says that Brainerd was "remarkably sociable, pleasant and entertaining in his conversation," [43] but we look in vain for actual instances of this aspect of his personality. Brainerd's contemporary, John Wesley, wrote a journal filled with notes on men, books, and events, but we find little hint in Brainerd of such things. In a period seething with political and national upheavals Brainerd has almost nothing to say of passing events. What books did he carry into his little cabins? What did he think of music? Of medicine? Indeed of horses (he rode them all his life)? We look in vain for answers to such questions.

How much it would mean to find related in the *Diary* just one tender anecdote such as that told by John Woolman, another contemporary, of how, as a child, he stoned a mother robin and killed her and then, sorry for the little birds left in the nest, climbed the tree and killed them and afterwards was hounded by a horrid sense of his evil. How much of the man Brainerd we might envisage if we saw him as we do Jonathan Edwards laboriously cutting out wooden blocks to demonstrate to a thirteen-year-old that a block two inches square is eight times as large as one an inch square. How good if Brainerd had given us ever so small a vignette of himself following the plow on his farm as did Robert Burns later in the same century. How human he might become if we could see some little foolishness in his life like saving bits of paper or one or two of those charming personal oddities in the life of still another of Brainerd's great contemporaries, Dr. Samuel Johnson. How revealing if we could know what he laughed at. Both *Diary* and *Journal* are untinctured by so much as one small touch of humor.

We do learn that Brainerd offered his patrimony to a struggling ministerial student at Yale and how afterwards he thought that perhaps he might have used it better in his Indian labors. We learn briefly of Brainerd's financial affairs, also how his teapot and bed-ticking were up for sale, but we are left almost totally in the dark as to what little oddments Brainerd liked to have in his room or what small foibles attracted him as a member of the human species. Did he try Dover's Powders or Tar Water, two famous "remedies" for disease in his time? Did he scramble for a copy of John Wesley's *Primitive Physick: or, an Easy and Natural Method of Curing Most Diseases,* which appeared in the year of his death?

There is almost no hint of the subjects he liked in college. Every student in those days studied Latin and Greek, and Brainerd was among the best of students, but we look almost in vain for traces that those languages, or indeed any other subject in college, entered the stream of his life.

Far more significant, since it can be explained as nothing less than a defection from Scripture itself, is Brainerd's seeming total disregard of the heavens and the earth as the handiwork of God. In the more than six hundred pages of the *Diary* and *Journal* there are fewer than a half-dozen instances in which the very suggestion of any regard for natural beauty occurs. Once in a state of dejection he envied the happiness of birds and beasts, once he went into "a pleasant grove" for prayer and meditation, and once he mentions the rainbow. That is pretty much the meager sum of it. It seems inconceivable that he could fail once to mention a sunset, a sunrise, the greenness of spring or the colors of autumn, the stars in the heavens, or any other eye-pleasing image in nature. So far as the record shows, never once did a bird's song pierce his ear as it did King Solomon's and never once did Brainerd feel, like King David, the tenderness of still waters and green pastures. Never once is it evident that, like Christ, he observed the lilies of the field. Saint Francis loved the very stones under his feet and spoke to "Brother Sun," but not so Brainerd. Tertullian could say, "I never get over how God moves tons of water around in perfect quietness and beauty as the clouds float by," and Perry Miller could say of Jonathan Edwards that no poet was ever more sensitive to the beauty of nature,[44] but not so Brainerd. There is nowhere the least hint of the attitude of John Wesley who, after riding all day over mountainous country, could still say in the evening: "I was surprised by one of the finest prospects . . . I ever saw in my life. We rode in a green vale, shaded with rows of trees, which made an arbour for several miles. . . . On the other side of the river the mountain rose to an immense height, almost perpendicular: and yet the tall, straight oaks stood, rank above rank, from the bottom to the very top." [45] Brainerd's contemporary Isaac Watts wrote a hymn about the mighty power of God:

That made the mountains rise;
  That spread the flowing seas abroad,
And built the lofty skies.

.   .   .   .

There's not a plant or flower below,
  But makes Thy glories known;
And clouds arise, and tempests blow,
  By order from Thy throne.

And John Calvin could look upon nature as "the garment we see God by," but not so Brainerd.

To be sure, Brainerd's experience was not that of a man who goes for an outing in nature. He knew what it meant to be lost at night in the forest (but for that matter so did John Wesley) and to hear the wolves howling around him. The wilderness was for him an enemy to be overcome. Brainerd's antipathy to mountains cannot be accounted for on the ground of his ill health, for he had unusually good health on his first visit to the frontier over the Blue Mountains and through the lovely Lehigh Gap, yet it was nothing more than "a hideous and howling wilderness" to him. If Brainerd ever remembered that Moses came face to face with God on a mountain, that Elijah talked with God on a mountain, that Christ was transfigured on a mountain, or that David said God's righteousness is like the great mountains, he leaves no word of it. The great questions put to God by Job concerning the visible world get no response in Brainerd. The sweetness of the word *Susquehanna* was itself sufficient to put Samuel Taylor Coleridge in an ecstasy of longing to found a utopia on its banks, yet no glint of light on its water and no prospect discovered around its winding shores ever drew a word of appreciation from Brainerd.

That he was not simply ignorant of Scriptural teaching about the natural world is pointedly suggested by Ebenezer Pemberton's sermon at Brainerd's ordination. Pemberton began: "God erected this visible world as a monument of his glory, a theatre for the display of his adorable perfections. The heavens proclaim his wisdom and power in shining characters, and the whole earth is full of his goodness." [46] It is impossible to escape the belief that David Brainerd's ignoring of nature is deliberate.

It is equally hard to avoid the conviction that for Brainerd the Bible was not the capacious book it was for Jonathan Edwards. Though both men abominated "imagination" in religion, this did not prevent Edwards from the employment of vivid Scriptural imagery as well as using striking parallels from the common life or from nature. On the other hand, Brainerd's imagery and figures seem studiously limited, as though he were afraid of the free, immense world depicted by Isaiah, Job, or the Psalmists. It is inconceivable that Brainerd should have written an essay like Edwards' "Images or Shadows of Divine Things" in which, citing St. Paul as his authority, Edwards argues that "the things of the world" are designed to "shadow forth spiritual things." With all his admiration for Brainerd, John Wesley was grieved that so good a man should be " 'wise above that is written,' in condemning what the Scripture nowhere condemns." [47]

On another score also the *Diary* and *Journal* are disappointing. While Brainerd the missionary is ready to sacrifice all for his people, one feels at the same time both a lack of tenderness toward them and a considerable unwillingness to take what we should today call a "psychological" view toward them. At times the very sight of the Indians seems to upset him. Visiting them at the eastern end of Long Island, Brainerd wrote: "Rode sixteen miles to Montauk and had some inward sweetness on the road; but something of flatness and deadness after I came there and had seen the Indians." Like many others of his time, he speaks of the Indians as "savages," "the heathen," "the poor rude ignorant Indians," "poor pagans," and "savage pagans." Yet there were hundreds of Christian Indians at the time and innumerable Indians who spoke fluent English. Even as far inland as Juniata he had found Indians who spoke English well. Moreover, Brainerd had been treated courteously by the various tribes he had ministered to, even those far back in the wilderness. He acknowledged that to his Christian message the Indians often put the most penetrating questions, and he was surprised to notice how quickly his converts learned the elements of Christian theology. Yet the epithets of "heathen" and "pagan" pretty well remain his common designation. The Psalmist had said of all the inhabitants of the earth that God "fashioneth their hearts alike," yet Brainerd and his fellow missionaries seldom raised the philosophical question of the Indian's status in the creation. In his time neither the Indian nor the Negro slave was strongly conceived of as made in the image of God. Hence there seems less of identification with these peoples than might have occurred otherwise.

An attempt to understand and capitalize on the favorable aspects of the Indian's culture, rather than to assume the Indian simply and hopelessly savage, might have made Brainerd a more effectual missionary. According to Albert T. Volwiler, one reason for George Croghan's great commercial success with the Indians was his learning the Delaware and Iroquois languages so well that he could "express himself in the figurative speech so dear to the Indian." [48] It seems apparent that Brainerd only reluctantly learned the Indian tongues and was never adept at them.

Another disturbing facet of Brainerd's *Diary* is its endless ups and downs. If in the *Journal* he is the man of action, in the *Diary* he is clearly the man of feeling. It is the record of his hearty, whole-souled yearning for a certain condition and attitude before God, with long hours or even days of effort to bring this condition about. What state of soul was it that Brainerd sought?

Perhaps the outstanding word to describe it is *sweetness*. He wished for a tender, melting, blissful ecstasy, "a sweet time . . . felt much of the sweetness of religion . . . was enabled to pray with a great degree of softness and pathetic fervour . . . had a melting sense of divine things. . . . O the tenderness I felt in my soul! . . . felt sweetly serious. . . . Afterwards was visited by some friends, but lost some sweetness by it . . . felt a little of the sweetness of religion. . . . O with what tenderness the love and desire of holiness fills the soul! . . . had some sweet thoughts . . . my soul was melted . . . spiritual sensation, in its soft and tender whispers . . . soft and tender affection . . . to feel our souls sedate, mild, and meek . . . sweet refreshment . . . praying incessantly, every moment with sweet fervency . . . my soul was melted . . . spiritual, warm, heavenly-minded . . . a sweet resigned frame of soul . . . blissful communion . . . a sweet melting season . . . sweetly resigned and composed." These are the states Brainerd constantly longed for, deliberately sought, and without which felt himself out of contact with God.

At the same time the *Diary* makes fearfully clear that Brainerd suffered all too often the opposite experiences of deadness, dejection, and melancholy. "My heart was sunk, and I seemed to have no God to go to . . . an awful distance from God . . . this world is a dark cloudy mansion . . . spiritual conflicts to-day were unspeakably dreadful, heavier than the mountains and overflowing floods." Sometimes this state remained with him for days and caused him to give up all for lost. Sometimes it took possession of him during his best endeavors for God. Once while administering the sacrament his soul was "filled with confusion, and the utmost anguish that ever I endured," and once he preached to his Pennsylvania Indians while under "inexpressible dejection." Another time he was "almost swallowed up with anguish" as he saw people gathering to hear him preach.

Brainerd finally came to recognize these fits of dejection as sinful. "I find discouragement to be a great hindrance to spiritual fervency and affection," he said. And again, "O that God would keep me from giving way to sinful dejection." He was in some measure relieved from these states toward the end of his life, though never fully. The reader who has followed Brainerd through page after page shares with him his satisfaction in recording, "Blessed be the Lord, that . . . for many days together, my mind is not gloomy as at some other times." Yet his own summary, written not long after his college years, is the correct one: "My life is a constant mixture of consolations and conflicts, and will be so till I arrive at the world of spirits."

Melancholy is of course a common experience of mankind and is biographically important only as it becomes pathological. Some of the great men of the world have suffered from it—Tolstoy, Coleridge, Bunyan, Goethe, Luther, Dr. Johnson, and Jonathan Edwards. Also King Saul of Israel. In his *Varieties of Religious Experience*, William James notes three manifestations of this condition, *i.e.*, melancholy from the vanity of mortal things, from the sense of sin, and from the fear of the universe. It was in particular the second of these which took hold on Brainerd's soul. His *Diary* is replete with the most abject confessions of his vileness. Since Brainerd's outward or manifest sins were few, it is obvious that his confessions have to do with what he regarded as inward or spiritual defects. These repeat themselves throughout the *Diary*. He saw himself as "exceedingly vile . . . worse than any devil . . . the greatest sinner in the land . . . little, low, and sinful . . . so vile and unworthy that I scarcely knew how to converse with human creatures . . . infinitely vile . . . so vile that I was ashamed to be seen when I came out of the meeting-house . . . the meanest, vilest, most helpless, guilty, ignorant, benighted creature living, with doubts and fears whether it was possible for such a wretch as I to be in a state of grace . . . viler, and seemingly more brutishly ignorant than the most barbarous people on earth . . . guilty of soul-murder . . . so vile and unworthy that I could not look my people in the face when I came to preach . . . inexpressibly loathsome and defiled . . . exceedingly polluted, like a nest of vipers, or a cage of unclean and hateful birds." Describing Brainerd's life during one period which he omitted, Jonathan Edwards says the *Diary* for that time contains "a sense of an unfathomable abyss of desperate wickedness in his heart, attended with a conviction that he had never seen but little of it."

What specifically did this vileness entail? Infrequently we get the record—self-exaltation, spiritual pride, warmth of temper, party spirit, shortcomings in duties, inability to be faithful for "one moment," barrenness, carnality, bitterness, want of a "Gospel-temper," "a kind of guilty amusement with the least trifles," spiritual blindness, indolence, trifling, wandering. It is very clear that in his last year at Yale Brainerd had a sharp tongue and deep resentment, yet those things he says he bitterly repented. Sometimes there seems an ominous suggestion of unmentionable sin, but all the evidence indicates no such conflict in Brainerd's life. The corruption he feels is that of a fallen creature before a sovereign and perfect God, also a conviction that he ministers inadequately to the spiritual needs of his people.

It is noteworthy that Brainerd appeared to derive satisfaction from bringing up sins of the long past, thinking them over thoroughly, and again repenting of them or seeking new depths in them of which to repent. The process seemed to accentuate his experience of God. He liked the "sweet and awful sense" of God "when I see myself as it were standing before the judgment-seat of Christ." Once he recalled as though just committed his childhood and youthful sins, "such follies as I had not thought of for years together," which appeared odious and made him feel "inexpressibly loathsome and defiled." Yet later the same day "the hand of faith seemed to be strengthened." It might be mere coincidence that the strengthening comes after the remembrance and renewed repentance, yet one wonders. The man of feeling recognizes that bitter repentance turns into sweetness. But is the sweetness thus sought for its own sake?

A parallel involves Brainerd's impulse to mental flagellation. "I long to be at the feet of my enemies and persecutors," he said, on his first return to Yale after his expulsion, as he abjectly remembered his former bitterness. "O it is sweet lying in the dust!" he exclaimed a little later. The process seems clear in another passage: "When God sets before me my past misconduct . . . it sinks my soul into shame and confusion . . . I have not confidence to hold up my face, even before my fellow-worms, only when my soul confides in God, and I find the sweet temper of Christ, the spirit of humility, solemnity, and mortification, alive in my soul." So the process involved is that the sin contemplated in all its hideousness brings on profound shame and spiritual flagellation, out of which comes the cry to God which results in the happiness and health of the soul. Again and again he is astonished that friends should show kindness or respect toward him, or even that the Indians should sit and listen to him. Do such things appear in part at least as "exercises" looking to holiness and even to the pleasure which holiness creates in the man of feeling?

There is also at times the martyr feeling in Brainerd, especially early in his thoughts of becoming a missionary to the "savages." On an April morning shortly after his dismissal from Yale he found himself willing, "if God should so order it, to suffer banishment from my native land, among the heathen, that I might do something for their souls' salvation, in distresses and deaths of any kind. . . . I felt weaned from the world, and from my own reputation amongst men, willing to be despised and to be a gazing-stock for the world to behold." [49] Such a commitment is all that could be asked of any young man thinking of God's service, and yet are there not some heroics in exaggerations like "banishment" and becoming a "gazing-stock for the world"? It is certainly true that Brainerd, as William B. O. Peabody points out, was neither physically nor temperamentally the sort of person to go alone into the wilderness, so that his real sacrifice lay in leaving the comforts of life, the warmth of a home fire, the shelter of a happy roof, and the refinement of books.[50] We should be happier for a simple acknowledgment of this kind by Brainerd, showing that he had a realistic view of himself, than for talk of banishment.

The truth is, I believe, that David Brainerd the man of feeling was never reconciled with the man of reason and common sense. In his depths he belonged not to the eighteenth century but to the early nineteenth, to the world of the mystical and imaginative. Or to the overcharged atmosphere of Madame Guyon and Fenelon in seventeenth-century France. It might have been better for him to have remained a hated "enthusiast," for then at least he would not have been afraid of nature and the natural channels of pleasure. As it was, he denied himself, unscripturally and almost as completely as a stylite living on top of a pillar, many of the legitimate joys of life.

What sort of man is it who, starting on a visit back home, fervently hopes that he "might not be too much pleased and amused with dear friends and acquaintances in one place and another"? Leaving the world, Brainerd nevertheless finds in his deepest heart the desire to feel. Hence he never quite accustoms himself to straightforward and stubborn missionary endeavor, even while performing it, but constantly seeks for "frames" [states of feeling] and suffers tremendous discomfiture when they are not forthcoming. It is interesting to speculate what might have happened had he felt the freedom to vent himself in great poetic utterances like those of David and Isaiah or even of contemporaries like Isaac Watts and the Wesleys.

Neither the *Diary* nor the *Journal* has the exultant tone of "God is for us, who can be against us?" or of Charles Wesley's hymn which declares, "Boldly I approach thy throne and claim the crown." John Wesley regretted that Brainerd suffered unnecessary sorrow and pain because when his sins were once confessed he did not put them behind him.[51] How good it would be to find an entry in Brainerd's diary similar to Edwards' for January 1, 1722–23: "Have been dull for several days. Examined whether I have not been guilty of negligence to-day; and re-

solved, No." Or to see Brainerd squarely confronted with the
advice of Miguel de Molinos to Christians who sin: "Would not
he be a mere fool who, running at tournament with others, and
falling in the best of the career, should lie weeping on the ground
and afflicting himself with discourses upon his fall? Man (they
would tell him), lose no time, get up and take the course again,
for he that rises again quickly and continues his race is as if he
had never fallen." [52] Brainerd is himself to some extent aware of
his problem. Once after talking with a friend at some length, he
said, "I find my soul is more refined and weaned from a dependence on my frames and spiritual feelings." Yet it is these feelings
which constitute the basic longings of Brainerd's soul throughout
his life.

THE MAN OF ACTION

We have now said a good many negative and conditioned
things about David Brainerd, and it is time to turn to some more
positive ones. And first we should note that Brainerd's journal
is so dissimilar from his diary that we can hardly believe the two
are by the same person. [53] In the journal we have the picture of
the busy missionary, the astute observer, the far-sighted strate-
gist, the systematic theologian, the splendid stylist, and the man
of confidence. Only rarely do the themes so prevalent in the
diary intrude—the melancholy and the spiritual ups and downs.
Even Brainerd's illness, significant as it was, plays a minor role.

We see Brainerd in his journal not simply as the preacher but
also as organizer, planner, and civilizer of the Indians. He is
busy settling them in one place where they can cultivate land and
establish habits of sobriety and proper commerce; he is anxious
to get both children and adults into organized schools and, above
all, to gain the encouragements of fixed practices in religion
through an established church and pastor. We see Brainerd as
the careful evaluator of the situation—the Indian's proclivity to

drunkenness, his good and evil contacts with white men, his civil rights, his poverty, his ingratitude for favors, his normal indolence and slothfulness, his inborn love of idleness, his lack of ambition or even of resolution, and his native shrewdness.

Explaining his failure to learn the Indian languages better, Brainerd wrote: "I am obliged to ride four thousand miles a year . . . to preach and catechise frequently, to converse privately with persons that need so much instruction and direction as these poor Indians do; to take care of all their secular affairs, as if they were a company of children; to ride abroad frequently in order to procure collections for the support of the school, and for their help and benefit in other respects; to hear and decide all the petty differences that arise among any of them, and to have the constant oversight and management of all their affairs of every kind." [54] We learn also of Brainerd's experience with unscrupulous white men, sometimes professing Christians, who tried to hinder the Indian work in one way or another.

One thing which appears with great clarity in the journal is Brainerd's interest in Indian anthropology. He inquires minutely into the legends and manners of the Indians, describes their tribal dances, and particularly endeavors to learn their religious beliefs. He is especially interested in the supernatural powers of the powwows. He had the unusual advantage of acquaintance with a diviner who had turned Christian, and he relates at length what this Indian told him of the source of his power which, said the diviner, he derived before ever he was born from a great man far above clothed in celestial brightness and all earthly beauty as well. [55]

In his journal we see Brainerd as the man of reason. He is particularly eager to have it known that in his evangelistic meetings there have been "no visionary notions, trances, and imaginations" but rather "rational convictions of sin and solid consolations." There has been no frightening of the Indians with "a fearful noise of hell and damnation," no "harangues of terror," but instead sound Christian doctrine and the love of a dying Savior. The Indians are, he says, "more affected with the comfortable than the dreadful truths of God's Word."

Perhaps more interesting than anything else is Brainerd's absolute determination to be sure of real rather than sham conversions. Descriptions of occurrences are manifestly cautious. It is correct, I think, to say that Brainerd simply did not believe in instantaneous salvation. In general conversion consists of a "misery" and a "remedy," and the remedy cannot adequately appear until the misery has been fully experienced. First, one must see oneself as utterly helpless and undone before God and thus emptied totally of dependence on self efforts. But this emptying must not then cause one to think that God will become pleased and bestow His blessing. Instead of some good frame of mind from loss of self-dependence, one must come to see his utter badness and the impossibility of ever making himself better. This state should shock one and make his true sinful nature clearer to him than ever before. Next must come the sharp recognition that it is entirely proper for God to send such a vile sinner to hell. The man must become naked and undone before God. This is the "misery" of conversion.

The remedy can then begin properly to appear. One sees something of the glory and beauty of Christ the Savior. Rather than giving away his heart, as he had originally supposed he could do, the man finds that his heart moves automatically toward that glory. Instead of bargaining with Christ, one's mind becomes occupied with His unspeakable excellency. A clear and wonderful idea of God's own way of salvation by means of free grace begins to appear. The sinner is then in position to be "comforted" and it is thus that a permanent foundation of true religion is established.[56] A good example of the process takes place in Moses Tattamy, Brainerd's interpreter. For a long period Tattamy simply carried on his work as interpreter. His first spiritual concern began in July and he continued in the various steps through the fall and part of the winter, and it was February when he was finally converted.

This process helps to explain Brainerd's practice of looking back at his own life. Why did he not, like St. Paul, having once confessed his sins, forget the things that were behind? The analysis of his past seemed at once to fascinate and horrify Brainerd. How shall we account for a busy missionary writing: "In the morning had as clear a sense of the exceeding pollution of my nature as ever I remember to have had in my life. I then appeared to myself inexpressibly loathsome and defiled; sins of childhood, of early youth, and such follies as I had not thought of for years together, came now fresh to my view . . . and appeared in the most odious colours. They appeared more in number than the hairs of my head; yea, they went over me as a heavy burden"? Yet he had made it perfectly clear that he was a youth of unusual sobriety and, by seven or eight years of age, deeply concerned with his soul.

Is the logic of this self-examination something like this: To be comfortable the soul needs to seek God. The soul seeks God only when it finds a need. The need arises from a sense of sin and the consequent misery. Therefore the sense of sin and misery are to be cultivated? "God," Brainerd wrote, "was pleased to give me a feeling sense of my own unworthiness; but through divine goodness such as tended to draw rather than drive me from God." This is the motif of much of Brainerd's self-examination. He is not satisfied with the confession of sin but needs to savor it for its curative, restoring, and comforting power. He needs to *feel* sin in order to *feel* the sovereign grace of God as forgiver of sin. The latter is accentuated according to the vividness of realization of the former.

Once over his period of enthusiasm at Yale, he was always thereafter the peacemaker among his brethren. The only issue on which he stood adamant was "false religion." He described this religion as the "sudden suggestion which many are pleased with, 'That Christ and His benefits are mine, that God loves me,' in order to give me satisfaction about my state." He greatly feared what he called "the imaginations and impressions made only on the animal affections." Jonathan Edwards described Brainerd's dying efforts to make perfectly clear the differences between a true and a false religion, the latter "consisting in or arising from impressions on the imagination, and sudden and supposed immediate suggestions of truths, and that faith which consists primarily in a person's 'believing that Christ died for him in particular.' " [57]

The world has had numerous illustrations of men practicing the extremities of evil; not so many of those seeking a noble holiness. Brainerd was a man of the latter kind. His endless confessions of sin make it clear that he knew the truly monstrous sins are in the recesses of the heart. Like a miner, he went down into its depths to explore, vein by vein, its structure, and the holiness of God was the light this miner hung on his cap. Many of Brainerd's contemporaries held that the heart is fundamentally good and only encrusted with defects arising out of the social system. Brainerd went inside and found rottenness at the center. Like Saint Augustine, he believed man was made for God and that all directions not Godward are devilish.

Above all, David Brainerd was the man of prayer. The medieval monk followed the canonical hours as reminders, but Brainerd needed no such. There is hardly a page of his diary that does not record the depth and persistency of his prayer experience. He spent days alone in the woods in fasting and prayer. Often on days not set apart for fasting his experiences with God became satisfying substitutes for food. "It was . . . my meat and drink to be holy," he wrote. He often prayed into the middle of the night and again would be on his knees at daybreak. Like Jacob with the angel, Brainerd knew what it meant to wrestle with God for blessing. When one looks at the floodtide of blessing on the Indians at Crosswicks, one should remember the great backlog of Brainerd's agonizing prayers for just such an occurrence.

As few other saints in history, Brainerd kept his hand to his ear for the breathing of the Spirit. He frequently experienced a tense expectation, hardly able to maintain the delay, that God would visit him. Brainerd's experience on Saturday, July 21, 1744, is an example. At the beginning of that day he felt oppressed with his vileness and pollution. About nine o'clock he retired into the woods to pray, but his oppression increased. During the day he learned that his Indians were planning a drunken feast and dance to be held soon. He felt he must attempt to break up these plans, but was baffled about a way of doing so. Toward nightfall, while still in this melancholy state, he returned to the woods. There God visited him. "I was exceedingly enlarged, and my soul was as much drawn out as ever I remember. I was in such anguish, and pleaded with so much earnestness and importunity, that when I rose from my knees I felt extremely weak and overcome. I could scarcely walk straight, my joints were loosed, the sweat ran down my face and body, and nature seemed as if it would dissolve." He continued through the long July twilight in incessant prayer that he might follow God's plan rather than his own in attempting to break up the idolatrous feast. "What I passed through was remarkable, and indeed inexpressible. All things here below vanished; and there appeared to be nothing of any considerable importance to me, but holiness of heart and life, and the conversion of the heathen to God." He went back to his cabin in this exalted state and that night frequently prayed again as he awakened. It is not surprising to learn that next day he had no difficulty in persuading the Indians to drop their plans and instead listen to the Gospel.

Another outstanding quality in Brainerd was his intention to serve God regardless of the cost. We notice this particularly in his fantastic indifference to his health. There is the repeated cry for "ministerial" gifts, the willingness to lay down his life for the cause, the desire like Paul to pioneer by going where the need is greatest regardless of conditions. He is wholly unafraid of any personal harm from the Indians. There is the constant wish and prayer not alone for his own labors but for the spread of Christ's work everywhere. To be sure, Brainerd reluctantly left civilization for the wilderness, but his steadfast putting of his hand to the plow is ultimately typical of the man. Brainerd's problem was not lack of a full-bodied intention to obey God but rather the uneasiness of his spiritual equilibrium.

Some feel that Brainerd ought from his college days to have been in a sanitorium. The same view might have put Saint Paul out of the Christian enterprise. Most of us take care of ourselves first, as though living to a ripe old age is everything. Brainerd's great wish was to be guiltless of "the misimprovement of time." There is only the steady intention to use his strength, such as it is, for God. Whatever explanations we care to make of Brainerd's motives, the indisputable fact remains that he did his work and that it was perhaps as substantial a work as was ever accomplished by any Christian in the same length of time. Let him criticize David Brainerd who has himself prayed and fasted and wrestled with God. The way of conformity, exigency, expedience, is only too clear in Christian experience. Shall we deny one young man the right to throw himself into the great experiment —no experiment actually to him—of living out his life wholly to God?

Whatever the precise cause, it is a fact of history that Brainerd's life has taken peculiar hold on the hearts of devout people. It may be his youthfulness, or his illness, or his unfulfilled love for Jerusha Edwards, or his holy purpose, or some combination of these, but the result has been an unending stream of Christian inspiration. Jonathan Edwards' *Life of Brainerd* is the most reprinted of all his works.[58] Ola E. Winslow says this *Life* made the name of Brainerd better known in the generation following its first publication than that of Edwards himself.[59]

While the biography is the major source of Brainerd's influence, it is worthy of note that a great educational institution had its immediate origin with him. The College of New Jersey (now Princeton University) was established as a result of Brainerd's expulsion from Yale. "The obstinate refusal," says Joseph M. Wilson, "of the authorities of Yale to admit Brainerd to his degree, after a humble submission and in disregard of personal repeated earnest solicitation of Dickinson, Pierson, Burr, and Edwards, satisfied them that it was time to arise and build a seminary suited to the times." [60] In an entry dated the day Brainerd should normally have received his degree from Yale, Esther Edwards, daughter of Jonathan, wrote in her journal that her father was "already in conference with Reverend Mr. Burr of Newark as to founding another college, perhaps in the Jersies, where young men can be safe from such [bad] influences." [61] The new college began its work in the year of Brainerd's death. Jonathan Dickinson, one of Brainerd's lifelong friends, was elected its first president, and David Brainerd's brother John was elected a trustee in 1755.

From the day of its publication in 1749, the biography of Brainerd became a spiritual classic. John Wesley, who had his own great experience of God in the chapel in Aldersgate Street, London, nine years before Brainerd's death, was so much impressed with the biography that he prepared and published a condensed version of it. Though he found fault with some of Brainerd's applied theology, nevertheless Wesley held him up as an example of utter devotion to God. "Find preachers of David Brainerd's spirit," he wrote in 1767, "and nothing can stand before them." [62] When asked later how to revive the work of God where it was decayed, Wesley gave a list of seven suggestions, the first of which was, "Let every preacher read carefully over the *Life of David Brainerd*. Let us be followers of him, as he was of Christ, in absolute self-devotion, in total deadness to the world, and in fervent love to God and man." [63]

Bishop Thomas Coke, another noteworthy Methodist of Brainerd's own century, wrote in his journal for September 24, 1784: "For these few days past I have been reading the life of David Brainerd. O that I may follow him as he followed Christ. His humility, his self-denial, his perseverance, and his flaming zeal for God, are exemplary indeed." The *Dictionary of National Biography* ascribes to Bishop Coke the creation of the worldwide network of Methodist foreign missions.

Still another Methodist of Brainerd's century who spoke warmly of the *Life* was Francis Asbury, first American Methodist bishop. He frequently read the biography and was consequently displeased with his own spiritual experience. In 1798 he expressed painful regret that the *Life* had never been published in America, and in 1805, after again reading the biography, he exclaimed that Brainerd's religion was "all gold, the purest gold." Later Bishop Asbury spoke of Brainerd as "that model of meekness, moderation, temptation and labor, and suffering self-denial." [64]

Perhaps the three missionary pioneers whose names are most frequently mentioned as having been inspired by the *Life* are William Carey, Henry Martyn, and Robert Murray McCheyne. Carey, writing late in the eighteenth century on the obligations of Christian missions, always mentions Brainerd alongside the great John Eliot, Indian missionary of the previous century. Carey not only admired Brainerd the young man praying fervently in the American forests for the souls of his Indians but also held Brainerd up to missionaries in India as an example of providing for the personal and agricultural as well as the spiritual needs of the people. To Carey, Brainerd's *Life* was all but another Bible.[65] Henry Martyn, says his biographer, "was made a missionary by reading the life of David Brainerd." [66] "I thought of David Brainerd," wrote Martyn, "and ardently desired his devotedness to God and holy breathings of soul. . . . I long to be like him; let me forget the world and be swallowed up in a

desire to glorify God." [67] Like Brainerd, the brilliant Martyn
died of consumption while still quite young, but not before he
had preached to Hindu, Moslem, and Briton, and translated the
New Testament into Hindustani, while serving in the same district in India with William Carey. "Let me burn out for God!"
was Martyn's missionary battle cry. Robert McCheyne was inspired by both Henry Martyn and Brainerd. In his diary entry
for June 27, 1832, McCheyne spoke of reading Brainerd's *Life*
and added, "Most wonderful man! What conflicts, what depres-
sions, desertions, strength, advancement, victories, within thy
torn bosom! I cannot express what I feel when I think of thee.
To-night more set upon missionary enterprise than ever." [68]
Though not actually at any time a foreign missionary, Mc-
Cheyne went to Palestine as a representative of the General Assembly of the Church of Scotland to gather information about
the Jews and was instrumental, by his saintly life, in sending
others forth.

And how shall we list the great additional cloud of witnesses
to the inspiration of David Brainerd? They come from America,
from Scotland, from England, and from Germany, and they
represent many religious denominations. There was Samuel
Marsden, the missionary to Australia and New Zealand and pre-
venter of the total destruction by white men of the Australian
aborigines. There was Robert Morrison, Scottish missionary to
China and spiritual father of Liang A-fa, a native who though
imprisoned, tortured, and banished for his Christian witness became the first native Protestant missionary in his country. There
was Samuel John Mills, who, along with four of his friends attending Williams College in 1806, was forced under a haystack
by a thunderstorm and there inspired them to thrust out to India
as a mission field. The site of this haystack, says Kenneth Scott
Latourette, "has long been marked as the birthplace of American
missions." [69] There was Christian Frederick Schwartz, a German missionary who arrived in India three years after Brain-

erd's death and because of his great service to the country became "priest-king of Tanjore," and left thousands of native Christians as his missionary fruit. There was Claudius Buchanan, another man known for translating the New Testament into both Hindustani and Persian and disseminating the Scriptures in India. There was Harriet Newell who died, at nineteen, while on the way to missionary service in Mauritius, but whose influence was nevertheless profound. All these testified to the importance of David Brainerd in their lives.

Most of these men and women were born or did their chief missionary work during the eighteenth century, but Brainerd's influence continued and perhaps increased in meaning during the following century. David Livingstone, for instance, the most famous of all in the history of missionary work in Africa, acknowledged his indebtedness to Brainerd. Among others who did the same were John Wilson, missionary and orientalist, of whom the *Dictionary of National Biography* says, "It is not easy to overestimate the importance of his labours for Christianity in western India"; Andrew Murray, first president of the South Africa General Mission which set up its work in the pioneer and dangerous Zulu and Podoland regions; and Sheldon Jackson, who "read with glowing eyes the story and diary of David Brainerd" and who in 1859 became missionary to the westward-moving Indians and pioneers and to the Indians and Eskimos in Alaska, in both cases building churches, originating mission stations, and opening schools, and who in 1885 was appointed by Congress as General Agent for Education in Alaska.

No doubt there were countless others who were moved to go or else to give to foreign missions through the inspiration of Brainerd. And of course no man, good or bad, can significantly influence one generation without thereby gaining some measure of lasting life. The pebble failing into the pond sends its waves onward until they are invisible and yet in the mystery of the physical world never end. If William Carey is stirred by David

Brainerd, and if then John Newton, the great hymn writer, says that Carey is more to him than "bishop or archbishop: he is an apostle!" it is obvious that the waves are in motion. Or again if Adoniram Judson is inspired toward missonary labors in Burma through Carey, it is evident that the waves go onward. And it is as hard to number the great company seen by John on Patmos as to count that company—red, brown, yellow, and white—brought into the Kingdom of God directly or indirectly by the young consumptive who burned himself out in the wilderness of New York, Pennsylvania, and New Jersey over two centuries ago.

Ola Elizabeth Winslow says that David Brainerd was the saintly example of the ideal missionary in an earlier time, but that to moderns "he is an example of the exact opposite." [70] At least one rather striking exception to the modern notion that Brainerd's influence has ceased occurred in 1956, fifteen years after her book was published. In that year Jim Elliot and four of his missionary companions gave up their lives while attempting to bring the gospel to the Auca Indians in South America. Brainerd's diary was one of the favorite books of Jim Elliot. That he was particularly stirred by Brainerd's search for true holiness is evidenced by a remark of his: "Confession of pride—suggested by David Brainerd's *Diary* yesterday—must become an hourly thing with me." [71] But Elliot was also moved by the drama of Brainerd's wilderness experience as a whole when he and his young friends entered the jungles of Ecuador to face a tribe far more warlike than any Brainerd ever met.

It is not Brainerd's accomplishments as a missionary, significant as they were, that have perpetuated his influence. It certainly is not his perturbations of spirit or his sense of vileness or his flagellation "complex" or his morbidity. I venture to say that it is not even his diary so much as the *idea* back of all which eventuated in moulding the man. In our timidity and our shoddy opportunism we are always stirred when a man appears on the horizon willing to stake his all on a conviction, even an antipathetic one such as Albert Camus' doctrine of absurdity, Nietzsche's idea that God is dead, or even Voltaire's triturating cynicism, providing we believe that conviction is real. Men, too often uncertain whether God is alive or dead, are inevitably excited by a brave spirit who sets out at all hazards to act on the proposition that He is indeed alive and in doing so proves that impossible things become possible.

There can never be enough examples of men willing to give themselves ineluctably to a goal nothing short of the touch of God's own hand. Thomas à Kempis, fifteenth-century monk who sought with all his heart to live to God, said: "There is nothing great, there is nothing precious or admirable, there is nothing worthy of repute; there is nothing lofty, there is nothing praiseworthy or fit to be desired, except what is eternal."

And D. L. Moody, the young Boston shoe salesman in the middle of the nineteenth century, heard it said, "The world has yet to see what God can do with a man wholly dedicated to Him," and set out to be that man.

In the long interval between Thomas à Kempis and D. L. Moody came David Brainerd saying, "I cared not where or how I lived or what hardships I went through, so that I could but gain souls for Christ," and because he did really mean it, we happily add his name to the list of those who left the world decidedly better than they found it and to that extent changed the direction of history.

NOTES

1. In 1734 Yale adopted a rule against card playing, and three years later forbade the drinking of "spirituous distilled liquors" in students' rooms during the week of Commencement. Franklin B. Dexter, *Documentary History of Yale* (New Haven, 1916), pp. 309, 325.

2. *Diary of David Brainerd,* p. 34. The manuscript of the first 44 pages of Brainerd's *Diary* (1732–1740) has been preserved in the Beinecke

Rare Book Library at Yale University, and this and other references are used by special permission.

3. "As for the Universities," wrote Whitefield after his visits to Harvard and Yale, "I believe, it may be said, their light is become Darkness, Darkness that may be felt, and is complained of by the most godly Ministers." Stuart C. Henry, *George Whitefield, Wayfaring Witness* (Nashville, 1957), pp. 66, 67. Even Jonathan Edwards, who was no particular friend of Whitefield, acknowledged that Brainerd probably spoke the truth about Yale and was himself greatly burdened, in the words of his daughter, at the "irreligion and wickedness prevailing there." *Esther Burr's Journal* (Washington, D. C., n.d.), pp. 26, 27.

4. Dexter, *op. cit.,* pp. 366–368.

5. *The Diary and Journal of David Brainerd,* London, 1902, I, 3. I shall hereafter refer to the two volumes of this work, my main source of information, simply as *Diary*.

6. Two years after Brainerd's death Edwards published *An Account of the Life of the Late Reverend Mr. David Brainerd . . . Chiefly taken from his own Diary, and other private Writings. . . .* Though this work consisted mostly of Brainerd's own words, Edwards frequently omitted portions, substituting his own summary of them, and he also changed Brainerd's wording at times.

7. Yale ms. of *Diary,* pp. 11–13, 20.

8. Yale ms. of *Diary,* p. 27.

9. Yale ms. of *Diary,* pp. 27, 28. In the margin beside this entry Brainerd added: "Lord's Day, July 12th, 1739, forever to be remembered by D. B." It is interesting to notice that the two sentences beginning "By the glory I saw, I don't mean . . ." were added later when Brainerd had come to fear the word *imagination*.

10. "I seemed to have power with God in prayer and power to get hold of the hearts of the people," he wrote of this experience. *Diary,* I, 60.

11. *Diary,* I, 90, 91.

12. *Diary,* I, 97, 98.

13. *Diary,* II, 273.

14. *Diary,* II, 271.

15. *Diary,* II, 241.

16. *Diary,* I, 100, 104, 107.

17. *Diary,* I, 140.

18. *Diary,* I, 135, 137.

19. *Diary,* I, 154. Brainerd kept two small notebooks covering the day-to-day events of his unhappy experience at Yale. Thomas Brainerd, the last known possessor of this notebook, declared that it was "justly severe on the college authorities; they broke his heart." See David Wynbeek, *David Brainerd: Beloved Yankee* (Grand Rapids, Michigan, 1961), p. 64. I acknowledge my special indebtedness to this study of Brainerd.

20. *Diary,* II, 247.
21. *Diary,* I, 155.
22. *Memoirs of Rev. David Brainerd,* ed. by J. M. Sherwood (New York and London, 1885), p. 99.
23. *Diary,* II, 249.
24. *Diary,* I, 169.
25. *Diary,* II, 250, 251.
26. *Diary,* I, 227; II, 52 ff.
27. *Diary,* I, 186; II, 212, 213.
28. *Diary,* I, 198, 214, 216.
29. *Diary,* I, 225, 252, 329, etc.
30. Wynbeek, *op. cit.,* pp. 148, 149.
31. *Diary,* II, 33.
32. *Diary,* II, 97, 98.
33. *Diary,* II, 19–32 *passim.*
34. *Diary,* II, 107–126 *passim.*
35. *Diary,* II, 124.
36. *Diary,* II, 24.
37. *Diary,* I, 318.
38. *Esther Burr's Journal* (Washington, D. C., n.d.), pp. 28, 29.
39. *Diary,* I, 343.
40. *Esther Burr's Journal,* pp. 34, 35.
41. *Ibid.,* pp. 37–39.
42. *Ibid.,* p. 41.
43. *Diary,* I, 332.
44. *Jonathan Edwards* (New York, 1949), p. 290.
45. Arnold Lunn, *John Wesley* (New York, 1929), p. 236. Wesley wrote a two-volume work called *A Survey of the Wisdom of God in the Creation.*
46. Jonathan Edwards, *An Account of the Life of the Late Reverend Mr. David Brainerd,* etc. (Edinburgh, 1765), p. 475.
47. *Works* (New York, 1840), III, 472.
48. *Croghan and the Westward Movement* (Cleveland, 1926), p. 44.
49. *Diary,* I, 36, 37. Jonathan Edwards records the fact that Brainerd on his second trip up the Susquehanna was "under a considerable degree of melancholy, occasioned at first by his hearing that the Moravians were gone before him to the Susquehanna Indians." One reason for his regret might be that the Moravians taught the immediate witness of the Spirit as a part of salvation. On the other hand, it is not difficult from time to time to read into Brainerd's diary a certain amount of forthright pride.
50. *Life of David Brainerd,* The Library of American Biography (New York), pp. 261, 262.
51. *Works* (New York, 1840), VI, 770.

52. William James, *Varieties of Religious Experience,* Mentor Edition (New York, 1958), p. 114.

53. The journal was written at the specific request of his missionary backers. Brainerd at times appears impatient with the amount of time consumed in writing it.

54. *Diary,* II, 186, 187.

55. *Diary,* II, 209 ff.

56. *Diary,* II, 101–104.

57. *Diary,* I, 343.

58. Thomas H. Johnson, *The Printed Writings of Jonathan Edwards* (Princeton, 1940), p. ix.

59. *Jonathan Edwards* (New York, 1941), p. 240.

60. *History of the Presbyterian Church in America* (Philadelphia, 1857), p. 258. We are told that no other college in the Colonies drew its students from so wide an area and that of 250 Presbyterian ministers ordained between 1758 and 1789, 120 came from Princeton and only 20 from Yale. William W. Sweet, *Religion on the American Frontier* (Chicago, 1936), II, 7, 8.

61. *Esther Burr's Journal* (Washington, D. C., n.d.), pp. 26, 27.

62. *Works of John Wesley* (Grand Rapids, Michigan), III, 294.

63. *Ibid.,* VIII, 328.

64. *Journal and Letters of Francis Asbury* (Nashville, 1958), II, 154; III, 218.

65. George Smith, *The Life of William Carey* (London, 1885), pp. 319, 450.

66. William W. Sweet, *Makers of Christianity* (New York, 1937), p. 21.

67. Constance E. Padwick, *Henry Martyn* (New York, n.d.), pp. 89, 90.

68. Andrew A. Bonar, *Memoirs and Remains of the Rev. Robert Murray McCheyne* (Philadelphia, 1844), p. 19.

69. *These Sought a Country* (New York, 1950), p. 46. I am chiefly indebted to this book and to Basil Mathews' *Forward Through the Ages* (New York, 1960) for the information in this and the following paragraph.

70. *Jonathan Edwards* (New York, 1941), p. 273.

71. Elisabeth Elliot, *Shadow of the Almighty* (New York, 1958), p. 105.

JOHN WITHERSPOON:
SON OF LIBERTY

❦

Henry W. Coray

John Witherspoon might properly be classified as the most underrated of all the signers of the Declaration of Independence. In the light that has blazed from that galaxy of superstars —names like Jefferson, Franklin, Hancock, John and Samuel Adams—the name of Witherspoon has quite naturally lost some of its luster. It is arresting that Moses Coit Tyler in his Literary History of the American Revolution *says of the only clergyman to sign that document: "Although John Witherspoon did not come to America until the year 1768—after he had himself passed into the middle line of human life—yet so quickly did he then enter into the spirit of American society, so perfectly did he identify himself with its nobler moods of discontent and aspiration, so powerfully did he contribute by speech and act to the right development of this new nation of the old cluster of dispersed and dependent communities, that it would be altogether futile to attempt to frame a just account of the great intellectual movements of our Revolution without taking some note of the part played by this eloquent, wise, and efficient Scotsman—at once teacher, preacher, politician, lawmaker, and philosopher—upon the whole not undeserving of the praise bestowed upon him as 'one of the great men of the age and of the world.' " This is high tribute coming from the Cornell historian. It is with the hope that Dr. Witherspoon's contribution to American statesmanship may be further recognized and appreciated that his story is here presented.*

On January 17, 1746, dashing young Charles Edward, "Bonnie Prince Charlie," trying desperately to recover the throne of England for the Stuart family, swept through the Scottish Highlands at the head of a small army. His objective: to gather recruits for the faltering Stuart forces. At Falkirk he was intercepted by the soldiers of George II, the established sovereign.

John Witherspoon, the youthful Presbyterian minister of the Kirk of Beith, fiercely loyal to the Crown, helped organize a company of Highlanders in an effort to support George. He marched at the head of this detachment, a hundred and fifty strong, from Beith to Glasgow, where the King's army was quartered. The Highlanders volunteered their services. For some unaccountable reason the men from Beith were never mustered in. Frustrated, they broke up and most of them stormed home in a temper.

Not Witherspoon. He and two companions, overpowered by curiosity, followed the army to Falkirk to watch the course of the fighting. Alas for the trio! To the astonishment of everyone, including the Bonnie Prince himself, he won a stunning victory over George's superior regulars. In the mad swirl of the battle's aftermath, a squad of Prince Charlie's soldiers seized and dragged them, violently protesting their civilian status, to the Castle Doune, near Stirling. There they were locked up in a "large ghastly room" in the castle tower.

In the adjoining chamber five other Scots who had been snared in the victor's net plotted their escape. At one o'clock the next morning they lowered a rope to the battlement seventy feet below and slid to safety. Witherspoon and his friends decided to follow them. The first succeeded, using the same escape method. The second, however, crashed to his death when the improvised rope snapped twenty feet from freedom.

John changed his mind, wisely concluding that "a living dog is better than a dead lion," and remained in the tower until hostilities ended two weeks later. The confinement proved bitter indeed. The castle was unheated, the stone floor on which he slept brutally hard, and the food wretched.

Witherspoon entered the world on February 5, 1723. He sprang from hardy stock. His father was an old-line Calvinist, his mother a descendant of John Knox. Milton once wrote: "The childhood shows the adult as morning shows the day." John provides a good example. At the age of four he was reading his Bible. While other bairns were trying to master the alphabet he was memorizing the New Testament, the Psalter, and the hymns of Isaac Watts.

At thirteen he matriculated at the University of Edinburgh. Three years later he was graduated and went on to study divinity, also at Edinburgh. On finishing his course, he received and accepted a call to the Kirk of Beith.

About that time he plunged headlong into the bittersweet experience of love. The object of his love, a resident of Edinburgh, he described as "an intelligent and excellent young lady." He proposed and was rejected. Presumably the disappointment was not greater than he was able to bear, for soon afterward he married Elizabeth Montgomery, daughter of George Montgomery of Craig House. She was his senior by two years. Curiously, John maintained a correspondence with his first love for most of his life.

Eventually the Witherspoons became the parents of ten children, only five of whom survived.

Witherspoon had hardly settled down as shepherd of the Kirk of Beith when he was drawn into a raging controversy. In his day the Scottish Church, like the veil of the temple when the Savior died, was rent in twain from the top to the bottom. The larger segment of the clergy, called the Moderates, had drifted from the moorings of historic Presbyterianism in two respects: they no longer proclaimed the doctrines of sovereign mercy, and they espoused the practice of paternalism. The first deficiency ushered a chilling wind of rationalism into the Church. The second, which in effect permitted influential citizens outside the congregations to install or remove ministers as they pleased, had produced a state of shocking worldliness. The minority group, known as the Popular Party, viewed with horror these signs of apostasy.

In that warfare John Witherspoon was no mere spectator, as at Falkirk. He came roaring out of obscurity, a wigged and black-robed Samson, to smite hip and thigh "those paganized divines, the Moderates." With the backing of the scholarly Erskine brothers he spearheaded the assault against the liberals. He published a pamphlet titled *Ecclesiastical Characteristics*. It spelled out the point he had made in one of his sermons: "A satire that does not bite is good for nothing."

The treatise was indeed a new sharp threshing instrument having teeth. Patterned after the satirical style of Jonathan Swift, it pounced on the unhappy Moderates like the ancient Assyrian army on Israel. Here are a few of its shafts:

I never knew a Moderate in my life that did not love and honor a heretic.

A moderate preacher must confine his subjects to social duties chiefly, and not insist on such passages of Scripture as will, by the very repetition of them, contaminate his style, and may perhaps diffuse a rank smell of orthodoxy.

One of our most famed preachers once chose for his text John 11:39, and of that verse the following words, *he stinketh*. He observed, "We had there (or thereabouts) a description of the three-fold estate of man: first, he sickened; second, he died, third, he stank." This I take to have been an accuracy in point of method, to which it will not be easy to find a parallel.

The sharpest arrow in his quiver he reserved for a fictitious doctrinal formulation he called the Athenian Creed. You find it in the heart of *Ecclesiastical Characteristics*. Here it is in all its caustic nakedness:

I believe in the beauty and comely proportions of Dame Nature, in Almighty Fate, her only parent and guardian; for it hath been graciously obliged (blessed be its name) to make us all very good.

I believe that the universe is a huge machine, wound up from everlasting by necessity, and consisting of an infinite number of links and chains, each in a progressive motion towards the zenith of perfection and meridian of glory; that I myself am a glorious piece of clockwork, a wheel within a wheel, or rather a pendulum in this grand machine, swinging hither and thither by the different impulses of fate and destiny; that my soul (if I have any) is an imperceptible bundle of minute corpuscles, much smaller than the finest Holland sand; and that certain persons in a very imminent station are nothing else but a huge collection of necessary agents, who can do nothing at all.

I believe that there is no ill in the universe, nor any such thing as virtue, absolutely considered, that those things vulgarly called sins are only errors in the judgment, and foils to set off the beauty of nature, or patches to adorn her face; that the whole race of intelligent beings, even the devils themselves (if there are any) shall finally be happy, as that Judas Iscariot is by this time a glorified saint, and it is good for him that he hath been born.

Ecclesiastical Characteristics rocketed its author to international fame. The piece rocked Scotland like an earthquake, and its resultant shock waves spread to England, the Continent, and eventually to America. In Witherspoon's native country the Popular Party hailed it with delight, while the infuriated Moderates consigned it to the lowest pit of the hell they said had no real existence. In all, ten editions were published.

Shortly after the appearance of the essay, two American churchmen, Samuel Davies and Gilbert Tennent, toured Scotland soliciting funds for the College of New Jersey. Tennent wrote to a friend back in the Colonies that *Ecclesiastical Characteristics* was a "burlesque upon the high-fliers under the inimical name of Moderate Men." He added, "And I think the humor is not inferior to Dean Swift."

Few writers wear their laurels modestly. John Witherspoon was no exception. Enormously flushed with the success of his first literary production he followed it with a second. This he called *The History of a Corporation of Servants,* and in it he tried to work out in allegorical form, à la *Gulliver's Travels,* the rise of Moderation. He located the action in Brazil, a territory about which he knew practically nothing. Unlike *Ecclesiastical Characteristics* this new effort turned out to be a fumbling failure.

Witherspoon now turned his attention to the development of Christian doctrine. His long tracts on regeneration and justification enjoyed an enthusiastic reception in the Church, and put him in the orbit of high scholarship. The University of Aberdeen conferred on him the degree of Doctor of Divinity.

Later, Ashbel Green was to pay Witherspoon glowing tribute by comparing him with John Calvin. "Between him and Calvin, indeed, in talents and improvements there was no inconsiderable resemblance. Both were men of great intellectual powers, both eminent divines, both distinguished heads of literary institutions, both erudite civilians, and both keen satirists."

Witherspoon was acclaimed as a splendid preacher. In truth, his printed sermons are notable for clarity of thought and purity of language, and his illustrations show a wide range of reading. He reveled in the rich truths of Reformation theology and proclaimed them boldly and joyfully.

In 1757, the Lehigh Kirk of Paisley extended him a call. The city of Paisley, a community larger than Beith and celebrated for its weaving industry, opened larger opportunities for service. His promised salary amounted to something over a hundred pounds, quite an advance over the stipend he was receiving at Beith. With true Scottish realism Witherspoon thought that the difference was a providential answer to the problem of supporting his rapidly expanding family. He resigned his pastorate and moved to Paisley.

At this point certain ecclesiastical politicians joined forces in an attempt to block his call. The Moderates in Presbytery, still smarting over *Ecclesiastical Characteristics,* saw a way of obtaining sweet revenge. They marshaled enough voting power to refuse to process the call. Thereupon the Council of Glasgow stepped in, overruled the negative vote of Presbytery, and to the infinite disgust of the liberals installed Witherspoon as pastor of the Paisley flock. It was a charade of classic irony. Those very churchmen who had advocated the cause paternalism stood helplessly by and watched a secular body paternalistically defeat an ecclesiastical action in favor of personal desire.

That same year Witherspoon released another thunderbolt. The occasion: the minister of Athelstaneford, one John Home, wrote a play, *The Tragedy of Douglas.* A theatrical producer staged it in a playhouse in Edinburgh. Home and seven other clergymen attended the premiere. Witherspoon, filled with moral wrath, heard about this and issued a stinging indictment against the eight. This was published in the form of a pamphlet, *A Serious Inquiry into the Nature and Effects of the Stage.* The writer followed it with *A Letter Respecting Play Actors.* In both publications he blistered the institution of the theater, actors, producers, directors, any and all who had anything to do with drama. The climactic salvo in his *Letter* is a masterpiece of invective:

I will conclude the essay by the comparison made by the French writer [Freneau] between the talents necessary to a good preacher or pleader, and those necessary to a good play actor. I wish he had mentioned the talents and qualifications, that we might have been able to examine his reasonings. As for my part, I can recollect but two which are essentially requisite to a player, memory and mimicry; and I have known both these talents possessed in great perfection by men who are not in understanding many degrees above fools; and on the contrary, some of the first men whom history records, that they were in no way remarkable in part of memory, and totally destitute of the other quality.

The effect of Witherspoon's diatribe was that Home demitted the ministry. The General Assembly endorsed the action. This caused Witherspoon and others of the Popular Party no little irritation. They believed that the Assembly should have censured the offender for his worldliness, and they said so publicly. Home's friends of the Moderate wing replied tartly that they did not "regard pleasure as wholly from the Evil One." On that plaintive note the matter ended.

Meanwhile, in the American Colonies, events unknown to Witherspoon were shaping up in a way that was to draw him into an unrehearsed drama far more exciting than any ever staged in the conventional theater.

Toward the middle of the eighteenth century the flames of religious revival burned brightly throughout the Colonies. The movement was known as the Great Awakening. George Whitefield, the English evangelist with the golden voice, pioneered the effort, preaching to huge crowds, often in open fields. Like the Wesleys he was an exponent of instantaneous conversion. His approach contrasted vividly with the quiet formality of the Established Church. Whitefield and his followers identified the illumination of the soul by the Holy Spirit with the experience of conversion. It was, they said, like the turning on of a great light: unless this conscious subjective experience took place in one, it followed that one simply was not saved.

The new thrust split both Congregational and Presbyterian

denominations into two camps. The New Side leaders branded those preachers who disagreed with their position—they became known as the Old Side—false prophets, wolves in sheep's clothing, blind leaders of the blind, who themselves as well as their people stood in need of conversion. The attitude is perfectly represented in James Russell Lowell's sly broadside:

> *The question of liberty simply means*
> *That light has been given me*
> *For deciding on you . . .*

This clash of conviction between the warring factions produced its effect in educational circles. In New England, Harvard and Yale were functioning as the hub of theological learning for the Old Side. In the Middle Atlantic states, the Log College at Neshaminy, Pennsylvania, started by William Tennent, served as the training school for New Side ministers. In 1756, after Tennent's death, the College of New Jersey—later renamed Princeton—was founded. To the chagrin of the Old Side, more young men flowed from Nassau Hall into the Church than Harvard and Yale combined were able to send forth. Envy widened the gap between the groups.

Ten years later, however, the bitterness had begun to die out. When death took Samuel Finley, president of the College of New Jersey, sentiment of both parties favored a reconciliation. The leaders called a conference and voted to set up a board of trustees to elect a successor for Finley. After some political maneuvering the new board decided to issue a call to John Witherspoon to fill the post. The Old Side, still smarting over the popularity of the New Jersey institution, grudgingly agreed to the choice.

One of the members of the body, William Peartree Smith, was assigned the duty of writing Dr. Witherspoon, urging him to accept the office. In his letter Smith apologized for the acts of God in removing by death the four former presidents "in the compass of four years." He explained that "Burr was infirm when elected President; Mr. Edwards dyed of Smallpox; Mr. Davies of mortal Fever; Mr. Finley of cirrhosis Liver and Dropsy. These things are so mentioned particularly to You, Sir, to remove any apprehension of the insalubrity of the Climate, which we can assure you is healthy here, as in any part of North America."

The promised salary amounted to two hundred and six pounds sterling, plus the fringe benefits of a home, a garden, a plot of land for winter fuel and pasturage, and a hundred guineas for traveling expenses.

Witherspoon read the communication with mixed feelings. He was immensely flattered, of course. And it so happened that at this precise moment in his Paisley ministry his stock in the community had taken a downward plunge. The reason: a group of boys had profanely simulated the sacred Communion service. Witherspoon, learning of their misdeed, had exploded against both culprits and their parents in a sermon titled *Sinners Sitting in the Seat of the Scornful.* He had said, among other things:

The late riotous meeting was without doubt the most audatious [*sic*] thing of the kind that ever was attempted in this place, and therefore calls for an open and vigorous testimony against it, by every person in this sphere. . . . Their worst enemies are those who trust them with indulgence, so long as they continue to justify or to palliate their offence. Nothing serves to harden sinners more than when no notice is taken of their crimes, and they find themselves just as generally and as well received as if they had done no evil.

He was aware of the resentment his sermon had aroused, and for that reason would have dearly loved to move on. But other factors militated against his going. After all, his background had not been in the field of education, and he seriously questioned his qualifications as a college administrator. Also, Mrs. Witherspoon was adamant in her stand against a change of climate, fearful for the health of her family, Smith's assurances notwithstanding.

Again, John had recently turned down overtures from three other churches, stating that he believed his labors in his present parish were not yet finished. Then too, being a native Scot, he nursed a burning love for the land of heather and gorse, majestic highlands and calm lochs with their haunting beauty.

Finally, there was the minor consideration of pecuniary interest. He was honest enough to bring this out in a parrying communication to the trustees. Referring to the proposed stipend, he wrote: "This is so greatly inferior to the offer which I received from Dublin last summer, where the work is much less burdensome, that when I come to explain Matters to my Wife and friends I know not what to say."

Back came an answer from trustee Archibald Wallace, who, it appears, had engaged in a bit of researching of the subject: "Provisions are cheaper by one half than at Paisley. Also we will provide a stately house and complements of sheep, Geese, Turkeys, hens, etc., etc., so that nobody has as yet been there who remained any time but has made money."

While this correspondence was being exchanged the trustees commissioned a friend of the college, Richard Stockton, then touring England, to visit Witherspoon and persuade him to come to America. Stockton resourcefully pointed out to John that not only would his educational services prove invaluable but that many discouraged church leaders in America felt him to be the key man to help stabilize colonial Presbyterianism.

Witherspoon was convinced, but a single barrier still stood: his wife's opposition to the idea. Not much information is available on the character of Elizabeth Witherspoon. A New Side clergyman, Charles Beatty, who once called on the family, confessed that he expected to meet "a poor, peevish, reserved, Discontented one." He found himself "agreeably surprised to meet a well-looking Genteel, open, friendly woman."

Because of Mrs. Witherspoon's unyielding opposition, Stockton reported the failure of his mission to the trustees. Disheartened, they proceeded to elect to the office of president a young man named Samuel Blair, a person altogether unqualified for the position.

While these developments were taking place, providentially a medical student, Benjamin Rush, a product of the College of New Jersey, was taking graduate courses at the University of Edinburgh. J. Kendall Wallis says of him that he was destined to become "America's most distinguished eighteenth century physician, the only Doctor of Medicine to sign the Declaration of Independence, the first American Professor of Chemistry, the writer of the first American text on psychiatry." This promising youth, anxious for the future of his alma mater, journeyed to Paisley to exert further pressure on the Witherspoons. He must have been persuasive with words, for he was able to overcome Elizabeth's objections. He sent a message to the trustees that Witherspoon was now willing to reconsider the invitation.

The trustees immediately went to Samuel Blair, knowing that only with great hesitation had he agreed to serve as president. They laid the matter before him. He said that he would be happy and relieved to step down in favor of Witherspoon. Elated, the board advised the Paisley preacher that he had been elected unanimously to the presidency. As a proof of their enthusiasm they raised the president's salary to four hundred and twenty-nine pounds sterling!

Unrestrained glee flooded the college, the American Presbyterian Church, and the Colonies in general when the news became known of Dr. Witherspoon's acceptance. All, that is, but in one quarter. A biased die-hard, William Patterson, on hearing the word, remarked to his friend John MacPherson: "Witherspoon is president. Mercy on me! We shall be overrun with Scotchmen, the worst vermin under heaven."

On crisp Friday evenings during the autumn months Princeton men get together at their traditional football rallies and raise their voices to chant:

Going back, going back
Going back to Nassau Hall,
Going back, going back
To the best old place of all . . .

Nassau Hall, according to Princetonian Henry Lyttleton Savage, stands as the most famous college building in the United States. "It was the center of American Presbyterianism; it suffered battle scars from both the British and American armies in the Revolution; it served as a meeting place for Congress in the difficult year of 1783; and since it has been recognized as the center of a great institution of learning."

There in November 1756, a hundred students and three tutors first gathered in the interest of higher learning. From the beginning the campus made itself known as a nursery for the cause of colonial liberty. As the heavy fingers of British oppression turned the screws tighter and tighter on the cover of colonial freedom, resentment mounted proportionately in Princeton. The 1765 graduating class, as a protest against "taxation without representation," refused to wear clothing manufactured in England. Two centuries before the University of California undergraduates thought of staging demonstrations in Berkeley, collegians at Princeton paraded up and down Nassau Street in the quiet New Jersey village and defied the authority of King George III, declaiming vigorously on such subjects as liberty and patriotism.

This was the mood of the College of New Jersey when President-elect Witherspoon moved in to take over the administration in August of 1768. Having passed a few days in Philadelphia for rest and refreshment, he arrived with Mrs. Witherspoon, five children, a male companion from Scotland, a complement of three hundred books for the college library, and a background of Old World cultural richness, plus a wealth of theological knowledge. Vice-President William Tennent, the professors, and the whole student body marched to the outskirts of town to meet his party. With lusty cheers and salvos of applause they ushered the Witherspoons to their temporary lodging at Morvan. The reception stirred the family to tears.

In his first sermon preached at the church the following Sabbath the good doctor voiced his appreciation in eloquent terms. He was forty-five at the time. His friend Ashbel Green, later to become the college president, has left this description of him:

> He was of middle size, fleshy, with tendency to corpulence. His limbs were well proportioned, and his complexion was fair. His eyes were strongly indicative of intelligence. His eyebrows were large, hanging down the ends next his temples;—occasioned, probably, by a habit he had contracted of pulling them when he was under excitement. . . . In promiscuous company he had more of the quality called presence than any other individual with whom the writer has ever had intercourse, Washington excepted.

At a special inaugural service held a few days after his advent, Dr. Witherspoon delivered a masterful address on the theme, *The Union of Piety and Science*. He spoke in Latin. The trustees and friends of the college heard him with unbounded delight, certain now that the choice of a president had been the right one.

Prior to leaving his Paisley parish, Witherspoon had gone to London to consult the leading English educators on such items as the latest textbooks and pedagogical methods. His foresight was to pay off handsomely. At once he made radical changes in the obsolete program of the school, thus becoming in a very real sense the pioneer of American educators. He instituted the lecture method, something unknown in the classrooms of the settlers. He introduced the study of Hebrew and French, languages with which he was personally familiar. It is said that he spoke French as fluently as English. He persuaded the trustees to add a teacher of Hebrew to the faculty. A man was appointed but never showed up, so Witherspoon himself took over the assignment. One of his outstanding achievements was to obtain the famous Rittenhouse orrery, an apparatus which, with the use of brass and ivory balls manipulated by wheelwork, displayed the motions of the solar system. He also broadened the department of philosophy to include civil government, politics, and international law.

Before his inauguration the curriculum had been geared almost exclusively to the training of students for the gospel ministry. With broad vision Witherspoon decided it was time to begin preparing young men for other professions as well. This would, he reasoned, increase the effectiveness of their service to the public. Dr. Harold Dodds, a former president of Princeton, has said of him:

More than a century and a quarter later Woodrow Wilson, in his inaugural address as president of the University, was to coin the phrase, "Princeton in the Nation's Service." But John Witherspoon anticipated him in directing students to the service of the nation, and set a tone to Princeton life which was never lost and which characterized his course of study throughout the intervening years.

Not the least of Witherspoon's contributions to the improved status of the college was his activity in fund-raising. At the time of his installation, the school was financially insolvent. Indeed, it could not even guarantee his full stipend. Immediately this shrewd son of Scotland launched a reform in the finance department. He directed the students to settle their back obligations, and encouraged them to pay their tuition fees, if possible, in advance. He traveled throughout New England, preaching in churches and soliciting donations from individuals. Apparently he was blessed with the Midas touch. So successful was his venture that he toured the South and returned to Princeton with considerable largess. He convinced the Synod of Philadelphia and New York that it should form a finance committee to collect monies for Christian education. Before long, the treasurer of the College of New Jersey was able to report that its enterprising president had moved that institution out of the red and into the black. In the board of trustees joy was unconfined.

Meanwhile Witherspoon had added to his numerous other duties the task of teaching students divinity and philosophy. The Presbyterian Church of Princeton called him to serve as its minister. Under pressure he accepted, and for several years when at home he preached two sermons every Sunday. By the time of the Revolutionary War, he was performing the work of three men.

He [Witherspoon] seems to have come at the right moment, to the right spot, in the right way. Being equally apt for thought and for action, and having quite remarkable gifts as preacher, debater, conversationalist, politician, and man of affairs, happily he found himself, in the fulness of his ripened powers, in a station of great dignity and prominence, near the centre of the new national life of America, in the midst of a kindred people just rousing themselves with fierce energy to the tasks and risks of a stupendous crisis in their history. Thenceforth, Witherspoon had in him to do, in things sacred or secular, in life academic or practical, in the pulpit, in the provincial convention, in the Continental Congress, for the shaping, in war and peace, of the thought and character and destiny of this primitive, passionate, indomitable people, he then had the opportunity to do. That opportunity so precious and so rare in the experience of men, he did not fail to use to the utmost.

So writes Moses Coit Tyler, noted American educator and historian.

Dr. Dodds, with equal perceptiveness, has put his finger on the key circumstance that explains the astonishingly quick adjustment of a middle-aged Scot, tough of mind and strong of will, to the tempo of American life. In the early years of the eighteenth century, wave after wave of Scotch-Irish immigrants swarmed into the Middle Colonies and the South. Pennsylvania in particular proved a haven for "those staunch Presbyterians, individualistic and land hungry, too intelligent and self-reliant to be serfs . . . and, in the name of the rights of man, challenged successfully the concept of proprietary government." The Quakers, long-suffering folk that they were, made room for them. Those stalwart, and sometimes irritating, Calvinists constituted the hard core of patriots who rallied round John Witherspoon. He had been intensely loyal to the Crown in Scotland. He had not conversed with these Scotch-Irish people long before his sympathies shifted wholeheartedly in their direction in their impassioned stand for freedom.

John Adams declared that the American Revolution began generations before the firing of muskets at Lexington and Concord. He was undoubtedly right. While the French and Indian Wars were going on, the British allowed the settlers to enjoy what Edmund Burke called "a state of salutary neglect." Gradually that happy condition lost ground as England came to realize what immense resources lay in the continent across the Atlantic.

In 1763, a standing army of seventeen regiments was sent over to defend the Colonies against the French, the Spanish, and the Indians. A tax was levied on the colonists to maintain these troops. Then, in rapid succession, the British Parliament legislated measures forbidding westward expansion beyond the Allegheny Mountains; making it illegal for colonial assemblies to issue legal tender paper money; imposing a heavy tariff on molasses imported from the West Indies; requiring the purchase of stamps for certain basic commodities; and finally passing the Declaratory Act, a law asserting Parliamentary authority over America "in all cases whatsoever."

In 1774, as a result of the Boston Tea Party, the port of Boston was closed to commerce, the government of Massachusetts reorganized to lessen resistance, and General Gage was sent to Boston with orders to enforce the regulations. The Americans rose up in holy wrath and decided that it was time to draw the line. John Witherspoon took his place in the vanguard of the revolutionists.

At this time a martinet named William Franklin, a son of Benjamin Franklin but estranged from his father, officiated as

Governor of New Jersey. He ruled with a fist of steel. The poor were not allowed to vote or to hold any public office. A puppet State Assembly, showing no interest whatever in the welfare of the people, backed Franklin to the hilt in his highhanded methods. When, in the summer of 1774, a Committee of Correspondence was organized to overthrow the old order of government, Witherspoon served on the committee. The committee met at Millstone, New Jersey, in July and drew up a list of resolutions. Witherspoon was the architect of the action. In the introduction he declared that neither the King nor Parliament nor the people of Great Britain had "entered into great principles of universal liberty nor were they willing to have discussion on points of right without prejudice." He proposed an eight-point program. Condensed, the program called for:

1. American loyalty to the King and a strong protest against Englishmen who hurled insults at him.

2. A statement that the British Parliament had passed unconstitutional laws to which the Colonies would never submit and that the aforesaid Colonies would prefer "war with all its horrors" than "slavery riveted on us and on our posterity."

3. Adherence "to the whole body"; a declaration that "we will continue united until American liberty is settled on a solid basis"; a demand that the rights of the Massachusetts Bay colony be restored.

4. A ruling which forbade the importation of merchandise.

5. Effective measures to be taken to promote private manufacture of goods.

6. A militia to be mustered in every colony for protective purposes.

7. A warning to be sent to the British army and navy not to function as instruments of enslaving America.

8. A plan of union to be set up for all the colonies in the interest of a common defense.

A year later the New Jersey Provincial Congress met at Trenton. Witherspoon served as a delegate. Most of the recommendations he had framed were passed.

That autumn the Assembly was dissolved and a new one put together. It was at this session of the New Jersey Congress that Governor Franklin, having been arrested by the patriots, was put on trial for subverting the cause of colonial freedom.

Witherspoon assumed the role of prosecuting attorney. He posed a number of pointed questions. Franklin refused to answer on the ground that the court which was trying him was functioning without any authority. Witherspoon replied in words shot through with thunder and lightning. The court thereupon voted to depose Franklin and sent him to Hartford as a prisoner of the Colonies.

Events were moving swiftly now. The American Colonies seethed in a state of ferment. War shadows hung heavy on the horizon. Impressed with the seriousness of the situation, the Continental Congress appointed May 17, 1776, as a day of national fasting and prayer, and requested John Witherspoon to deliver an appropriate sermon. With moving solemnity he spoke on the theme *The Dominion of Providence over the Affairs of Men.*

The pulpit is sometimes referred to as Coward's Castle. Witherspoon was always careful not to use it as a whipping post. He had previously made known his convictions on the relationship of the Crown to the Colonies. "You shall never hear from me in the pulpit what you have never heard from me in conversation," he said in his introductory remarks. He went on to articulate his views, based squarely on Scripture, of God's eternal purpose as unfolded in the drama of historical development. He also defined clearly the issue that was bound to split America from England: "Neither King nor Parliament nor people of Great Britain have entered into the great principles of universal liberty or are willing to have discussion of points of right without prejudice."

With true Scottish sagacity Witherspoon capitalized on the opportunity to advance a word of practical counsel to the leaders of the island kingdom:

For every shilling they [the British] gained by taxes they would lose ten in the way of trade. For a trifling addition for the sum of public money to be applied or wasted by ministers of state, they would lose ten times the quality distributed among useful manufacturers, the strength and glory of a state. I think this has sometimes been compared to the difference between the draughts of spirituous liquors to intoxicate the head or weaken the stomach, and the cool refreshing food to give soundness, health and vigour to every member of the body.

His message received tremendous applause on this side of the Atlantic. In Great Britain, however, where it was widely circulated in print, accompanied by notes, it raised the temperature of most citizens several degrees. Witherspoon was branded a rebel and a traitor.

The Provincial Congress of New Jersey now elected Witherspoon, together with four other members, to represent the Colony of New Jersey at the Continental Congress scheduled to convene in Philadelphia to consider a resolution of independence. They arrived there on July 1, 1776, in time to participate in a momentous event, one that was to profoundly affect the destiny of their country.

Rain clouds hovered over Philadelphia and war clouds over the American colonies generally as delegates to the Continental Congress converged on the City of Brotherly Love. A powerful British army was attacking Benedict Arnold's wretchedly equipped force on the shores of Lake Champlain. It was only a matter of time before Arnold would have to retreat to the lower Hudson Valley. In New York, George Washington was making frantic preparations to engage a loyalist fleet of a hundred warships cruising down from Halifax. In the Deep South, another of

King George's armadas had launched an assault on Charleston. General Charles Lee, in charge of the defending army, pleaded for Congress to send him reinforcements.

The three-pronged British offensive was calculated to cut communications between New England and the Middle Atlantic provinces, and between the North and the South. The men who came together in Philadelphia on Monday morning, July 1, 1776, were grimly aware of the situation. In consequence, feverish excitement charged the air.

The Congressional figures represented a fair cross-section of colonial life. There was bespectacled Dr. Benjamin Franklin, who came riding in a sedan chair borne by his servants. He had already attained his allotted three-score years and ten, and carried them jauntily. His multifaceted talents had produced kaleidoscopic changes in young America. He wore the several hats of printer, author, inventor, postmaster, crackerbarrel philosopher, political troubleshooter, and statesman, and wore them well. His contemporaries classified him as a deist: his God had forever detached Himself from the world of His creation. If true, Franklin dramatized a strange form of deism indeed. At a later session of the Constitutional Convention he was to advance a plea for a season of public prayer, stating, among other propositions, that "if a sparrow cannot fall to the ground without His notice, is it probable an empire can rise without His aid? We have been assured, sir, in the sacred writings, that except the Lord build the house they labor in vain that build it. I firmly believe this; and I also believe that without this concurring aid we shall succeed in this political building no better than the builders of Babel."

There was handsome thirty-three-year-old Thomas Jefferson, a lawyer from the Blue Ridge Mountains of Virginia and the author of the Declaration. Jefferson was tall, athletic, and possessed "all the attributes of the mind, and the heart, and the soul which are essential to eloquence of the highest order." Paradoxically, he would not say half a dozen words during the assembly. His contribution was to be in writing.

John Adams, representing Massachusetts, was there. A Harvard graduate, a Presbyterian elder, by profession an attorney, a dedicated advocate of the cause of liberty, he would stand as a tower of strength when the going got rough. Of him Jefferson said, "John Adams was our Colossus on the floor; not graceful; not elegant; not always fluent in his public addresses, he yet came out with a power, both of thought and of expression, that moved us from our seats."

Judge Roger Sherman from Connecticut was there. In his earlier years he had roamed New England as a surveyor. He was also a student of astronomy and a brilliant mathematician. Blessed with rare perceptiveness, he had long anticipated trouble with the Crown and had spoken his warning with vigor.

Robert Livingston was there—but not for long. Actually, even before Congress opened, that overly cautious youth from New York had folded his tent and silently slipped back home.

These five constituted a committee previously appointed by Congress to edit the proposed Declaration of Independence and submit it for possible adoption.

John Hancock of course was very much on the scene. He officiated as President of Congress with pleasure and with supreme confidence. In no wise plagued with a sense of inferiority, the wealthy Boston shipowner delighted in reminding anyone who would listen that in King George's black book he headed the list as England's public enemy number one—with a sizable price on his head.

Present too was Samuel Adams, cousin of John, a devout Christian, a rigid Sabbatarian. He had engineered the Boston Tea Party in December 1773 at the head of an incendiary organization known as the Sons of Liberty. Before John tapped the gavel calling Congress to order, Samuel remarked to Benjamin Rush: "If it were revealed to me that nine hundred Americans out of every thousand will perish in a war for liberty, I would vote for that war rather than see my country enslaved. The survivors of such a war, though few, would propagate a nation of free men."

Benjamin Harrison, destined to serve as chairman of the board of war, a huge mountain of flesh, was abundantly in evidence. He would be called on to spell John Hancock in the chair many times before Congress adjourned. He owned a scalpel-sharp wit. After signing the Declaration, he spied slender Elbridge Gerry of New York standing near him and said, "Elbridge, when the time of our hanging comes I'll have the advantage over you. It will be all over for me in a minute, but you will be knocking in the air half an hour after I'm gone."

Pennsylvania's John Dickinson, an orator of no mean ability, was recognized as spokesman for the conservatives, that block of voters favoring conciliation with Britain. A Quaker trained in the school of the Inner Light, his watchword was, "Gentlemen, look into your hearts." Notwithstanding the fact that he debated heatedly for rapprochement, two years later he would leave Congress and take command of a brigade of Pennsylvania soldiers in the Battle of New York. After the war Delaware would choose him to be its governor.

Of the fifty-odd legislators gathered to hammer out their manifesto, there were twenty-four attorneys, fourteen agriculturists, nine manufacturers, four physicians, one clergyman, and three individuals trained for the ministry but currently struggling in the political arena. These were all said to be "men of proud vision and men of violent passions, a mixed assembly of rebel leaders from thirteen separate provinces—from the granite-faced mountain farms of New Hampshire to the swampy rice fields and tobacco plantations of Georgia. They formed a senate unlike any the world had seen before."

A perceptive writer, R. J. Rushdoony, has brought to light two important features, commonly overlooked by historians, that colored the convictions of the Continental Congressmen. One, they knew very well that the provinces they represented had functioned as free, independent, self-governing units. Only when the Crown claimed divine right and absolute power of rule and insisted on forcing these principles on their people did most of the leaders feel that the time had come to take action. Then, also, the religious angle figured as a contributing factor in the forthcoming revolt. Parliament, operating with a high hand, had tried to force bishops on the colonial churches. John Adams stated that the reason for the resistance movement, "as much as any other," lay precisely there. "The objection was not merely to the office of bishop, though even that was dreaded," he wrote in a letter to a friend, "but to the authority of Parliament, on which it must be founded."

Congress met in the State House, or what is now known as Independence Hall, a building erected forty-two years before at the cost of $28,000. After the Battle of Brandywine Creek it was converted into a hospital for wounded soldiers. Here George Washington delivered his famous Farewell Address.

The meeting place was a large room—soon to be "smoke-filled"—east of the main entrance. White-paneled walls split by oblong windows endowed the chamber with a cheerful look. The Speaker's table adorned the platform up front.

Promptly at nine o'clock John Hancock stood back of the Speaker's table and said, "Gentlemen, the assembly will come to order." Secretary Charles Thomson, a merry-eyed Irishman, a classical scholar in his own right, called the roll. All the delegations responded except the one from New Jersey.

The morning was taken up with routine items. After lunch the real business of the day came before the council. In the interest of greater freedom of expression it was decided to go into a Committee of the Whole. John Hancock summoned Benjamin Harrison to the platform, handed him the gavel and took a chair in the front row.

John Dickinson rose to speak for the conservative cause; namely, for delaying action. He was known to have the backing of the middle provinces. On the other hand, the majority of Southerners and New Englanders were known to be strong for resistance to the Crown. The house was thus divided.

The Pennsylvanian bowed his head and prayed audibly: "I implore most humbly, Almighty God, who is wisdom itself, to enlighten the members of this house; that their discussions may be such as will best promote the liberty and safety and prosperity of these colonies. . . ." He ended his prayer, faced his fellow members and said: "Some of us believe that we ought to wait for the information which is on its way from England. Others, trusting in fortune more boldly than Caesar himself, assert that we ought to brave the storm in a paper boat. . . . I fear the virtue of the Americans. Their resentment of injuries may irritate them to counsels and actions harmful to the cause which they would die to advance. . . . I say, let us wait. Let us wait for an answer to our applications to France. Let us know how they might regard the strange new star among the states of the world."

Dickinson went on to advise his hearers that eventually America, if it forced the issue, would have on its hands not "only Britain as an enemy but also France. The French will play the waiting game until England bleeds white its wayward American child, then rush in for the kill."

John Adams leaned over and whispered to Cousin Samuel, seated next to him, "I'm afraid it won't go through. Dickinson will have his way."

The gentleman from Pennsylvania continued his address, soaring to heights of brilliant oratory. He seemed to be carrying the body of Congress with him. He wound up with an impassioned plea: "Declaring our independence at a time like this is like burning down our house before we have another in the midst of winter, with a small family; then asking a neighbor to take us in, and finding that he is unready. How will we answer our people at home? When they find themselves in a battle made more savage by such a declaration, will they not prove changeable? In bitterness of soul, will they not complain against our rashness? Why did we not first form an alliance? Why did we not first settle the differences among ourselves? Why did we not wait until we were prepared? Gentlemen: look into your hearts. How will you answer them?" Dickinson sat down. A dramatic silence closed in on Congress. Many a wigged head bobbed up and down approvingly. The extreme Northerners and Southerners appeared depressed. Those in favor of independence waited for someone to answer Dickinson. Nobody moved.

At last twenty-six-year-old Edward Rutledge of South Carolina, youngest delegate in the council, went to John Adams and whispered, "We're waiting, Mr. Adams." The barrister from Braintree got up reluctantly. He had hoped someone else would carry the torch for the policy of aggression. In that moment he longed for the gift of expression he felt he lacked.

Speaking slowly, brokenly, Adams pointed out that every one of the colonial grievances and wrongs laid before the King had met with stony apathy. America, in actuality, was already in a state of armed conflict. The Crown had officially pronounced that fact. The British army and navy even now were crowding native shores and native waters. This was most assuredly not the time for vacillation. Brethren of Congressmen had already moistened American soil with their blood. To back down at this crucial hour would spell ruin, disaster, slavery.

At this point the door of the room opened to admit the tardy delegation from New Jersey, "high-charged with independence." In stepped John Witherspoon, Richard Stockton, Francis Hopkinson, John Hart, and Abraham Clark, very wet and very apologetic. Every head in Congress swung toward the quintet.

"We are sorry to be late," said Dr. Witherspoon. "We have been held up by the storm."

They shed their greatcoats and were formally enrolled.

"May we ask for a review of the arguments," Witherspoon said.

No answer.

He repeated his request.

"You already know the arguments," John Adams said.

"That is true but we have not heard them *in Congress*."

Wearily, Adams summarized the case. As he talked on, it became clear that the delegation from New Jersey was with him to a man. Their moral support seemed to invest him with new vitality. He concluded his speech with an unexpected burst of eloquence that rocked the council. He cried: "We have been duped and bubbled by the phantom of peace. We have been caught asleep. We continue between hawk and buzzard while every day furnishes us with fresh reasons for an external separation. [*Applause.*] For myself, gentlemen, I can only say this. I have crossed the Rubicon. All that I have, all that I am, all that I hope for in this life, I stake on our cause. For me, the die is cast. Sink or swim, live or die, survive or perish with my country, this is my unalterable resolution!"

He had no sooner finished than John Witherspoon was on his feet. Waving his right arm in a circular motion, a familiar gesture, he called out, "New Jersey is plump for independence."

"The oratory is fine but the facts show we're not ripe for it," said John Alsop of New York.

Granite-faced John Witherspoon fixed his flashing eyes on Alsop and thundered, "We are more than ripe for it, and some of us are in danger of rotting for want of it!"

"Hear, hear!" roared Samuel Adams.

"Hear, hear!" rang out from all sections of the room.

Harrison ordered Thomson to call the roll for a trial vote. The result was surprisingly one-sided. Nine delegations voted for the adoption of the Declaration, two voted negatively, Delaware was undecided, New York abstained.

Edward Rutledge then moved to postpone the final vote until Tuesday. It was so ordered.

The next day Congress again convened at nine o'clock, and again under heavy skies. Before resuming the discussion on the Declaration of Independence, other pressing items on the docket called for consideration. There were communications from Washington, Arnold, and Henry Lee begging for more ammunition and reinforcements. Provincial assemblies had sent up messages asking for counsel on civic problems. Certain Congressional committees had to give reports. Current bills were awaiting settlement.

Besides all this, a committee of thirteen, one delegate from each colony, had drawn up a plan of union in the form of twenty Articles of Confederation, and committed it to Congress for study. Furiously, the men worked over this report. Questions came up as to the basis of representation: should it be according to colony or should it be according to population? And on the matter of taxes, what ought to determine the amount required of the colonies?

"My idea is that taxation should be assessed on the basis of the value of property," Witherspoon said.

"Not so," John Adams protested. "People are the true unit and therefore taxation must be according to the population."

"Then what about slaves?" another demanded. "Should we include them in the census?"

This posed another thorny question and triggered a prolonged controversy. The delegates from certain areas of the South wrathfully objected to the notion of a tax on slaves, arguing that such an imposition would wreck their economy. In many of the Dixie communities the Negroes outnumbered the whites fifteen and twenty to one.

"But Negroes eat food," a Northerner pointed out. "Any creature that eats food deserves to be taxed."

"Mr. Chairman." The familiar burr of John Witherspoon's *r*'s identified him. As he rose slowly the assembly could tell from the florid character of his complexion that Princeton's president was not enjoying good health. In point of fact, he had recently sustained a serious dizzy spell in the Princeton pulpit on a Sabbath morning and had fallen from the chancel into the family pew. Dr. Rush diagnosed the mysterious affliction as a type of apoplexy. "Mr. Chairman, may I answer the gentleman?"

"Dr. Witherspoon may," John Hancock said, pointing the gavel.

"Then, sir, let me suggest that I have in my stable a horse that eats food. Should he not be taxed?"

This plunged the assembly into convulsions of laughter, and produced the wholesome effect of relieving the tension. Minutes passed before Hancock was able to restore order.

The debate continued until noon and, following lunch, into the afternoon. At four o'clock John Hancock cut off further discussion on the Articles of Confederation. The hour had come, he ruled, for Congress to make up its mind on a resolution forwarded by the Virginia colony. That resolution, if approved, would then become the steppingstone to possible acceptance of the Declaration of Independence. The overture was known as the First Article of the Virginia Bill of Rights, and had been passed by the Virginia legislature early in June. Placed in juxtaposition with the Introduction to the Declaration it can be seen that striking similarities exist between the two documents.

Hancock turned the chair over to Harrison. Harrison ordered Secretary Thomson to read the preamble to the Virginia Bill:

A declaration of rights made by the good people of Virginia, assembled in full and free convention; which rights do pertain to them and their posterity, as the basis and foundation of government.

SECTION 1. That all men are by nature equally free and independent, and have certain inherent rights, of which, when they enter into a state of society, they cannot, by any compact, deprive or divest their posterity; namely, the enjoyment of life and liberty, with the means of acquiring and possessing property, and pursuing and obtaining happiness and safety.

Disallowing debate, Benjamin Harrison said to Thomson, "You may call the roll."

The New England colonies, the first polled, declared themselves. New York abstained. By a majority of one Pennsylvania voted in the affirmative. The Southern representatives all said, "Aye."

John Adams turned to Jefferson and held out his hand. "Tomorrow we shall take up the Declaration," he said triumphantly. "You can count on me to fight for every single word of it."

Adams was mistaken in his prophecy. The Declaration of Independence was indeed read before Congress on the next day but so late in the day that no vote could be taken. Action was postponed until the morning of the fourth of July.

Even then, slashing cuts and sharp revisions had to be effected before it came up in final form for ratification. At one point in the paper Jefferson had referred to George III of England as a tyrant. Immediately on hearing the slur cast on his former sovereign, Witherspoon struggled to his feet.

"Mr. President, I consider the description wholly false and undignified," he said. "It is false because George has the respect of his subjects in England, and undignified because it ill becomes one sovereign power to abuse another sovereign power. I say let us substitute the word *King* for *tyrant.*"

It was so decreed.

On another occasion Witherspoon's temperature hit the boiling point when his ear picked up a statement condemning "Scotch and other foreign mercenaries" for taking part in the British invasion. Both he and James Wilson of the Pennsylvania delegation, a fellow countryman, jumped up simultaneously and claimed the floor. The chair recognized Witherspoon.

"I resent the term 'Scotch and other mercenaries,'" he boomed. He was obviously unacquainted with the fact that certain soldiers in kilts, together with a band of Hessians, hirelings of George III, were at that very moment fighting with the Redcoats against General Washington in New York. "Highlanders, sir, are not mercenaries."

"I move that it be deleted," said James Wilson.

The assembly, in no mood to engage in a cold war with the pair of fiery native sons, voted to strike out the phrase.

"Well," Witherspoon whispered, winking at the delegates seated near him, "I perceive that we scotched that one."

The paramount issue that all but wrecked the congressional session turned on slavery. In the original draft Jefferson had incorporated in the list of grievances against King George a statement indicting him for initiating the slave trade.

He has waged cruel war against human nature itself, violating the most sacred rights of life and liberty in the persons of a distant people who have never offended him, captivating and carrying them into slavery in another hemisphere, or to incur miserable death in their transportation hither.

Most of the representatives had already taken their stand against the institution of slavery. As a convinced abolitionist, Benjamin Franklin fought courageously against the evil of slavery. Jefferson himself hated it with a perfect hatred. The Virginia legislature had repeatedly petitioned King George to put a stop to the flow of slaves from Africa. As the discussion raged, it became evident that the majority of Northerners and a number of Southerners as well favored the retention of Jefferson's statement.

The crash of verbal artillery reverberated for an hour. The denunciation was too violent, some said. Others said that it was not violent enough. Still others said that it was too undignified, or the style too vulgar. John Witherspoon took the floor to state that he thought it was unfair to pronounce judgment on the King for an evil which had been in existence before His Majesty's birth.

After nearly three and a half days of solid concentration on great issues, the bodies and minds of the Congressmen had grown tired. Tempers flared, friend snapped at friend, Southerners glowered at Northerners, Northerners frowned at Southerners. Jefferson listened to the disputation in silence, jotting down notes on a pad, and devoutly longing to see the section kept intact. In this, he was to meet with grievous disappointment. South Carolina and Georgia made it clear that should the paragraph be approved they would vote against the adoption of the Declaration of Independence. And so, in deference to the two hold-outs, the section was dropped.

Thomas Jefferson, the alleged deist, entered his reaction to the decision in his notes: "I tremble for my country when I reflect that God is just, and that His judgment cannot sleep forever."

The last obstruction blocking the way to a roll call vote seemed now to have been removed. But, even so, the issues involved in the dramatic decision about to be made prompted some of the more conservative of the delegates to question the wisdom of approving the Declaration *at this time*. Would it not, they wondered, be advisable to wait for a more propitious hour?

John Witherspoon then delivered the speech that once and for all settled the fears of the most timid in the council room. With a true Churchillian roll to his words, he moved his right arm in the well-known circular motion and said: "There is a tide in the affairs of men. We perceive it now before us. To hesitate is to consent to our own slavery. That noble instrument should be subscribed to this very morning by every pen in this house. Though these gray hairs must soon descend to the sepulchre, I would infinitely rather that they descend thither by the hand of the executioner than desert at this crisis the sacred cause of my country." No one present attempted to reply to the speaker.

John Hancock, in the chair, nodded to Charles Thomson. Thomson stood up and began to read the draft of the Declaration in its refined form:

When, in the course of human events, it becomes necessary for one people to dissolve the political bands which have connected them with another, and to assume, among the powers of the earth, the separate and equal station to which the laws of nature and of nature's God entitle them, a decent respect to the opinions of mankind, requires that they should declare the causes which impel them to the separation.

We hold these truths to be self-evident: that all men are created equal, that they are endowed by their Creator with certain inalienable rights; that among these are life, liberty, and the pursuit of happiness. That to secure these rights, governments are instituted among men, deriving their just powers from the consent of the governed; that whenever any form of government becomes destructive of these ends, it is the right of the people to alter or abolish it, and to institute a new government, laying its foundation on such principles, and organizing its powers in such form, as to them shall seem most likely to effect their safety and happiness. . . .

The reading concluded, the secretary called on the various delegations to cast their votes. He began with the New England colonies and moved south. With monotonous regularity chairman after chairman called out, "Aye." There was not a single dissenting vote. After thirteen replies, John Hancock said quietly, "The Declaration by the representatives of the United States of America has been adopted unanimously." *

An almost reverent hush followed his pronouncement. Men stared at the ceiling or at the floor or at the flow of traffic outside. Some prayed.

Charles Thomson placed the document on the Speaker's table and looked at the President of Congress. That proud man sat down and fingered his goose-quill pen. Then with a flourish John

* Cornel Lengyel, *Four Days in July,* p. 249.

Hancock proceeded to write his signature on what would take its place in history as one of the greatest declarations of liberty put together by any group of freedom-loving men.

"There," he said with a smile. "His Majesty can now read my name without glasses. And he can also double the price on my head."

The price was five hundred pounds.

In his monograph on John Witherspoon, Thomas Jefferson Wertenbaker, the well-known historian, calls him "the Father of American Presbyterianism." There can be no doubt that he was instrumental in breaking down the partition that separated the New Side from the Old Side. Also, in synodical meetings he consistently served on various important committees. The wealth of experience he had garnered in Scotland proved of inestimable value. He was as much at home in dealing with problems of ecclesiastical law as with civil jurisprudence. "He was a powerful thinker," wrote Ashbel Green, a Presbyterian clergyman and president of Princeton, "When he took hold of a subject, he searched it to the bottom; and in discussing it, he treated it both analytically and synthetically."

The influence of the Presbyterian community widened as tension increased between America and Britain. No less an authority than historian George Bancroft has said:

The Revolution of 1776, as far as it was affected by religion, was a Presbyterian measure. It was the natural outgrowth of the principles which the Presbyterianism of the Old World planted in her sons, the English Puritans, the Scotch Covenanters, the French Huguenots, the Dutch Calvinists and the (Scotch-Irish) Presbyterians of Ulster.

A Tory living on colonial soil, much upset over the revolt against the Crown, wrote George III: "I fix all the blame of these extraordinary proceedings upon the Presbyterians. They have been the chief and principal instruments in all these flaming measures. They always do and ever will act against government from that restless and turbulent spirit which has always distinguished them everywhere." And when word of the signing of the Declaration of Independence reached England, Horace Walpole said in Parliament, "Cousin America has run off with a Presbyterian parson."

In the heat of the Battle of Elizabethtown, in New Jersey, the infantrymen of the colonial army found themselves running out of cotton wadding for their muskets. Presbyterian chaplain James Caldwell, realizing their predicament, dashed into a church, seized a supply of hymnals, handed them to the defenders and shouted, "Put Watts into them, boys! Give 'em Watts!"

John Witherspoon, the Presbyterian leader—"Our old Scotch Sachem," Benjamin Rush called him—came in for his share of criticism. "What right has a clergyman to dabble in politics?" some of his enemies demanded.

On this point historic Presbyterianism had made its position perfectly clear. In the Confession of Faith the section on Synods and Councils declares:

> Synods and councils are to handle or conclude nothing but that which is ecclesiastical; and are not to intermeddle with civil affairs, which concern the commonwealth, unless by way of humble petition, in cases extraordinary; or by way of advice for satisfaction of conscience, if they be thereunto required by the civil magistrate.

John Witherspoon defined his views in a sermon in which he set forth his obligations as a Christian citizen over against his duties as a Christian minister: "Ministers [should] take care to avoid officiously intermeddling in civil matters. A minister should be separated and set apart for his own work; he should be consecrated to his office. . . . It is still more sinful and dangerous for them to desire or to claim direction of such matters as fall within the province of the civil magistrate. When our blessed Saviour says, 'My kingdom is not of this world,' he plainly intimates to his disciples that they have no title to intermeddle with state affairs."

It was a source of sorrow to him that the war forced him to curtail many of his ecclesiastical pursuits as well as his educational activities. In the fall of 1776, the British drove Washington's army from New York and en route south penetrated New Jersey. On November 29, Witherspoon called the Princeton students together and with no little emotion announced that classes would be discontinued. Between president and student body a strong tie of affection had built up. Both dreaded the separation, but both knew there could be no other course. Witherspoon said good-by and with his family withdrew to Philadelphia.

A week later the loyalist forces under General Howe stormed into Princeton. They took over Nassau Hall and converted it into a barracks, but their stay turned out to be short-lived. On January 3, 1777, Washington fiercely counterattacked and in one of the critical battles of the Revolution drove Howe out of Princeton.

The Continental troops then settled in the college buildings. It was a case of the last being worse than the first. The behavior of the patriots was inexcusably bad. They burned the flooring and furniture for firewood, despoiled the library with its two thousand books, wrecked the costly Rittenhouse orrery, knocked out the plaster walls, broke up the organ in the chapel, and otherwise made a shambles of the campus.

In his *Diary* and *Autobiography,* John Adams noted:

Dr. Witherspoon enters with great Spirit into the American Cause. He seems as hearty a Friend as any of the Natives—an animated Son of Liberty.

That New Jersey elected Witherspoon to Congress for four terms shows the esteem in which he was held by the people of that state. The war years were critical ones for the United States, still an infant wrapped in swaddling clothes, testing its lungs and cutting its teeth on hard foodstuffs. In Philadelphia, nerve center of activity, the Continental Congress faced prodigious problems: the forging of the Articles of Confederation, liaison with foreign powers, the delicate business of financing the war, the establishment of a department of state, eventual settlement of peace terms. Thomas Paine's plaintive cry, "These are the times that try men's souls," echoed and re-echoed through the council chamber of the State House during those stirring days.

The name of John Witherspoon is inextricably bound up with these affairs of vital importance. He was appointed to serve on such influential bodies as the Committee for Foreign Affairs, the Committee to Reorganize the Board of Treasury, the 1777 Finance Committee, and others. And, following the surrender of Cornwallis at Yorktown, Congress drafted him to help draw up the armistice terms. Historian Lyman Henry Butterfield says: "The responsibilities Witherspoon was called upon to shoulder and the opportunities spread before him were precisely those best calculated to draw forth his powers and talents."

Baffling as were the military aspects of the Revolution, its financial complexities weighed even more heavily on Congress. In that organization there existed many false and foolish theories about money and its relation to the war. Witherspoon, in good conscience, felt that he had to fight certain money changers in the temple of the state. Asks historian Tyler:

Under such circumstances, what greater service to the American cause could have been rendered by a man like Witherspoon than by exposing, as he did, the financial sophistries of Revolutionary demagogues and blatherskites, and by putting into pithy, livid, and fearless words the essential and immutable truths as to what is possible and desirable in public finances?

One evil Witherspoon believed needed correcting involved the extravagant method of supplying the army by commission. Congress had sanctioned the practice of granting a certain percentage of all funds invested to agents who purchased equipment for the military. It followed that the more money the commissioners spent, the more capital lined their pockets. Unscrupulous individuals did not hesitate to take advantage of the situation, with the result that costs of financing the struggle mounted to astronomical figures. Witherspoon lined up with those delegates who worked for reform. By virtue of strong and persistent agitation they managed to bring about a sweeping change. Congress voted to authorize the Secretary of Finance to have all sales to the army and navy negotiated by contract, thus practically eliminating graft.

Too, the doughty Scot threw all his influence to kill the fixing of commodity prices. He publicly scored the custom of "price-fixing by authority." It was, he contended, both illogical and absurd. "So many of one kind of provision and the scarcity of another, the distance of one place and the few days or weeks, good or bad roads, good or bad weather—these and a hundred other things which cannot be foreseen actually govern and ought to govern prices at markets."

With equal firmness Witherspoon opposed the practice of the government's issuing paper currency. Here he was a voice crying in the wilderness. His views on the subject came out in a treatise, *Essay on Money*, a summary of his speeches in Congress. Dr. Dodds subtly suggests that "it might be worthwhile to supply some of our modern statesmen with a copy."

Witherspoon laid down a dozen basic principles. Some of the more important ones, condensed, are:

1. The quantity of gold or silver is the criterion of natural wealth.

2. No paper money is, properly speaking, money. It ought not be made legal tender. It should not be forced on anybody unless it can be bound on everybody.

3. The increase of paper currency not negotiable in other na-

tions raises costs and lowers profits. Wherever paper is introduced in large amounts, gold and silver vanish universally.

4. Excessive quantities of paper money issued by different
states will result in losses to the whole, and the state issuing most
will lose most.

5. The cry "scarcity of money" is putting the effect for the
cause.

6. Those refusing doubtful paper money are friends and not
enemies of their country.

His opponents, infuriated, were ready to nail him to the wall.
On Staten Island he was burned in effigy. Nevertheless he stuck
stubbornly to his convictions, and America was blessed indeed in
having a man with his acumen to help pilot the ship of state
through troubled financial waters into its desired haven. "It was
a tribute to the versatility of Witherspoon that Congress should
entrust to him a large share of the responsibility for financing
the Revolution." Nor are there wanting today serious economists
who are persuaded that his doctrine of currency, if applied,
would guarantee for the United States a healthier financial structure than that conjured up by the men of Harvard Yard.

The role of France in the prosecution of the war was important. Benjamin Franklin persuaded Louis XVI to grant both
financial and military aid to the hard-pressed colonists. This provided an enormous lift to American morale. But when Louis saw
that the current of battle was flowing against the patriots he
weakened. The promised loans did not come through. The effect
of his hesitation on the Revolutionists was all but disastrous. A
groundswell of discouragement set in. Some of the leading statesmen talked in terms of surrender.

The Committee on Foreign Affairs swung into action. Its
members were fully aware that they must convince France's
ruler he would not be backing a losing cause, that he would suffer neither financially nor politically in his choice of investments.
It was a difficult assignment. Providentially, at the very hour

Louis wavered, word reached him that Washington had turned back the British at Princeton and Trenton, and Gates had defeated Burgoyne at Saratoga. The double victory insured the eventual success of the colonial forces. The committee was able to obtain the needed loans. Says Tyler:

Witherspoon's part in securing the treaties of 1778 with France, without which the cause of the Revolutionists might have been lost, is one of his greatest contributions to the nation.

History records a rather sad sequel to American dealings with the French nation. For John Witherspoon it must have been a disillusioning experience. When the war ended, he and other leaders counseled the peace commission to have Louis XVI approve the final terms of settlement before they should be ratified. How were they to know that France was secretly negotiating with Spain on the conditions that would be offered England, terms that were inimical to the interests of the colonies? When the bitter facts came to the surface the knowledge drove a wedge between the two nations that had stood shoulder to shoulder in the conflict against Britain. Franklin, Witherspoon and other loyal friends of Lafayette suffered deeply in spirit. Years were to pass before the wound finally healed.

The delightful stratum of humor in Witherspoon, even in those tempestuous years, continued to flash in the Congressional chamber like shafts of light in darkness. On one occasion a delegate, becoming intoxicated with the music of his own voice, soared in flights of rhetorical speech with the use of long words and complex sentences. It was plain to everyone that he was impressed with his own eloquence. When he had finished, Dr. Witherspoon rose to ask for a point of privilege. It was granted.

"I am acquainted with a physician," he said, "who sitting with a lady in his office was asked by her, 'Doctor, are artichokes good for children?' He answered, 'Madam, they are the least flatulent of all the esculent tribe!' 'Indeed, doctor,' said the lady. 'I do not understand a word of what you have said.' "

After the thrilling triumph at Saratoga, General Gates dispatched one of his officers to Philadelphia to convey the news to Congress. The courier proceeded to travel on horseback in such a leisurely fashion that word of the victory was announced in Congress three days before he arrived. It had been a tradition of long standing to honor faithful army messengers with some sort of recognition. In this instance one of the delegates proposed that a souvenir silver sword be awarded the officer. Dr. Witherspoon asked for the floor and was recognized.

"Mr. President," he said sonorously, "I should like to offer as a substitute motion that the gentleman in question be given, not a silver sword, but rather a pair of golden spurs."

He all but broke up that session of America's most dignified body.

When the Revolution ended, John Witherspoon retired to Princeton and resumed his duties as president of the college. He took up his residence on a farm two miles north of town. He called the place Tusculum in honor of the ancient Latin town near Rome.

He assigned himself the work of rebuilding Nassau Hall, which he found in wretched shape due to the erosive effects of war. He managed to persuade Congress as well as the New Jersey legislature to allocate limited funds for that purpose. These not being enough to complete the program, the trustees requested him and a friend of the college, Joseph Reed, head of the Supreme Executive Council of Pennsylvania, to visit England and Scotland in an effort to raise money. The move turned out to be unwise, really, for the island population still nursed a stout resentment against Witherspoon for what it considered an act of treachery on his part against King George. The mission resulted in almost total failure.

He was invited to preach only once. The elders of his former church at Paisley opened the pulpit to him. It proved to be a sad experience. Gone were many of "the old familiar faces." A number of his former parishioners would not attend the service. Of those who did, not a few greeted him coolly. He left the city, the scene of so many joyous memories, despondent, wishing he had not accepted the invitation.

On his return to America, through sheer persistence he succeeded in securing enough funds, chiefly through private donations, to finish the task he had undertaken. In time he was rewarded by seeing a renewed and improved college rise up to serve the nation.

In the summer of 1783, an unexpected twist of events made it necessary for Congress to get away from Philadelphia. Several hundred of Washington's troops, about to be mustered out of the army, raised a violent protest against the legislators because, they said, they had been robbed of their back pay. They organized a demonstration, angrily marched on the State House and laid siege to it. When Congressmen tried to remonstrate the troops turned on the politicians not only deaf ears but loaded muskets also. Some even took hold of President Elias Boudinot, John Hancock's successor, and shook him roughly.

Alarmed, Congress appealed to the Pennsylvania Council for protection. Nothing was done. The Trustees of Princeton learned of the trouble and immediately voted to invite the Assembly to meet in Nassau Hall. Congress lost no time snapping up the offer. And thus for four months Princeton functioned as the capital of the young American nation.

One of the first pieces of business the body transacted was to invite George Washington to visit Princeton. The commander-in-chief of the army, fresh from his victory over the British, sent back word that he would be overjoyed to come. Congress appointed Witherspoon to act as chairman of a committee to accord him a fitting reception. On Washington's arrival Dr. Witherspoon held forth with a masterful speech of welcome. He congratulated Washington on the happy culmination of the conflict with the enemy. He assured the celebrated soldier that he was certain that he, General Washington, had been indeed God's choice of a military leader for the young nation he had so successfully defended. Washington replied by thanking Dr. Witherspoon for his courtesy. He went on to promise that he would pray for the blessing of heaven on the college, its head, its trustees and its faculty, that God would be pleased to prosper the institution and use it increasingly in promoting the cause of religion and learning. And, to show his appreciation of Princeton's worth, he contributed fifty guineas to the treasury.

In September the first postwar commencement exercises were held in the Presbyterian Church, a stone's throw from Nassau Hall. Present were General Washington, the college trustees, a host of dignitaries including many Congressmen and, representing France, the Marquis de la Luzerne. Dr. Witherspoon gave the invocation, and senior Ashbel Green, one of his brightest products, the valedictory address. It was a delightful affair. For years the good citizens of Princeton Town boasted of the renowned men who had graced their church that glorious afternoon.

Later, further honors came to the community when Peter John Van Berckel, prime minister of The Netherlands, paid a visit to the campus. The Witherspoons entertained him at Tusculum. Congress requested him to deliver an address, and had Witherspoon introduce him. In his remarks the Scot pointed out that the very name *Nassau,* borrowed from Holland, suggested the close relationship existing between The Netherlands and the college. Berckel responded, speaking in fluent French. Many present understood not a word but would have sacrificed an arm rather than admit it. They put on a great act, nodding, smiling and applauding at the right points in the speech. The Assembly would have done well to have asked Witherspoon to interpret.

By the first of November the military difficulties had been smoothed out. Congress then voted to end its sessions in Princeton and adjourned, to meet later at Annapolis. Before leaving Nassau Hall, however, the Congress passed a resolution thanking Dr. Witherspoon and the other college authorities for granting it permission to convene there during the emergency.

The Witherspoon children meanwhile had grown up and scattered.

The oldest son James, a youth of unusual promise, had enlisted in the army at the outbreak of the war. Washington recognized his skill and promoted him to serve as aide to General Francis Nash. Both Nash and James were killed in the Battle of Germantown.

The second boy, John, studied medicine and after graduation began his practice in South Carolina. While he was making a trip from New York to Charleston on a coastwise ship a storm wrecked the vessel. John was among the passengers who went down with the ship.

David, like his father, was precocious. At fourteen he was graduated from Princeton and took up law. He married the widow of General Nash and settled in New Bern, North Carolina. There he enjoyed rare success in his profession.

Anna married Dr. Samuel Stanhope Smith, who would succeed his father-in-law as president of the college. A scintillating mind, Smith was elected an honorary member of the American Philosophical Society, an institution noted for profound scholarship. In 1779 the Princeton trustees appointed him to the chair of Moral Philosophy. His addition to the faculty brought the college no small distinction.

Frances, Witherspoon's second daughter, became the wife of the soldier-historian David Ramsay, field surgeon in the army during the war, member of the Continental Congress and its president in 1785 and 1786, and author of two excellent histories of the American Revolution, as well as a biography of Washington.

Tragedy struck the Witherspoon home again in 1789. Elizabeth Witherspoon passed away in the twenty-second year of her emigration to the land she had so dreaded to adopt. These had been exciting and tumultuous years. In the darkest hours of the war, when shadows lay deep on John and the tensions and responsibilities seemed almost too much for one man to bear, she had encouraged and sustained him.

Witherspoon's massive labors had begun to take their toll on his body, even though his mind continued to throb like a dynamo. Wisely he turned over many of the administrative duties to his son-in-law. He did keep up his preaching and lecturing, however, and derived great satisfaction from both activities.

Henry Lyttleton Savage, who calls Witherspoon "unquestionably the best known educational figure in the America of his day," writes:

The history of Nassau Hall of the period divides itself about him into three periods: pre-Witherspoon (1756–1769), Witherspoon (1769–1794), and post-Witherspoon (1794 to, say, the fire of 1800).

It is small wonder that Dr. Savage is so impressed with Witherspoon's administration, labeling it the "golden age of Nassau Hall." The young men who sat at his feet would constitute a miniature Who's Who in American life during and after the Revolution. One of them, James Madison, became President of the United States, and another became Vice-President; two were signers of the Declaration of Independence; ten were Cabinet members in the infant republic; twenty-five were delegates to the Continental Congress; eleven were members of the Constitutional Convention; thirty became senators and fifty were members of the House of Representatives; seventeen became state governors; four were justices, with one becoming chief justice of the Supreme Court; and numerous others were public figures.

Nor was Witherspoon's contribution to American life secular only. Many of those who came in contact with him, fired by his enormous zeal for the cause of Christ's Kingdom, went forth to preach in established churches or to engage in missionary activity in the expanding West. Some pioneered in that exciting and heroic movement known as the "circuit riders," men who scaled mountains, braved storms, encountered wild beasts and otherwise risked death in order to evangelize settlers and Indians, found churches and start schools. Not until that momentous hour when "the books are opened" will it be known how far-reaching was the influence of Princeton's illustrious president.

Of Witherspoon's personal piety, Dr. Ashbel Green says: "Few men were ever more anxious to walk with God, and by a solid, righteous and pious life to adorn the doctrine of the Gospel. Besides the daily devotions of the closet and the family, he regularly set apart with his household the last day of every year for fasting, humiliation, and prayer. He was also in the practice of spending days in secret exercise of this kind, as occasion required."

John Witherspoon's closing years were a chiaroscuro of light and shadow. In 1791, at the age of sixty-eight, he married the lovely twenty-seven-year-old widow of Dr. Armstrong Dill of York County, Pennsylvania. The joy of this second marital union so transported him to the clouds that, when he and his bride returned from their honeymoon, he declared a three-day vacation for his students. They had expected only one.

"Great men," said Job's friend Elihu, "are not always wise." Even with his canny sense of the value of coin, Witherspoon invested injudiciously in a real-estate project in Vermont and sustained considerable loss. He accepted this reverse with philosophical calm, believing it was the will of God that he should suffer the loss.

To the end of his life he retained the ability to see the humorous side of life. He derived great pleasure from working the soil on his Tusculum farm. He aspired to be a scientific agriculturist, a role at which he was more enthusiastic than successful.

"Scientific farmers," he once remarked to a friend, smiling, "can always give good and plausible reasons why they are *not* successful."

Witherspoon was fond of horseback riding. Curiously, no one ever noticed his steeds gallop. An acquaintance asked him why.

"In Scotland it is considered a breach of decorum to put one's horse to a gallop," he answered.

"Have you never done so?"

"I will admit that I have," he said. "When the British army was approaching Philadelphia and Congress adjourned to meet at Lancaster I put the spurs to my nag."

"Wasn't that indecorous?"

"Ah, yes. But that was a case of necessity—a breach of etiquette for which, even in Scotland, I would have been granted a special dispensation."

On another occasion a lady who lived near Tusculum spotted him in his garden ruefully viewing his withered rosebushes.

"Well, Dr. Witherspoon, I do not see any flowers in your yard," she said.

"You are right, madame," he said drily. "Nor in my discourses, either."

Shortly before his death Witherspoon was deprived of the sight of both eyes. Again, he interpreted the loss as the disposition of his Heavenly Father, and grace enabled him to maintain a cheerful disposition even though the affliction was, to an extrovert like John Witherspoon, catastrophic.

On November 19, 1794, at the age of seventy-one, he was seated in a rocking chair at Tusculum when God sweetly kissed away his soul.

In a quiet cemetery in Princeton, one can read on the tombstone over his grave this information:

Beneath this marble lies interred the mortal
remains of John Witherspoon, D.D., L.L.D.
A venerable and beloved President of the
    College of New Jersey
Exceeding in every intellectual gift
He was of pre-eminent piety and virtue
And deeply versed in the various branches
    of literal and liberal arts
A grave and solemn preacher
    His sermons abounded in the most excellent
    doctrines and precepts of holy Scripture
Affable, pleasant and courteous in familiar
    conversation
He was eminently distinguished in concerns
    and deliberations of the Church
And endued with the greatest prudence in
    management and instruction of youth
He was for a long time conspicuous among
    the most brilliant luminaries of learning
    of the Church. . . .

BIBLIOGRAPHY

Dodds, Harold Willis, president of Princeton University, 1933–1957. The lecture, *John Witherspoon*, was delivered at the National Newcomen Dinner in New York on April 26, 1944.

Lengyel, Cornel, *Four Days in July*, the detailed story behind the Declaration of Independence.

Lyman, Henry Butterfield, *Witherspoon Comes to America*, a documentary account based on New Materials, issued under the sponsorship of the Friends of the Princeton Library.

Savage, Henry Lyttleton, *Nassau Hall*, edited for the bicentenary of the foundation of the hall by the Archivist of the Princeton University Library.

Sprague, William B., *Annals of the American Pulpit*. The article on Witherspoon was written by Dr. Ashbel Green, president of Princeton College from 1812 to 1822.